Still Woman Moving

Eunice Russell Schatz

To Val
for life at your center

Eunice Schatz

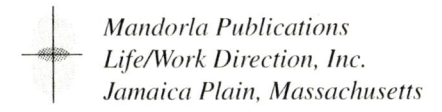

Mandorla Publications
Life/Work Direction, Inc.
Jamaica Plain, Massachusetts

Copyright © 2002 by Eunice Russell Schatz

Still Woman Moving
by Eunice Russell Schatz

Printed in the United States of America

Library of Congress Control Number: 2002100916
ISBN 1-591600-04-9

All rights reserved under International and Pan-American Copyright Convention. Published in the United States by Mandorla Publications, Life/Work Direction, Inc., Jamaica Plain, Massachusetts. No part of this publication may be reproduced or transmitted in any form or by any means without written permission of the publisher.

The Scripture quotations contained herein are from the New Revised Standard Version, copyright © 1989 by the Division of Christian Education of the National Council of Churches of Christ in the U.S.A. Used by permission. All rights reserved.

Xulon Press
11350 Random Hills Road
Suite 800
Fairfax, VA 22030
(703) 279-6511
XulonPress.com

Some of the names in this book have been changed.

for

Donald Gregory Schatz

*one of those rare human beings
who maintains total consistency
between his public and private self.*

*I love you for always being who you are
and for encouraging me to be the person I am.*

CONTENTS

Prologue .... *ix*

PART ONE: Growing Within Pleasant Boundaries

  1 *Born Into a Tradition* *3*

  2 *A Goodly Heritage* *9*

  3 *Uprooted* *27*

  4 *Wheaton, My Third Parent* *43*

  5 *Mirror to the Self* *67*

PART TWO: Moving Into Freedom

  6 *Born Again in Therapy* *85*

  7 *Window to The Other* *99*

  8 *The Seventies* *123*

  9 *Sabbath Time* *143*

 10 *The End of Ideals* *149*

 11 *The Beginning of a Life Work* *163*

 12 *The Preacher's Daughter Comes Home to Church* *179*

PART THREE: Becoming Still

 13 *The Inner Journey* *191*

 14 *De Profundis: Breakdown and Breakthrough* *207*

 15 *Mothering My Mother* *223*

 16 *Life With a Jewish Christian Poet: For Better, For Verse* *239*

Epilogue *255*

Acknowledgments *259*

Bibliographic References *263*

Prologue

"WHY HAVE YOU come to me?" I put the question to the young woman before me. It was Carrie's first counseling session. She had been seeing an expensive psychiatrist in the suburbs for several years and I was not sure why she was now choosing to do a piece of work with me. Her eyes were large with distress and longing.

She sat quiet for a moment, curling her crossed legs in front of her, a favorite pose she would assume over the coming months. Then she spoke, tentative and thoughtful.

"Because you're so *still.*"

I looked at her, startled. How had I deceived her? Did she not know the person I had been and to some extent still was? The young woman leaping on table tops in camp dining halls, clowning and telling stories to a wide-eyed camper audience. The evangelical leader who knew "the answers" and preached them with eloquence. The task-oriented co-founder of an organization geared toward college students, and which hovered on the margins of acceptability by the Christian educational establishment in the wake of the political and societal turmoil of the Sixties. How could she call me still?

Did she sense the deep changes I was at that moment undergoing in my approach to spiritual life, my growing attraction to silence, that I now loved to listen more than to speak? I was following the advice of a mentor who instructed: "If you can be still and wait, the person you are counseling will tell you what is on her mind. And if you continue to wait, she will tell you what is in her heart. And if you wait still longer, she may share her soul." It was soul work into which I was now called, and Carrie had sensed it.

I am writing this story because I want you to know that change is possible, continuous and significant change from one stage in life to another as long as one lives. I write this to encourage the fainthearted who know deep dissatisfaction with themselves and who despair of seeing a different self, wrapped in grace and love and hope. This new self is possible no matter how futile your efforts to change seem; no matter how caught in the contradiction of recognizing personal abilities but lacking the confidence to attain a full and complete life; no matter how carefully you work to conceal your doubts and failures, or how much you fear exposure as an impostor in the community of faith. All these conditions are familiar ones and can become grist for the mill of hopeful change.

What prescient instinct in adolescence made me choose II Corinthians 3:18 as life verse:

> *And all of us, with unveiled faces, seeing the Lord as though reflected in a mirror, are being transformed into the same image from one degree of glory to another; for this comes from the Lord, the Spirit.*

Mirrors have fascinated me all my life, for they seemed to give me back myself. But I only saw what I had set in place behind my own eyes as I looked at my image. Often what I saw was distorted. One time, I spent a week in a wilderness retreat hermitage which was not equipped with a single mirror. I wondered if I would be able to tolerate not knowing what I looked like, because I have been so dependent all my life on how others responded to me. It has been a hunger, and I have often come up empty. I have longed to look into that mirror which is the Lord of glory and see myself as God sees me. It is a lifelong quest to know the truth of God, of life, of myself.

As I have written this story of my life journey, I have strained to see and speak the truth, to lay bare my process before God and whoever happens upon this book. I am grateful for God's delete button, forgiving and forgetting many moments of blindness and folly, but I am even more thankful for the moments of transfiguring penetrations of grace which shaped my life, changing me "from one

PROLOGUE

degree of glory to another."

I am inviting you to walk with me through the pages of my story, to meet some of the persons who have been moving forces in my life, beginning with the mother who birthed me and whose legacy to me was both strong and complex. I also invite you not to fear the part of my journey which took me into the dark night, and which required solitude for a season before the phoenix of hope could rise from the ashes.

Stillness is the fruit of that dark night. You can walk there without fear too.

PART ONE

Growing Within Pleasant Boundaries

The boundary lines

have fallen for me in pleasant places;

I have a goodly heritage.

Psalm 16:6

one

Born Into a Tradition

It is a balmy Sunday evening in a quaint brick church on a hill in the center of Ashland, New Hampshire. I am just three years old, seated in a pew next to my mother, my brother Philip flanking her on the other side. My father stands erect, as always, behind the pulpit. The sun dips low in the western sky, casting a golden glow through the stained glass windows. Soon night falls, the singing stops, and my father begins to preach. My head, nestled against my mother's cushiony shoulder, rolls automatically over onto her lap. Mother strokes my hair absentmindedly, her hand pausing to caress my brow. Soon I am fast asleep, utterly secure.

Suddenly, the sermon is over, and the last hymn is being sung. Mother remains seated, honoring the burden on her lap. The sound of the music startles me to consciousness, and I begin to cry. I am sure, at this writing, that my reaction is not just a startle reflex but an instinctive response to the music which is already so "home," so familiar to me.

I STILL CRY in church at the music. A vision sweeps over me of the heavenly throng, "lost in wonder, love, and praise." It is part of the primal vision of my life.

Cradled by mother and father, by mother church, I never knew anything but unwavering trust in the God of heaven and in these lesser gods of earth. I was a Christian; I didn't need to "get saved."

It was puzzling when people asked me, "Are you saved?" Saved from what? From hell? I knew better. My Dad was a preacher, but not of the sort to preach hellfire and damnation in order to scare people into faith.

I wasn't converted as a child, either. I used to envy people at church who told riveting stories of a life in sin until they met Christ and radically changed. I had no such story to relate.

Nor did the term "born again" register with me.

I was born into the Christian faith. All my life I have felt a gravitational pull Godward. The bedtime stories my parents told me made Daniel and Joseph and Ruth and Esther and David and Samuel as real to me as my childhood playmates. It became utterly natural for me to adopt the words of the psalmist in Psalm 22 as my own:

> *I have been entrusted to you ever since I was born; you were my God when I was still in my mother's womb.*

Another disturbing strand appeared in the tapestry of my life quite early. Parents and teachers talked of "original sin," making it sound as though sin were ingrained in my nature. The words of Psalm 51 reinforced this thought:

> *I have been wicked from my birth, a sinner from my mother's womb.*

I instinctively shrank from these words, not wanting to take them in as true. My "mother's womb" harbored a conflict: was I God's child from birth, or desperately wicked?

My contemporary Episcopal friends escaped this conflict. They were carried into the church as infants and held over the baptismal font as the priest placed the sign of the cross on their forehead, intoning the solemn words:

> *"You are sealed by the Holy Spirit in Baptism and marked as Christ's own forever."*

But my parents were Baptist, my father a minister, and our doctrine declared that I was born in sin and must wait until I reached the "age of accountability" to make a clear conscious choice. Baptism was not something being done to me and sponsored by my parents; I would walk into the baptismal waters voluntarily. It was presupposed that baptism was the sign of a previous personal encounter with Jesus Christ.

I wrack my brain to conjure up a memory of such an encounter, but the mind draws a blank. Rather, I must rely on my mother's story which she has told over the years. How shall I own that which I do not remember? Conversely, why should I question that which she recalls with such assurance?

As she tells it, on an April Sunday afternoon during nap time I came into the room where she and my father were resting. I was six years old at the time. I crawled up onto the bed, crying. When my parents asked me what I wanted, I said I wanted to ask Jesus into my heart. There did not seem to be any clear antecedent to this expressed wish—like a recent punishment for something I had done wrong.

It sounds like a Samuel experience, whom God called in the night by name. Like Samuel, I had been prayed for before conception. His life growing up in the temple was not totally unlike my life in the minister's family, immersed in the life of the churches Dad pastored.

I take my mother's story at face value, and wonder about the resonance of the experience within my own child mind and heart. In retrospect, I see it as one of a long series of experiences in my life which speak to an inner sense of belonging to God. But to my parents, it was a watershed. For me, the ensuing ritual was etched indelibly on my consciousness. A baptism was planned for a Sunday in June—the earliest possible in that cold New England climate since baptisms took place in a lake.

My brother and I awoke before dawn; we slithered out of our beds, our bare feet hitting the cold wooden floor of our parsonage home. There would be no fire in the pot-bellied wood stove until later, so I hurried to get dressed. I pulled on my scratchy wool bathing suit, then Mother slid a white organdy dress over it—sign of a special occasion. I went along with the preparations cheerfully, a little excited, not fully aware of what lay ahead. The impact of entering the waters of a New

Hampshire lake at six o'clock in the morning of the sixth of June had not yet registered in my six-year-old brain.

My brother and I huddled in blankets in the back seat of our '29 Chevy as it bumped its way along a woodland track toward the lake. We pulled into a clearing, making room for other cars which began to appear. I jumped out of the car and stepped onto the narrow beach. Soon a small cluster of church people gathered and my father began wading cautiously into the water.

My brother and one or two others preceded me. Soon my turn came. Guided by my father, I waded into the frigid waters, shivering and trembling. Dad held me in his arms and gently lowered me under the water, slowly repeating the ancient words,

> *"I baptize thee in the name of the Father, and of the Son, and of the Holy Ghost."*

For a moment I panicked, as the water swirled over me, though I felt the strong comfort of my father's arms. Then I was lifted clear of the waves, and I burst into tears. On the shore, my mother stood watching, as shafts of sunlight slanted through the tall pines, glinting on the surface of the lake. She was singing "Sunrise Tomorrow." Hand in hand with my father I walked back to shore, where he spoke the ritual words which were his signature at baptisms:

> *Lord, it has been done as thou hast commanded; and yet there is room. What hinders thee from being baptized? If thou believest with all thy heart, thou mayest.*

Then Mother shuttled me into the car quickly to change clothes.

An odd detail imprints the occasion on my memory. The organdy dress I had worn for the baptism was given me by twins, so I had received two identical dresses. I now donned the second one, which was dry. At church later that morning, friends who had seen me at the baptism gasped, seeing the same dress, but completely dry. I took wry pleasure in this little trick.

The following Wednesday evening, I was received into membership of the church. This meant giving my testimony before the group assembled. I rehearsed carefully, and when my turn came, I stood up, grasped the railing of the chair in front of me and blurted out the words I had been taught, "I'm glad I'm saved," and began to cry.

Now I would no longer be passed over on communion Sundays when the little squares of bread and cups of grape juice were distributed. It was the consummate *rite de passage* in the Baptist tradition, which only celebrates communion once a month, not weekly like the sacramental confessions.

I do not know what to name my experience. None of the usual metaphors seemed to fit—being converted, saved, born again. I had a foggy notion that what I needed to be saved from was my willful tendency to disobey my parents. I was too young to have any concept of rebirth. I had simply knocked on a door, asking to be let inside. I wanted to be where my mother and father were, and this seemed to be where Jesus was. All I had to do was ask, and the door had opened and I had been enfolded in loving arms. My tears tell me that it was a movement on my part that deeply mattered, but I could not have said why.

Amy Dyer Russell with firstborn son Howard, 1926

two

A Goodly Heritage

LIKE TWO MOUNTAIN streams rushing down a hillside, twin currents of life bore me into the world with tender force. Each current had its own unique power: the one, a river of life arising within my mother's womb where I gestated during the months of pregnancy and continued as I was cradled in her arms and listened to her songs; the other, a more mysterious force coming from my father, locking my soul to his while I was still young.

THE MOTHER I NEVER KNEW

I have spent a lifetime unraveling the powerful influence my mother exerted upon me. Beginning in her body, knit in her womb, I absorbed something of the complex strength and tenderness in her character. I would need both in order to survive and become myself. Recently I came upon a photograph in an old album which startled me into a new consciousness of this woman who became my mother.

The delicate shading, the lighting, and the gesture of Mother's body, the tilt of her head, and the way she looks at the contented face of her newborn baby—all of these things move me. I wonder how my father, "legally blind" and using an old-style box camera, obtained such results. The picture is full of love, warm and deep. Love from my father who held the camera, and love from my twenty-six year-old mother who looks at her firstborn son, and through the mirror reflection is viewed by my father holding the lens.

What is her life at that point? Coming from the simple confines of her Maine farm, to marry my father whose future would seem uncertain, with his poor eyesight, and then to travel across the world to a foreign country to birth a child within the first year of arrival—how did she experience this moment, caught in freeze frame by the camera? She stands erect and tall, her face bent tenderly over the sleeping child, her long garments cloaking her body gracefully.

The mirror allows me to see my mother's face from both sides. Does she yet know that her firstborn son, Howard, has spina bifida and will survive only a few months? That this brother whom I never knew, will be laid to rest in a cemetery in North China near the sea? This womanly figure is not the Devouring Mother of ancient myth. She is young and hopeful, and the image of her is art.

I was a much longed-for and prayed-for child, arriving four years after my second brother Philip was born. My parents took care to tell me how, in the days before my birth, they would climb a pine-laden hill in the town of Epsom, New Hampshire, on fall afternoons, stretch out on the soft pine needles to rest, my brother playing nearby, my father writing sonnets. Mother remembered me at birth as "so pink and white, different from many newborn babies." Then she added: "You were born more contented than many." After a short time had passed and my temperament emerged, she wrote again in my baby book, "Eunice is strong-willed." By adolescence, that strong will of mine was seen as a direct challenge to her authority, whereas I felt completely dominated by this powerful woman, especially by her ability to make me feel shame and guilt.

I look at this picture now, a decade after her death at the age of ninety-five, and I see an independent young woman, softened by the suffering of labor. She is a mother in this picture, but not yet of me. I can detach, and receive her motherhood as an objective reality—as someone else's mother. I can let myself identify with her fully. I have her body structure, many of her bodily strengths and weaknesses. We come from the same stock.

The Good Mother

Another image presents itself, this one embedded in memory.

It is early on a frosty January morning in Northwood, New Hampshire. I am five years old. I awaken in my bedroom, the windows open to the wintry cold. I am used to finding snow on my coverlet by morning. I scurry out of bed and race down the stairs to the pot-bellied stove in the front room. There by the fire, Mother is kneeling frog-like in her maroon bathrobe, her Bible open on the chair before her. I wriggle my shivering body underneath her arm, forcing her to embrace me and to acknowledge my presence. She gathers me in, even as I understand that I must not interrupt the divine service going on.

I was vaguely aware as a child that other mothers were more stylish and slim. But I was puzzled, "Where were their laps?" I loved curling up into the capacious softness of my mother's body. Her large-boned frame was cushioned, perfectly designed for holding my wriggling form. I nestled in her lap while she crooned.

She was a comforting and ideal mother in my early childhood, always present, able to soothe, and full of games to entertain. She burst into song as she worked around the house. Her presence was physical and palpable as she busied herself in the kitchen. She dug her arms up to the elbows in bread dough, kneading with force and skill. The pungent smell of freshly baked whole wheat bread filled the kitchen. On special occasions, she treated us with cinnamon buns or cookies plump with raisin filling. When I was sick—twice with pneumonia in the frightening days before antibiotics—Mother hovered near with an endless array of liquids to nurse me back to health: juice, ovaltine, egg nog, warm milk, lemon fizz. Food was comfort for both giver and receiver.

On Sunday afternoons I was allowed the treat of combing Mother's long hair. The pleasure was mutual, for Mother loved the sensuousness of having her hair brushed and combed. In later years, I complained about her lack of style. I wished she looked like the other women with their permanents and short cuts. I think she kept her hair long because of my father's fondness for it; perhaps it was part of their own private love ritual.

Mother was trained not to speak of, or even see, the shadow side of life. And it cried for acknowledgment. As a four-year-old discovering the responses of my own body in an innocent moment of pleasure, I encountered my mother's shocked and agitated response. Though very young, I knew I must keep certain things secret from this person who was my mainstay and comfort, in whose lap I snuggled with cooing contentment. A tiny barrier had arisen.

Parenting was a loving duty for my mother, one which required her to quash sentiment in favor of the long-term goal of subduing my inherently sinful nature. She took her instructions primarily from her own experience as a child in a late nineteenth century farm household headed by her father, Howard Dyer, a patriarch in the noblest sense. Mother adored her father and described him to me in glowing terms. He may have assumed saintly status because he died of a stroke when Mother was sixteen. The loss was crushing, enveloping earlier times with a roseate glow by contrast. Although she talked of playful times with her father, she frequently repeated stories about his punishments, which seemed arbitrary or severe to me. Mother saw his strict and loving traits as totally compatible and absorbed his hatred of lying without question.

It then becomes ironic that I told my first lie to my mother—an act which took considerable courage and ignorance. We were squeezed together in the tiny pantry off the kitchen in our Northwood, New Hampshire, home, making cookies together. As a four-year-old, I was immensely proud of being able to be included in this mysterious matriarchal process. At one point, Mother left me alone while she went to fetch an ingredient elsewhere in the kitchen. "Don't touch those raisins," she cautioned me as she disappeared through the pantry doorway.

As soon as I was alone, the delicious thought that she herself had planted in my head overwhelmed me. I reached my pudgy fist into the jar and scooped out a handful of raisins and crammed them into my mouth. Sooner than expected, Mother returned. She took one look at my bulging cheeks. "Eunice! Did you eat any raisins?"

If only she had not asked. My reply was instinctive, and protective. "Nope," a word uttered with some difficulty through the yet-unswallowed raisin goo in my mouth. "Open your mouth," commanded Mother. I opened wide, revealing the sticky mass inside. Caught!

This posed a dilemma for my mother, who had been taught that lying is a serious sin, sins must be punished, and spanking is an act of love in such an instance. So she spanked me, likely one or two swats, but they left a sting on my soul. I felt betrayed, not being privy to the set of beliefs of this righteous school of parenting. I am not sure that I consciously adopted the new strategy which emerged—that of hiding unapproved behavior—but it became my way of coping from that point on.

It was tempting to induce Mother's reactions by occasional bursts of outrageous behavior. I could count on her shocked, "Eunice!" coupled with a frustrated whimper, indicating her loss of control. Something in me wanted to punctuate the seriousness with which she took small offenses, and to provoke a more whimsical response. Something else in me was deathly afraid of her disapproval. I became a master of deceit very early. For I must have her love, a love which was as palpable as her judgment, despite the fact that I did not consistently please her.

Whereas Mother took her child-rearing strategy from the example of her father, a benevolent and just master of discipline, her mother became the model for her relationship to her husband—unquestioning love and devotion, and an attitude of servanthood. I would find in my grandmother, Bessie Shepard Dyer, the unconditional love I craved.

Bessie was a Cockney, born "within the sounds of Bow Bells", a church in London. At sixteen, Bessie came across the Atlantic, and settled in Charleston, Maine, fifty miles northwest of Bangor. She became live-in hired help for a farmer named Herb Howes. We always heard him called 'Erb 'Owes in Grandma's Cockney accent.

She scrubbed floors and cooked meals, and did the laundry in galvanized iron tubs for the family and for their hired hands.

In time, Howard Dyer came courting and soon Bessie and Howard married and set up housekeeping on a farm. When Howard suddenly died in 1912 in his early fifties, Bessie picked up the reins of management of the orchard and animals without missing a beat. But a bleak sorrow hovered over the home. Soon Bessie moved away from the farm, to a cottage in the village, the place where I spent many happy summer vacations as a child. The memories come back readily through my childhood's heightened sense of smell.

The kitchen was often suffused with a floury odor laced with a hint of molasses whenever Grandma made cookies or gingerbread. As soon as they were laid out on racks to cool, my brother and his cousin would swoop up a handful, with Grandma scolding them, but in such a way that I could tell she was more pleased than angry.

There was no underground drain for waste water from our sink and the laundry tubs sitting in a side room, so a slightly putrid smell arose from the swirling gray residue in the yard outside whenever we washed dishes or clothes. In contrast, the sweet spring water which we trudged a quarter mile up the road to fetch smelled fresh.

A friendly burn smell filled the kitchen whenever my mother and aunt heated the heavy "sad irons" on the back of the wood stove. The ironing board cover was always covered with scorch marks. I was proud when I was old enough to be trusted to use these clumsy appliances.

We loved these family times in Grandma's home. I remember seeing her scrunch up her face as she wrung out the laundry by hand. I hovered near as she painstakingly sewed quilts, working the stitches inch by inch with her gnarled work-worn fingers. She sang in a high nasal crooning voice, her piercing dark eyes crinkling with a smile. On a Sunday morning she would clip the stray hairs on her chin, sweep up her white hair in a bun, plunk on a straw hat, and set out for church. Everyone loved her there, and the men, especially, treated her gallantly, offering help with an arm as she struggled down the steps or got into a car for the ride home. In her own eyes, she was simply an 'umble person.

Grandma's presence in our home was a constant when I was growing up. Although she made regular trips to visit her other daughters, she considered our place to be her home. When I came home from college for Christmas my senior year, I remember Grandma pushing me away from the sink when I started doing the dishes.

"You're tired. You've been working hard at college," she chirped. "I'll do the dishes."

I took one incredulous look at her diminutive eighty-three year old frame planted firmly at the sink. It took all my force to put my arms around her and carry her into the living room.

Two years later when I went home for Christmas, I saw that Grandma's health had deteriorated. Soon Grandma stopped eating. She had always served others; she had taken care never to be a burden. This was her only way to quietly ebb away.

A few weeks later my mother wrote me that Grandma had died. I laid my head on my desk and sobbed. The finality of death caught me by surprise. I did not want to be without my grandmother. Like so many other daughters, I had instinctively moved past my own mother to get to the "Grand Mother" in order to receive acceptance and approval. Getting this direct from the preceding generation was too fraught with expectations and judgments and fears. Writer Naomi Lowinsky notes that a woman "is easily polarized with her mother. She needs the power of the. . .grandmother, the one who is a generation removed. . .to help her find her way."[1] Grandmother love was safe and enveloping and I basked in it.

Tensions with my mother put my own capacity for maternal warmth at peril, as I grew. It was easy to turn against all that my mother represented, and in the process unwittingly destroy a precious legacy mothers give their daughters—the power to nurture. I would need that capacity in the life calling which later emerged, that of encouraging others in personal spiritual growth. The heritage my grandmother imparted saved some of that motherly legacy in me.

THE WISE FATHER

The other current of life bearing me into the world came from my father, Emmet Russell. My mother carried more of the shadow elements of our family. She was naturally quick to pick up faults in a situation, often attributing them to her own deficits, leaving my father to shine in the reflected light of her unquestioning love and adoration of him. For much of my life, my father became the Hero, my mother the Villain, and I took care to keep my interpretation of life in those simplistic terms.

It was extraordinarily easy to do. My father had a remarkable history of impressive accomplishments, especially literary ones: his command of nine languages, his achievement of a Harvard degree in Philosophy, his three-year stint of teaching in a private university in north China in the 1920's, his lifelong devotion to scholarship and reading in a wide variety of fields. I thought he was a genius.

Can it be, however, that my father's real genius lay in the way he dealt with the most obvious of his characteristics: Dad was "legally blind," in today's governmental parlance. And that made all the difference.

It is not easy to admit the centrality of my father's handicap in our home life, because this is something our family ignored. Sometimes friends I brought to the house would be shocked and say to me privately, "You didn't tell me your Dad was blind!" I never thought to. Our entire life had been worked efficiently around his condition. To us, he was not handicapped. Dad took us out into nature and encouraged us to look at the colors—which he could see and enjoy. He was able to read holding the book or newspaper near his chin, moving his head back and forth as he went over the lines from left to right. It is hard to explain how normal this appeared to us.

Now I wonder at my self-deception in this regard. Wasn't I secretly pleased when my friends were surprised? I knew how to slip into the conversation his Harvard degree (earned in three years rather than the customary four), his law degree (not so easily earned, I later learned), his seemingly limitless knowledge of so many subjects in which he was well read.

I was curious to know what had happened to his eyes but I could not pry much information from him. I discerned that the topic was *verboten,* probably because he liked to think of himself as "fully compensated" and firmly distanced himself from others' pity. The story gradually sifted through in fragmentary conversations. He had been born with limited sight in his right eye. But a shadow fell over the circumstances leading to total loss of sight in the left eye. It had to do with a doctor who had been drinking, whose instrument slipped when putting in the silver nitrate required by law for newborns, and the firm decision of his parents not to pursue that legally, a course of action unthinkable in today's litigious society and insistence on malpractice insurance.

My father made sure that his handicap would not become a burden on us. My brother and I became serenely oblivious to any limitations in my father's functioning as our parent. Sunday afternoons, Philip and I devised a game we called "Pester Daddy" in which we landed square on Dad's tummy as he lay on the floor, presumably trying to rest from his Sunday morning labors. Since he prepared his sermons in a study set apart for him at home, he was unfailingly available to us, never giving a hint that we were intruding.

I loved the way he kept his study in order, a necessary habit for a person with limited eyesight. He owned so many treasures inherited from his forebears—an expensive watch on a gold chain, a leather-bound book of Longfellow's complete works of poetry, a microscope and opera glasses. There was always the sense that my father had partaken of the world of genteel persons who were savvy to a more luxurious lifestyle than we experienced in the Depression era. He knew how to order meals in the dining car of a train, how to hail taxis and make hotel reservations and tip porters. His father had left him some parcels of real estate when he died, and Dad occasionally took trips to Kansas and Missouri to inspect them. Eventually Dad sold the farms, one by one, to pay my college tuition, then costing $400 a year. Such marks of worldly acumen effectively masked any fears my father may have entertained about his competence to care for his family.

THE FATHER-DAUGHTER BOND

How shall I explain the father-daughter bond—that strong sweet connection which arose early in my life? That it existed for me is not surprising, given the character of my father whose sensitivities were aesthetic and emotional. There was a natural fit, a gently sloping incline of matched temperaments that made it easy for us to move toward one another. A subtle unspoken communication of emotion developed between us like a tide, a current that affected my childhood in a particular way. It was more amorphous than concrete events. It was the whole sense of his person, as it unfolded before me through the years.

I remember myself as a five-year-old, standing on tiptoe at the end of the piano keyboard in our Northwood, New Hampshire, living room. I was just tall enough to peer over the edge watching my father's fingers fly over the keys, playing Schumann's "Happy Farmer" while I danced up and down gurgling with delight. My father's pleasure in my chirping glee was evident. I saw that I had the power to bring happiness to this person.

As I grew older, Dad and I engaged in extended conversations about issues that mattered to me. Lacking keen eyesight, his ears became the sense organ which connected him to the world. He listened intently and I knew I was heard. He treated my questions seriously; he was not afraid to say, "I don't know." He would not give me false surety that would thwart the possibility of mystery; he would encourage me to go beyond the confines of the known, the sure.

Such conversations made time spent with my father sheer poetry. One evening when I was sixteen, Dad and I took a walk together on the outskirts of the town where we lived. My thoughts were long and deep as we walked and looked up at the star-studded sky. In halting and half-formed phrases, I tried to describe to my father my notion of infinity. It was my first stretch toward the thought of endless time, and I felt original in talking about it, sure that my father would understand. He listened patiently, as though it were a

A GOODLY HERITAGE

new thought—which it was to me, but surely not to him.

I know now, from reading his journals, that my father was often gripped by somber moods. I could not ignore my father's unexpressed feelings. I was caught in the circle of his embrace and would not desert him to his sorrows. I remember evenings in my youth, when instead of being in the kitchen with mother busy with supper preparations, I preferred the company of my father in the living room. Dad would sit quietly in his rocking chair, head bowed deep in thought as dusk fell, while I played hymns on the piano. There would be that inevitable moment when he let out a deep sigh. I knew he was feeling what I played, for that is how I played—with feeling. I sensed very early in my life that I was the child who could lift his spirits. Before his marriage, it was his cherished young cousins in Idaho whom he visited from time to time. Now I would serve.

It was a role I would reluctantly surrender. Electra dies hard.

To say that we are deeply affected by our parents is a truism, and most of us can trace the influence of our parents' conscious attitudes upon our own lives. However, as Marie-Louise von Franz writes in *The Feminine in Fairy Tales*, we are just as powerfully influenced by their unconscious attitudes. This was the legacy from my father. Von Franz goes on to caution: "A daughter who is more fascinated by the figure of the father than by the mother in her youth tends more to the fate of being separated from life."[2] In my case, for a long time I was blind to the need for any other male figure in my life, because I was inundated by the waves of attachment to this very special person. It would be hard for a male peer of mine to compete with the adored father image etched in my psyche.

When the time came for me to navigate my teens, I needed different kinds of help from each parent. I think my mother felt inadequate for the task of bringing me into young womanhood. I turned to my father instead, and was often rewarded.

One day he surprised me by giving me one of the special treasures

*Emmet Russell caught in a
whimsical moment after
graduation from
Harvard Law school, 1919*

*Emmet Russell
Pastor, 1942*

*Grandma Bessie Dyer,
Amy and Emmet Russell*

he had inherited from his father. It was a slim silver case containing a razor and blades. I was old enough to want to shave my legs and under my arms like a proper lady. Although Mother looked askance at such an unnecessary vanity, Dad indulgently admitted to me that such a desire might indicate suitable feminine progress. I was more overwhelmed than I let him know, for it signified that he understood my need of his support as I moved toward womanhood.

There is such a subtle line in the father-daughter relationship as a young girl blossoms into womanhood. In so many ways, my father propelled me forward and filled me with confidence. But the idolization which I felt for this man, and which he unwittingly permitted, would hold me back. The perfection of this relationship would be hard to match in a man twenty years his junior. This, coupled with my mother's ineptitude in helping me adjust to teenage feminine culture in the 1940s, left me with an outcome which was a mixed blessing. On the one hand, I felt like a WASP princess, and on the other, a woman consigned to the destiny of a Protestant nun.

Two Streams Join

Although the effect of each parent on me was decidedly different, my parents' marriage was one of seamless unity. It became clear very early that I would never be able to pit one against the other in order to get my way. For different reasons, my parents' devotion to each other bordered on fusion. Mother viewed my father with uncritical admiration. For his part, my father needed the rocklike strength, the practical New England Yankee thrifty sensibility which my mother provided.

As a young man, my father was something of a Victorian, naturally inclined to idealize women. He was preternaturally shy, always aware that his limited eyesight might prove a barrier to sustaining a normal courtship. His youthful journals reveal deep currents of wistful longing for romance, although his social contacts were few and did not suggest likely success in his quest for a mate.

My parents met at Gordon College, then located on the Fenway in Boston. My mother, Amy Dyer, had come from her farm home in Maine to prepare for Christian service. My father, Emmet Russell, must have seemed an unlikely match—fresh from Harvard Law School, a man with a strong literary and cultural bent, at home in the world of ideas. But they were kindred spirits in two areas: the world of nature, and in their earnest faith.

Unlike my mother, my father had come to evangelical faith without the support of a family or religious community. Raised Universalist and Unitarian, his faith had been formal, founded on ethics, not personal experience of belief. His was a questing mind, and Harvard intensified his search by the sheer absence of reassurance about the metaphysical world. Science and reason faltered in preparing students for religious faith.

His conversion came in solitude the summer he turned twenty-two. He had spent time in Goshen, New Hampshire, with a family whose faith was warm and simple. They had spoken his name around the breakfast table at morning prayers, kneeling while he sat listening in awkward silence, deeply moved. When a friend gave him a copy of Moffat's version of the New Testament, he sat up all night beside a kerosene lantern in order to read it through to the end, gripped by the power of the words in modern English.

A few weeks later, traveling in the West by train, and continuing his reading of Scripture in the Gideon Bibles placed in hotels wherever he stopped, he came upon a verse which stopped him in his tracks:

> *For our light affliction, which is but for a moment, worketh for us a far more exceeding and eternal weight of glory; while we look not at the things which are seen, but at the things which are not seen: for the things which are seen are temporal; but the things which are not seen are eternal.* (II Corinthians 4:17, 18)

For my father, coming to faith meant seeing some purpose in his "light affliction," his partial blindness. His dependency on a highly developed intellect was aborted by this fresh perspective on the possible purpose of a loving God. Over subsequent months, he moved into a community of like-minded warmhearted Christians who nurtured his budding faith. Soon he made the transition from a career in the law, for which he had never felt temperamentally suited, to a vocation in Christian ministry.

This new vocation required theological education, so he turned to Gordon College of Theology and Missions, as it was then called, at precisely the same time that my mother arrived from Maine after two years of teaching school. They met at a meeting of Student Missionary Volunteers, where Amy addressed the meeting talking about her experiences on a mission field in Manitoba during the previous summer. As she told of harnessing and driving a horse about her field, Emmet saw how competent she was in things he could not do, as well as involved in preparing for some form of Christian ministry just as he was. He worried that this woman whose voice spoke of a rich interior life, could not look at a half blind young man with more than pity.

Emmet began to linger in the college library every evening, because Amy was there, sometimes outstaying all others. He began to feel that if she were not in his life, it would be empty without her. When he returned from Christmas vacation, it only took the warm handshake of welcome she offered to give him just the encouragement he needed. Maybe the woman who could harness a horse was not out of reach. Indeed, writing at eighty years remove, I would say that a woman who could harness a horse would prove a strategic choice for my father, who often had frail health and would need another's eyes and strong body for many of life's tasks. He was making a wiser choice than he acknowledged.

Emmet grew bolder. The library was a nice place to sit; but one had to be quiet there. The couple began to go places together—to Ruggles Street Church where Amy was a Church Visitor, as well as to places of interest dear to him and new to her: the art museum, the symphony, historic sites in Concord. Hesitation was over. Amy was giving indication that she cared. Emmet must only find the right time and place to declare his love.

It turned out to be the beach at Marblehead, a cave by the sea, with waves washing over the gravel, friendly stars winking out as the sun set. Together they settled the question. Amy was already a Christian from childhood, dedicated to the service of Christ, even if it meant foreign service; now they gave themselves to one another.

The following spring, in a private ceremony at the home of Gordon College President Wood in Arlington, Massachusetts, my mother and father were married. Their honeymoon took place in their first apartment in Roxbury, on a street not far from where I live in Jamaica Plain eighty years later. My parents were to enjoy their love for the next fifty-seven years.

China became home for the first three years of their marriage. Dad had a three-year contract to teach sociology and English at Nan Kai University, the only private university in North China at that time. Mother was already four months pregnant. Five months later, Howard Dyer Russell was born, looking healthy and beautiful.

A few days after the birth, my mother and father learned that the baby had a condition known as *spina bifida,* for which there was no known cure. He would not live; even if he did, he would be helpless. Six months later, he was laid to rest in a Japanese-owned cemetery by the sea. Many years later, I would occasionally sense the shadowy sorrow in my mothers' eyes whenever she spoke of my oldest brother.

My parents came home to America at the end of three years and settled in New England. My father began fulfilling his dream of becoming a country pastor, first in Maine, where my brother Philip was born in 1925, and later in Epsom, New Hampshire, where I appeared on the scene in 1929 during one of their happiest pastorates.

Thus rural New England became the cradle that embraced me for the first seven years of my life. I accepted its primitive amenities as natural. In many ways I was totally unprepared for the adjustment to city life which was thrust upon us the summer of 1937, when Dad's mother became terminally ill. A telegram came for my father and he boarded a train for Kansas City. Mother watched him go with foreboding, knowing we would soon be following and it would be up to her to take his place in the pulpit for a few weeks (she too was an ordained minister), and then pack up our belongings to make the long journey to an unknown future in the midwest.

three

Uprooted

THE ABRUPT CHANGE from my Edenic life in rural New Hampshire to the bustling city streets of Kansas City was a rude shock. I entered a new world with a maze of concrete pavements and houses jammed so close together I could hear the neighbors fighting. The constant wail of fire sirens and clang of trolleys were an assault on my primitive consciousness, attuned to the bucolic atmosphere of bird song, green earth, and pine-covered forest floors. I was encountering an alien world for the first time.

On the physical plane, there were marked improvements in Kansas City: our lifestyle moved forward a decade in one leap. We had a bathroom in place of an outhouse, a porcelain sink with faucets instead of the old black cast iron sink with its pump, a kerosene stove and a furnace which meant we no longer needed to chop wood and build fires in order to cook our food and warm ourselves.

We only spent a year in Kansas City, waiting as my grandfather died, and settling matters of my grandparents' estate, so I dismissed it as an interim in my life, waiting to get back to normal. The year sped by, a blur of fast frames, images of violence and death, sounds of sirens and shrill cries of horror.

> *—I am playing out front of our house in summer, barefoot in the rain. I am still not used to streets with heavy traffic. I see a model A Ford is coming down the hill. Two women are inside, properly attired in fancy hats. The driver is screaming, trying to gain control of the relentless descent of the car to the intersection at the foot of the hill. I watch*

in stupefied horror, seeing a street car move slowly across the intersection, just as the Ford narrowly misses the tail end of the trolley. But something in my seven-year-old brain knows that the brick wall at the end of the street holds doom for the occupants of a car whose speed is ever-increasing. A loud thud, and then silence. I did not go down to see the wreck.

—It is dusk, and my parents have gone out for the evening, leaving us in the care of Grandma Dyer, who is staying with us. My brother and I are lying in our beds in the slant-ceilinged attic room where the whole family slept. Grandma kisses us goodnight, and starts thumping heavily down the treacherous crooked stairs toward the landing, when I hear her fall, crying out in agonizing pain as she tumbles to the floor. Somehow Grandma manages to drag herself down the remaining steps, spending a troubled night before getting treatment for what turns out to be a broken hip. Lying in the dark upstairs, paralyzed with fear, I hear the ever-present fire sirens wail.

—I enter the gym for class, where folk dancing is the activity planned for the day. A girl named Gail and I sit forlornly on the sidelines as our classmates do the Virginia Reel. Gail tells me that we don't participate in the dance because we are Baptists. This makes no sense to me. I sit and watch with unspoken longing.

Heretofore, life had been secure and predictable, the surrounding community a replication of the warmth of my family and the parsonage, with few exceptions. It was what James Hillman calls a situation of "primal trust"—my own garden of Eden. Expulsion from that garden was a necessary development, even as it was for Adam and Eve long ago. I felt betrayed by the removal of expected supports and the consequent floundering in a social context which I did not understand and for which I was unprepared.

Hillman sees such a betrayal as necessary for growth:

> *Primal trust will be broken if relationships are to advance; and, moreover, . . primal trust will not just be outgrown. There will be a crisis, a break characterized by betrayal, which. . .is the sine qua non for [entering]. . .the world of human consciousness and responsibility.*[1]

My uprooting at the age of seven was the kind of break of which Hillman speaks. I had experienced earlier small betrayals—my mother's unexpectedly stern disapproval, and a first grade teacher's false accusation on one occasion when I was innocent—but this was a more profound break. I was leaving Eden, and it felt risky and unsettling.

Death hung like a pall over our year in Kansas City. Grandpa was bedridden, and slowly wasted away until he died in January. Sometimes, in his delirium, he would call for "Iola"—Grandma's name. My father, probably not knowing what to do, would ask me to go in to Grandpa, since my middle name was Iola, named after Grandma. This confused me. I stood there by his bedside, seeing his beautiful strong face and snow white hair, but I knew he was weak and helpless now and I did not know how to be in his presence. It was my first and only acquaintance with him.

Grandpa's death freed us to move on in our lives. My parents chose to make our home in Wheaton, Illinois, a suburb of Chicago, where my brother could begin high school at Wheaton College Academy, a prep school for Wheaton College. Dad would look for another pastorate, and meanwhile complete his doctoral dissertation in Sacred Theology. I hoped that the year in Kansas City was an aberration which I could erase from my memory.

Social Life in the Suburbs

In suburbia, rural security was long gone. The confusing melange of Kansas City noise and bustle was also gone. I was thrust into a peer culture with bewildering and complex layers of social interaction. I instantly felt at sea. I waded in naively, trying to carve out a niche for myself, but found life could be even more cruel. As an eight-year-old entering fifth grade, I was younger and smaller than my classmates, and also less sophisticated when it came to social mores. Cliques had already formed among my classmates, reinforced by geographic proximity which was missing in both of my previous school situations where I had been bused to school in the country, and part of a heavily populated area in the city. Everyone in my suburban school lived a few blocks from one another.

At first, I was only the new girl, an unknown who could be tested and found wanting or not. I soon learned the subtle distinctions—the ones who arrived at school disheveled, the slower learners, the ones who lived south of the tracks. I managed to maintain an uneasy balance between the included and excluded by placing myself on the margins where I could safely observe, only venturing out occasionally.

Two sisters in my class, Annie and Beth, took over my socialization. We began spending time after school together, sewing doll clothes and engaging in girlish chatter. Having lacked social contact with peers, I was like a sponge, trying to learn how to participate. Beth, especially, lacked no assurance in this area, and was the clear boss. I was a willing follower.

Like all pre-teen relationships, our threesome went through peaks and troughs of congeniality and distance. At one point, we embarked upon a miniature business enterprise together. We found a box of tongue depressors that had fallen on the floor, ruining the contents for sterile use. The three of us huddled together with our little treasure trove, wondering what use could be made of them. We decided to make Scripture verse plaques, using alphabet soup letters.

We set upon our venture with a high degree of business acumen for our age. Beth was the leader, and the one to suggest we sell these plaques to college students when they came into the lobby of the gym building for their daily mail. Annie and I bought paint and glue and the alphabet soup letters and we were in business. Beth was unabashed in hawking our product, and college students humored us, plunking down the fifteen cents we charged.

Beth soon tired of the wooden plaques, and discovered plaster of paris, and using old dishes for molds, she expanded the business to include these more expensive and elaborate items. When she got bored with that as well, she dropped out, but Annie and I continued. Whereas Beth's interest in the enterprise was primarily social, Annie and I had an economic goal: to buy roller skates. So we continued with our project until we had earned sufficient money to buy us each a pair. My natural entrepreneurial flair was in bud; the blossom would appear throughout my professional life.

A climax to the equilibrium of our triumvirate occurred in eighth grade. All three of us attended Wheaton College Junior Academy, a small "lab" school managed by the local college for the benefit of students who were working toward a teaching certificate and needed a place to student teach. The entire school consisted of less than twenty-five students. One day Beth came up to Annie and me and announced authoritatively, "There are two groups here, the Liked Group and the Unliked Group." She paused a significant moment. "And you're in the Unliked Group—you two and Jessie Rice."

That sent the three of us into a huddle. After school we hatched a plan. Okay, if we were a group, we would *be* a group. I wrote a secret code for communicating with each other and wrote it into tiny code books which we carried around. Jessie was an artist, so she drew the design for a crest. In the center, large and bold, the letters T - U - G stood for The Unliked Group. We named ourselves Tuggies at that moment, priding ourselves on our secret, and thereby undoing the sting Beth inflicted.

Finding a New Home in Camp

I was a country girl at heart. Amid my awkward attempts to navigate the intricacies of suburban social life, I found reprieve at the end of every school day by retreating into the familiar and friendly world of nature. I developed a daily ritual of circling the house, taking note of each flower and shrub as it appeared in season.

Summer camp became a perfect solution by providing me with the aesthetic and unspoiled natural surroundings familiar to me in childhood, while at the same time a social context which embraced the shy loners as well as the extroverts. The egalitarian ethos, produced by the absence of established social groupings and the mix of girls from various communities but with common interests, meant that I felt fully accepted by my peers. It changed everything for me as a twelve-year-old. I began to grow into a distinct social self: my awkwardness began to heal, I developed an array of outdoor skills, and over time my leadership emerged.

Attending camp was not part of our family's habitual routine. It would not have occurred to either of my parents to send me to summer camp. Mother's childhood on a farm gave her ample exposure to primitive outdoor life. My father's parents would never have considered turning him loose in rugged circumstances. Therefore it took the slender thread of destiny to bring me to my first encounter with camp.

In the winter of 1942, a winsome college senior, Miss Louise Troup, was assigned to teach literature to our eighth grade class of five girls. We found Miss Troup delightfully vulnerable to our attentions. She laughed irrepressibly at our antics, dimpled engagingly when teased. We did everything in our power to unsettle her, and because she responded, we had no inclination to stop.

Troupie was intent on teaching us to love literature, by means of the big green volume entitled *Prose and Poetry Adventures*. One day, when we found Miss Troup sufficiently engrossed in her reading performance, at a prearranged signal all of us opened our desktops at once, creating a row of five wooden barriers. But Miss Troup only laughed. Here was a teacher who apparently enjoyed pupils who went against the grain.

Amid this atmosphere of admiration and antics, Miss Troup invited us to consider attending Camp Cherith, the summer camp sponsored by a recently-formed club organization called Pioneer Girls. We had attended one club meeting at our church and in the manner typical of early adolescents, had arbitrarily decided "thumbs down." Our resistance was a challenge sure to draw our teacher in, for she had become deeply involved in the formation of the fledgling Pioneer Girls program.

As time went on, and our interest in our teacher increased, we began to reconsider her proposition. If Louise Troup was going to be at camp, we might take a different view of it. It took a good deal of convincing for my parents to approve this adventure away from the home nest, but Louise was adept at "mommering and poppering" as she termed her recruiting efforts, and eventually I was permitted to go.

Camp convened in Lemont, Illinois, for one week, and it was love at first sight for me. A new world opened up—music and nature and campfires and woodscraft and skits and laughter and a cabin of new friends—all accompanied by a bevy of college-age counselors who were having as much fun with each other as with us. We sensed the love and caring, and lapped it up.

It was here in camp that I first tasted the meaning of the Pioneer Girls slogan, "Christ in every phase of a girl's life." I could not have articulated it, but I was feeling it, sensing it, living it. It became for me a consciously self-articulated philosophy of life as a teenager.

Since all of the counselors were young college students, a spirit of play pervaded their approach to the task of running a camp. The attitude was contagious and, shy as I was, I found myself being drawn in to this undiscovered world of campfires and rituals and mealtime boisterousness. It was my first time away from home, and I was not homesick. I relished the freedom, and being at home with peers, a new experience for me, so used to rural isolation in New England.

I was not a typical camper—always awkward in sports, totally unfamiliar with hatchets and cookouts at first, only marginally interested in the names of birds and plants and trees (looking at them was satisfaction enough). But music and stories touched me, in the universal way Christian educators later taught me. To experience these around a glowing campfire under the trees or in a recreation hall, under the guidance of women just ten years my senior, constituted a kind of bliss new to me.

I would return for the next twenty years, reveling in camp's unique combination of deeply rooted earthiness and a mystical quality associated with God's presence in fire and song and sunsets. It taught me that I could survive in the wilderness with minimal equipment—even when I forgot the salt or the flashlight. I could carry all I needed on my back and walk all the way to a mountain top and look over the world spread out in all four directions in a magnificent panorama.

I snuggled in my sleeping bag with nothing between me and the winking stars; I might rouse occasionally to stir the embers of the flickering fire left glowing for warmth, then spend much of the night whispering my deep thoughts to a friend curled up close by. At dawn I rose shivering, unwound from my twisted bedroll, and moved to the crackling flames of the revived fire where a frowzy-headed counselor was beginning preparations for breakfast.

I learned how to add just enough water to a box of Bisquick to form a "doughboy" around the fat end of a stick I had fashioned from a tree branch. I twirled it carefully over the coals for what seemed an eternity until it turned biscuit brown and I could remove it, pour in butter and honey, then savor each crumbly dripping bite until it was gone. For the first time, I knew hunger, for life in the out-of-doors does that. As I became more proficient in camp cookery, my experiments became more adventuresome. There was nothing to equal the risk of throwing a slab of juicy raw steak directly onto glowing coals, giving it a quick singe on one side, then turning it and letting it sizzle and cook, sending its incredible aroma to my nostrils. When it was ready, I would slide the steak through a pan of melted butter and onions to brush off the ashes and bits of charcoal, before eating it the only proper way—with my fingers.

As campers, we were free of parents, yet under the watchful eye of adults just enough older to provide role models with whom we were willing to identify. We were with peers, but in a context less fraught with competition over looks or brains. There was time and space to be alone, as well as to experience the alternately devastating and blissful intimacy of a cabin setting bereft of conveniences. We were within a safe world, cordoned off from movies and headlines.

After a time, I learned the extra privileges of becoming one of the counselors, engaging in after-hours horseplay. On a moonlit night, we would make our way down to the dock, slide into the water which felt warm under the surface, slither out of our swim suits and toss them into a heap on the dock, floating free in our naked bodies, hearing the echo of our giddy laughter reverberate across the lake.

Camping in War Time

These adventures were still ahead of me in 1942 when I began attending camp. I came home that summer overflowing with stories which I recounted to Nancy Wareham, the only girl my age at the Glen Ellyn, Illinois, church my Dad pastored. We became pals and decided to go to camp together in 1943.

World War II was in full scale operation during this time, and it became an undertone to camp life. One day a Navy chaplain in full uniform came to visit his daughter in camp, a reminder of the tremendous dimensions of the war—the sacrifices people were making. Gas and food shortages impinged on camp life around the edges. One day the camp cook approached the director in distress. Food had been ordered from Sexton, but it had not come, and there was no food for the next meal.

"We have to have something," the cook told the director, who replied, "We don't have anything. Do what you can." The cook always managed to come up with something. This was the year I remember raspberry chiffon pie for dessert, made from jello and graham crackers, an example of a "something."

But in general, the horrors of the war were only dimly felt, and as yet we had no glimmering of the massacre of millions of Jews. We were immersed in the protected freedom of life which occurs in the wilds.

The following summer of 1944, I eagerly boarded a train to

travel to Kalamazoo, then proceeded by bus to the shores of Gull Lake, and to Gull Island by launch, where Camp Cherith was held that year. Although I was still living a protected life in suburban Wheaton, at camp I was exposed to a cross-section of girls from the inner cities of Chicago, Detroit, and Cleveland, whose life experience was quite different from mine. I remember sitting at the supper table the first evening when a noisy flock of kids from Cleveland City Mission arrived late. They were sporting the fashions of war time, carrying big purses, walking on high heels, and wearing lipstick smeared on thick. They bragged about flirting with sailors on the way up by train. They weren't necessarily tough kids at all, but I could see that they were more worldly-wise, having survived more of "life" than those of us from suburban Christian homes. I felt young and naive beside them. I could not have articulated it then, but I was experiencing some of the breakdown of barriers of class and geography produced by the war.

Camping on an island meant a lot of attention to waterfront activities. The pride of the waterfront was two long "war canoes" which could be propelled by twenty-four of us, paddling in unison, as the counselor in charge called out, "Forward Dip! Forward Dip!" in rhythm. A few of us took a certain amount of perverse pleasure in paddling water into the lap of the person directly behind us. Amid these kinds of capers, a paddle stroke from the camper in front of me swooshed off my glasses one sunny afternoon. I watched in alarm as they went down into two hundred feet of water, irretrievable.

I was nearly blind without those glasses. That night we went on an overnight trip across the lake. My partner, Ellen, and I beached our canoe on shore, and I began tossing our blanket rolls and gear to her. Just for fun, after catching my blanket roll, Ellen playfully tossed it back—to see if I was keeping alert. Without glasses, alertness lost its meaning, and into the shallow water went my blanket roll. This was before the days of waterproof sleeping bags. These were army blankets, and mine were sodden for the remainder of the night.

After campfire, a counselor took us out into an open field to show us the constellations in the evening sky. I gazed up into the starry blur, struggling to see the outlines of Orion and Cassiopeia as they were being pointed out. But without my glasses, stars were just fuzzy flashes of light. Still, something about that evening spoke to me, and I have remembered it always. Perhaps I got a wee taste of my father's experience in seeing the heavens, for despite his partial blindness, he appreciated the sunsets and stars more than most sighted persons.

We were promoted to the rank of junior counselors the following summer of 1945. Counselors were named for birds at Camp Cherith. Being only junior counselors, Nancy and I were permitted half a name so we divided Tufted Titmouse. Nancy became "Tufty" and from that point on I was known in Pioneer Girls camp and throughout my later career in the organization as "Mouse."

After serving as counselors to younger campers in July, Nancy and I decided to attend senior camp as campers in August back on our beloved island. Later, we were told this was a mistake: once we had tasted the role of leadership, it was difficult to return to camper status.

Another factor had intervened. In May that year, at the age of fifteen, I finally had my first menstrual period. I was ecstatic. I was tired of wearing undershirts instead of bras, of being the only one in gym class who could not get excused absences each month. A marked shift occurred in my personality.

When I arrived, I was no longer Mom and Dad's "good girl," but an adolescent ready to rebel. Something in my shy nature had snapped. I became a clown and a ringleader. I was not interested in keeping the rules; I was interested in testing the limits. Nancy was shocked, and she told me so. "What has happened to you?" Her tone was reproachful.

It was a week of pranks and hilarity for our cabin. We were convinced that we were the life of the camp. When we had dish duty, we were not content to simply wipe the dinner plates dry and put them away; we took pleasure in stationing ourselves ten feet apart, one of us by the dish drainer, throwing the plates, one by one, to the other who was standing by the dish cabinet to put them away.

One day, during the camp session, word came that the Japanese had surrendered. There was a celebration at camp. I was a young patriot then, innocent of the complexities of war. Vietnam later turned me pacifist. By the time of the terrorist attacks on September 11, 2001, so close to us in the northeast, I was no longer naive about the suffering that members of the world community can inflict on each other. I could only cringe in sorrow and horror.

In the months following camp, I began to learn of the unspeakable atrocities perpetrated against the Jews. In subsequent years, I would feel inexplicably drawn to stories about the Holocaust. I felt that Jews were my people too, perhaps because I had been immersed in the biblical stories of the patriarchs and prophets, instilling a tenderness in me toward these people of God.

> *That fall, Louis and Allen Alport, uncles to Donald Schatz, returned from the European theater of war with a story to tell and lots of photographs taken of the concentration camp at Buchenwald, which they had helped liberate. Donald, then a boy only eight years old, but someone who would one day grow up and become my husband, stared at the haunting images of corpse-like figures, and heard the adults speak in horrified and angry tones. The images would forever change him.*

Learning to Lead

I should have been surprised, perhaps, that when plans for a traveling caravan of camp counselors was announced for the following year, I was asked to join. I was to learn later that the caravan director, Rachel, had been shocked by my behavior that week of camp. I remember earnestly and sincerely arguing with her that it was "fun to break rules," something she adamantly refused to believe. Lee, a camper from Cleveland who had shared a number of escapades with me the previous summer, agreed with me that a counselor could not properly understand campers unless she understood their basic urge to test the limits of authority. The issue was never resolved. Nevertheless the bond with Rachel was a sturdy one, and became even stronger during the two summers we traveled together. We called our team the Conestoga Caravan, named for the Conestoga wagons used by pioneers heading west more than a century earlier.

The idea of developing a caravan of camp counselors to tour the country for a summer, contributing their leadership and energy to the fledgling camps springing up in many areas, emanated from Pioneer Girls headquarters in 1946. There was a promotional edge to the idea. Between camps, this team would have speaking engagements in churches—presumably to generate support for the tiny organization, in money and interest. Nancy had talent as a singer, I played the piano, Lee was an artist who did "chalk talks."

The church engagements we endured. But the camps we loved. We began with Ohio Camp Cherith that summer. It was announced in a brochure as taking place "on beautiful Lake Odell." As we pulled into the site, the lake lay before us, brown and muddy. The dining hall, a grotesque, sprawling structure, sinking on one end, was next to the administrative building we came to call the "control tower," a rigid, rectangular box with an unusable first floor.

The worst was yet to come. One Sunday afternoon, the Caravan returned from a church service we had conducted in a nearby town to find that the bathtub on the second floor of the dining hall had crashed through the floor boards and now hung precariously midway between the two floors. Thankfully, no campers had been near to be hurt.

In many ways, this first caravan camp was an initiation rite for me as a budding counselor. I realized I was a leader now. Sometimes the distinction between camper and counselor was not great, for as young teenage women we engaged in a lot of horseplay around the edges of our responsibilities. I experienced a conscious shift in thinking about myself. Campers were now investing the same kind of trust in me as I had placed in counselors before. Something clicked inside. What I said and did mattered to my young charges.

I was assigned a cabin of five lively African American girls from inner city Cleveland. My zany antics and fun-loving spirit made it easy to establish rapport. Camp was new to them; counseling was new to me.

I soon found a natural role in camp life—that of song leader. It became my specialty for years to come. Music was integral to the spirit and soul of camp. It was not just in the evening campfires, where the mood was set by the darkness and firelight. I led rollicking songfests in the dining hall after the noon meal as well. I loved to make a fool of myself, leaping up on benches or tables, directing the campers in crazy fun songs, folk songs from all around the world. It was all *a cappella*—the pure sound of voices without instrumental support. I became a magician conjuring up an atmosphere of hilarity, then of melodic sweetness when we slowly began to sing the quiet, more thoughtful songs. The group responded instantly to my slightest gesture that indicated "softly now." And then the great hymns would roll out. I was creating a moment of worship for us all, worship such as we rarely experienced in church.

Part of the thrust of camp was evangelistic. The strong emotions generated in the camp setting brought many girls to the decision point in following Christ, but I was always aware that the groundwork had been laid in the devoted work of their club leaders back home. My counselor training had given me some idea of how to "lead a girl to Christ," but I was distinctly uncomfortable in the evangelizing role, having more enthusiasm about helping campers grow spiritually, making their faith a positive force in everyday life.

I was asked to go on a special overnight hike planned for the older campers. We had been paying special attention all week to three fourteen-year-olds from inner city Cleveland—Joy, Jackie, Corny—girls with a story to tell, a story of rough home backgrounds and experiences that had made them grow up too fast.

As we set out on our hike, Joy fell into step beside me, talking as we walked. When we arrived at the overnight site, she sidled up to me as I was unrolling my blanket roll.

"Mouse," she began softly. "Could you talk to me about becoming a Christian?"

I was grateful for the darkness which covered my strong reaction. I was both thrilled and terrified. This was my first experience of leading someone to faith in Christ and I didn't know how to do it. I had been trained in formulas, but this felt different. Joy was a person in my care. She was asking me, a person just two years her senior. I felt weak.

I turned to her, "Of course. How about tonight after campfire?"

That night we walked together under the stars, and in my stumbling way I tried to explain something I could barely articulate myself. I had been so immersed in the language and culture of faith. Joy's life experience was in stark contrast. What would it mean for her to follow Christ?

Two days later, we gathered around the bus that was to return the campers to Cleveland. As counselors, we were poignantly aware of the contrast between this week in camp and the city streets to which they were returning. Joy approached me, put her arms around my neck and whispered a sad goodbye. Before boarding the bus, she put an envelope into my hand, her eyes bright with tears. After the bus pulled away, I opened the envelope. In it was a red ribbon with a letter thanking me and asking me to keep the ribbon as a token of her new life in Christ.

We wrote during the winter following, but soon lost touch. I kept the ribbon.

My two years on the Caravan were formative in my spiritual life. The six of us became a tightly knit team, meeting together for prayer and conversation all summer long. During one of these intimate gatherings Rachel, our director, introduced us to the poetry of a British priest called "Father Andrew." It was my first exposure to a mystical tradition and I felt strangely drawn to the tender passionate intimacy of Father Andrew's cry for his Beloved in page after page of his poems. This tiny volume is still on my shelf, dog-eared and held together by tape. The last poem in the booklet captures the sense of his poetry which would reverberate in me for years to come. Here are the first lines:

> *Jesu, Jesu, Jesu,*
> *All my being flows to Thee,*
> *As the white moon draws the sea*
> *So my life's tide yields to Thee*
> *In this mighty Mystery*
> *Jesu, Jesu, Jesu.*[2]

There are many times now when the cry, "Jesu, my being flows to Thee," comes flooding up unconsciously in my spontaneous prayer. Such an impulse was a portent of a later ripened experience of God the Beloved. The seeds were planted long before the fruit appeared.

four

Wheaton, My Third Parent

WHEATON WAS A third parent to me—Wheaton as a college, and Wheaton as the surrounding evangelical community. Town and gown were not so separate in 1938 when I moved there as an eight-year-old girl. A town with a population of 8,000 could more easily be dominated by the college than is the case today, with its 55,000 inhabitants.

There was a distinct ethos about Wheaton for our family, after years in rural New England. We were received in a climate of warmth and friendliness: people spoke to us on the streets. Accustomed to Yankee reticence and reserve, we were attracted by the new openness and feeling. It was to change our lives.

Our move to Wheaton fulfilled a dream of my father's. Long before, he had carried on a brief correspondence with Charles Blanchard, second president of Wheaton College. Blanchard was known for his impassioned stand against secret societies, and had built this prohibition into the principles of the college his father had founded. My father was a relatively new convert to Christianity, and as a Mason was troubled about Blanchard's published articles against the evils of freemasonry and similar secret societies. My father took it upon himself to write Blanchard a letter for advice. An answer came back, signed in Blanchard's own hand. Dad became convinced that his Masonic connection was a hindrance to his spiritual life, so he severed his connection with all Masonic bodies—leaving behind an investment of several hundred dollars in life memberships. My father was so impressed with President Blanchard that he determined to send his children to Wheaton College some day.

The influences of my home were now being reinforced by school and community. It was a powerful combination, and I was not alone in being affected by it. Wheaton wrapped its protective arms around us all, shielding us from "the world." We were warned of sin (most clearly identified by drinking, smoking, dancing, movies and sex) and called to repentance.

One overwhelming image captures the essence of those Wheaton years for me. It is the altar call. There were hundreds of them (some preachers thought it a grievous omission to neglect even one opportunity to invite sinners to repent). A particular occasion lingers in my memory. It was a cold February night. As was customary, the college was having its semi-annual "evangelistic services."

I was eleven years old at the time, and was sitting in a pew with my friends. I scarcely remember the sermon, preached by Howard Ferrin. I only remember the final hymn. We were standing, hundreds of bodies close together in the college chapel, singing softly. Between each stanza, Dr. Ferrin spoke in loving, imploring, tender tones. My heart melted.

"Softly and tenderly Jesus is calling," the congregation sang slowly, beseechingly. "Come home, come home." The lady in front of me bowed her head, her lips moving in silent prayer. I felt a movement in the pew behind me. Out of the corner of my eye, I saw a young man slip out and down the aisle, his face working in obvious emotion.

"Praise God," the evangelist said quietly, with deep feeling. "Is there another?" Everything quiet and dignified, worshipful. No shouting, no raucous noise, no emotional display. "Don't resist the Spirit of God. He's calling you. There'll never be a better time."

I had my theology straight. I was "saved" and baptized, so these appeals did not apply to me. But there was always a second invitation—for the backsliding sinner, the lamb in the fold but gone astray. In this category, I felt I fit.

I swallowed my pride, impulsively burst out onto the aisle, and walked to the front—careless of the many eyes upon me, little caring that people might be surprised that a minister's daughter needed spiritual help.

Back in the "inquiry room" where I was sent, a college student was assigned to "deal with me." I only wanted to be left alone, and she was too solicitous, too concerned. For weeks thereafter I avoided her on campus when I saw her. It seemed as though she didn't understand why I had come forward. I didn't know clearly myself. I stuttered, "I want to be sure I am saved." More than one Christian tradition has recognized the importance of "confirming" a young persons' earlier religious experience or status at that age.

I was crossing the threshold into a Wheaton-defined world. Whereas earlier I had looked for full acceptance by my parents, I now was searching for inclusion by this third much larger parent—Wheaton, and all that it embodied. The enveloping warmth of religious experience in this atmosphere drew me powerfully and spoke of a God who was a kindly father.

How could I feel included in this Wheaton world? It wasn't like joining the Catholic church, or being bar mitzvahed, or being inducted into the Army. There were no clear boundaries or formal entrance requirements for this amorphous spiritual community. This left me with continual uncertainty. Was I all right? Was I in? Another altar call would raise those doubts afresh. I longed to please this father-like God with all my heart. I marched down that chapel aisle and others like it again and again and again over the next nine years I spent in Wheaton, each time hoping for a rock-like certainty that would ease my distress at not measuring up to the standards held before me.

Although the definitions of this Wheaton world were not clear, there was a distinct atmosphere there in the 1940s, heavily influenced by the presence of the college and its fourth president, V. Raymond Edman. It was an atmosphere characterized by a powerful blend of Holiness and Calvinist influences bound together by Pietism. Wheaton College's founder, Jonathan Blanchard, had originally decided on a loose connection with the Congregational church for the precise reason that this tie offered the greatest degree of institutional flexibility. In the absence of a single strong tradition like some of its sister Christian denominational schools, Wheaton College found itself developing an eclectic brand of evangelicalism.

The Holiness influence came through Edman's attachment to and reverence for Charles Finney, his ties with the Christian and Missionary Alliance, and his own personal warmth and emotionality. His wife was even more so inclined. I was awed, as a teenager, listening to her preach and pray and agonize. I had never heard such impassioned preaching; her strong emotion made me afraid of her.

The custom of semi-annual revival services was another mark of Holiness influence, in part. These services usually included one evening focused on the importance of the Holy Spirit. However, the position of both school and community was solidly against "speaking in tongues" and similar charismatic or emotional displays.

The Calvinist influence was more evident: the respect for Christian scholarship, the emphasis on "sound theology" and building a rational basis for belief all fit naturally into an academic environment. In addition an intangible Puritan influence came through in the prohibitions against and preoccupation with "worldly" activities and behavior.

These streams of influence came together in a spiritual climate I can only call Pietistic—in its historical nonpejorative sense. The admonitions to personal holiness and experience were constant, and came out in specific teachings on Bible study, and prayer in a daily quiet time, the watermark of spiritual attainment. Neglecting to pray and read the Bible daily constituted spiritual failure.

A fiery young British evangelist, Stephen Olford, held the college student body spellbound for seven days of chapel messages in January of 1948. He directed us in the details of the "quiet time", suggesting we use notebooks to record our morning and evening meditations on Scripture. "Impression without expression is depression," he thundered. A new sound system had just been installed in the chapel; even without it, Rev. Olford would have been able to make himself heard in the remotest corner. With its assistance, none could escape. I was profoundly affected by his messages that week. Along with perhaps seventy-five per cent of the student body, I began a little "quiet time" notebook.

Over the years the issue of "quiet time" was to haunt me, and others I in turn influenced. It was a habit hard to maintain in a disciplined way and I found that its satisfying fruits were not guaranteed. I never could understand a certain perversity in my life which made it seem the days went best when I forgot the ritual. I labeled those occasions as discrepant exceptions to the rule and went loyally on with the habit, until one day I decided to risk finding out what my heart would teach me, not my head. If I loved God, I would talk to him often, wouldn't I? It was refreshing not to be bound by legalism, to feel the liberating cords of love instead.

Legalism is the unintended legacy I received from the Wheaton world. Whereas my mentors propounded the paradox of law and grace, judgment and mercy, it was easier for me to absorb the God of high demands than the God of unrelenting encompassing love. I failed to grasp these grand, overriding principles, which were the emphasis and intention of my teachers, and instead ingested the detailed formulas pointing the way to the victorious Christian life. I was young and impressionable, unable to sift out the subtleties in the messages delivered from church and chapel pulpits.

I agonized over the exhortations to witness as a "Christian responsibility." If I were truly saved, why wasn't I talking about it joyously to others, and snatching them from the path to destruction? Since I had no logical answer that would stand the test of my teachers, I figured the problem must be with me. When I could dredge up no known unwillingness to share my faith, I decided to simply plunge in and do it. I cringe, when I remember the Sunday afternoon I went calling on total strangers in the Wheaton area, ostensibly to invite them to church, but hoping to engage them in a spiritual conversation. Being socially shy and awkward, I found the whole experience to be excruciatingly painful. I could not bring myself to continue.

It would take another two decades before I would grasp the spirit of witnessing. It occurred in the wake of six months of intense and liberating therapy. My enthusiasm for that life-changing experience was evangelistic as I talked about my experience. I glowed with radiance, and the words tumbled out in profusion and authentic power. Something tangible and real had happened to me, and I lost my shyness for the moment as I got wrapped up in the experience again in the retelling.

While I got lost in the tangle of legalisms on an emotional level, intellectually I was free-thinking compared to the rigid fundamentalism of the 1940s. Wheaton scholars ventured to criticize a literal interpretation of the Genesis account of creation occurring in six days. These "days" could be understood as enormous geologic periods, Professor Paul Wright told us. This reputation of moving toward a more "open-minded evangelicalism" has persisted (with important exceptions in the late 1960s and early 1970s), as evidenced by an October, 2000, *Atlantic Monthly* article examining this trend in the wider world of evangelicalism and using Wheaton as a generally positive example.

Even in my time, Wheaton represented the finest in the scholarly evangelical tradition of the mid-twentieth century—with its genteel reasoned approach, the richness and resonance proceeding directly from the balance of mingled traditions. The daily college chapel became a national crossroads for the most literate and articulate preachers and scholars of the evangelical world of the day. Unfortunately, they always began their messages the same way: "I'm happy (honored, privileged, humbled) to be here on the campus of the greatest Christian college in the country." (Or was it "world?") We grew accustomed to seeing ourselves at the top of the evangelical hierarchy.

Unconsciously, and without malice, we looked down on other colleges, the ones that accepted the students Wheaton turned away. We learned to be critical ("discerning?") of the less-intellectual, the more emotionally expressive, groups and movements. There were whole categories to be disposed of with a shrug of the shoulder: Bible schools, dispensationalists, charismatics, socially concerned liberals, evolutionists, divorcees, Communists, people making money off religion, missionaries in dowdy clothes and square-heeled shoes, actresses—even when converted they were still suspect. If college is supposed to develop a critical mind, it certainly succeeded with many of us. And we were so well-intentioned about it. I am inclined to defend myself, remembering how earnestly I thought I was right. Wheaton taught me to fear the fate of narrow-mindedness. But Wheaton itself was too closed an environment for me to see how small a world it was. Its connections entwined themselves around me for years to come.

Life in a Christian Prep School

My life on the college campus began in 1942 when I entered Wheaton College Academy, prep school for the college at the time. As a small private boarding school, it was able to shelter me from certain situations faced by my contemporaries in public high school. The prohibition against movies, dancing, and card playing precipitated the creation of a complete array of permissible social activities which insulated us from the secular culture. This meant that I didn't notice the absence of *verboten* activities. Instead, with a frenzy, we turned in upon our tiny world and organized substitute activities. Cheerleading and roller skating were female substitutes for dancing, and were considered fitting adjuncts to male sports. Parties and clubs took the place of movies, with a frenetic emphasis on dating and the accompanying necking and petting on which adults looked askance.

Secretly, I would have loved to go to the movies. The prohibition against them must mean something, since so many of my fellow students took pains to break the rules. My brother, four years older, felt repelled by these strictures, and found his way to resist them along with a cadre of others familiar with Wheaton cinema's back door entrance.

I felt too awkward to consider dancing as an option, although I often fantasized myself caught up in some man's arms and whirled around the floor. Since it was the sexual aspect of dancing which was emphasized in the taboo against it, this aspect preoccupied me. Dancing as an art form, or a creative expression, was unknown and

The Wheaton Years

8 years old

12 years old

16 years old

incomprehensible to me. The irony became that prohibitions against sex made it all the more enticing. It was a force to be ignored at one's peril.

I had the opportunity to observe that sexual innocence in a girl can leave her vulnerable to a harder fall. When I was fifteen, a college senior named Grace came to room at our house. Grace was a model of chaste behavior, wearing her long black hair in braids wound around her head in a fashion approved by her straight-laced mother. Grace's boyfriend Will came often to visit, which gave me a chance to see courting in action up close. As they sat on the porch of a spring evening, I would scurry past them quickly, then dart into the living room to watch them furtively from behind the window curtains.

Grace's demure appearance veiled a passionate flame within, easily kindled by Will's eager advances. Grace would perch on his lap, her soft womanly body sinking into his embrace, as they talked and cuddled into the night until curfew. It was not surprising when they announced their plans for marriage, but it was unsettling when they set a date much earlier than first announced.

I remember the morning Grace's mother arrived to help Grace put on her white velvet wedding gown. Her mother seemed distressed, as she slid the gown over Grace's mounding belly. "You're getting so fat," she complained. Six months later, a baby was born. My mother and father shook their heads sorrowfully. The message was clear: sexuality is dangerous and must be avoided. I kept my peace. I was a little envious of Grace's demonstrative passion.

SCREWING UP THE DATING SCENE

Dating was a major preoccupation on the Academy campus. It was not an arena in which I could compete. I was a year younger than my classmates, and slow in physical development, as well. The result was extremely distorting. I hid in religious piety and in academic accomplishment—both of them safe havens.

There were compensatory experiences for me, moments when I could safely enter the social domain. Some encounters with young men in high school opened a door of hope. I remember feeling a momentary bond with Ernie, bespectacled and on the margins of social life, who confided in me as we walked together one evening that he loved to walk in the rain. I figured that made us soul mates. And Bob, my chem lab partner, who once drove me home from an Academy function, was softly gentle and attentive, making me feel like a princess. I had sequential crushes on any boy who paid me a minimal level of attention.

It was not until my junior year at the Academy that I officially entered puberty with the arrival of my first menstrual period. I had tried to hurry things along my sophomore year by buying my first bra with my own money—my mother didn't believe in such things. Also, she could fairly point out that there was little need for such a garment in my case. It never occurred to her to pay attention to my bodily development, and consequently I felt bound to compensate by focusing on my slowly emerging profile as I imitated cheerleading poses, arching my back provocatively before the full-length mirror in the bedroom.

In May, I helped plan a roller skating party for our Girls' Athletic Association. I made it through most of the evening; then came the dreaded slow skate. Lights dimmed. Everyone began pairing off. I watched the graceful movements as a boy would swoop down past the line of waiting girls and reach for someone's hand, and swoosh!—off they went across the floor entwined lightly together. In terror, I gradually realized that one by one, girls were being picked off the line. Even the fact that some pairs had to be two girls (not enough boys), did not allay my growing panic. Then I saw him—Mark—heading for me, the lone girl left. I was paralyzed. Mark was only a sophomore (and that made a difference) and I carried an impression of him as not being cool. Astonishingly, I was transferring my own self-deprecation onto him. But I was desperate, and there was no time to equivocate. He came rushing toward me at a terrific pace—and encircled my waist with his arm. "Oh, no," I remonstrated prudishly, and made him change position to cross-arm skating. It was somehow a bit more "pure."

Oh, how we skated. I was trembling, uncertain. But he was so skillful, so sure. I floated on the thrilling memory of that brief moment when his arms had encircled me.

That same year, at fifteen years of age, I had my first date. I belonged to a club for commuter girls. Students living in the girls' and boys' dorms had periodic dorm parties. To equalize the commuter girls' opportunities for coed events, we formed a club whose sole function was to plan parties to which we invited boys. It was to be a progressive dinner, ending up at my home. I chose a red-headed boy named Dan.

The final entertainment in our living room was a Truth or Consequences Show, emceed by Conrad, a feisty little Italian fellow I was to come to view with heightened respect in the course of the evening. Dan's and my turn came before the mike, and as maneuvered, we "failed to tell the truth," and so had to "pay the consequences." Right there, on my very first date, Conrad unwittingly put his foot in it. "Eunice," he directed, "This is your consequence: tell us about your first date."

I was rarely at a loss for words, but the complexity of this moment undid me. I was painfully self-conscious about this being my first date. I had tried hard all evening to act experienced, sophisticated, not to make any mistakes—walk on the inside of the sidewalk, let Dan open doors, be demure, chatty, interested in him—I had read the articles in *Ladies Home Journal* well.

I stood there, staring at Conrad—how could he do this to me?—wanting the floor to swallow me up. I gulped, started to squeak, stopped in red-faced discomfort.

Conrad scrutinized me for a long moment, seeing me splutter and try to speak. There was only an instant's hesitation before he announced importantly, "I've changed my mind. Instead, make love to your date in French."

I looked at Conrad with inexpressible gratitude. He knew I was good in languages, and had placed me safely at home in the realm of the intellect, and in French. My date understood not a word, as I rattled off clusters of French phrases about anything that came to mind.

That was not the only time Conrad showed extraordinary understanding toward me. One day before History class, as we sat around in the classroom talking, Connie nudged me with his elbow. "Hey! Eunice." He lowered his voice. "Saw your brother last night at the Prince Castle."

I looked up, startled, wary. My brother was rebelling against the strictness of his home and community standards, which meant doing terrible things like going to movies, smoking and drinking. In that sheltered monolithic community of Wheaton, such behavior was easily discovered and quickly condemned. What would Connie say next? Some of my classmates had made "knowing" remarks, and I could sense a distance and disapproval developing. A minister's family isn't allowed much leeway from group norms.

Connie put his two fingers to his lips in imitation of holding a cigarette, and pretended to take a long draw. Then his face broke into a grin, and he winked at me. His eyes told me, "It's O.K. I know, and it's O.K."

My whole body untensed, and a rush of appreciation for Connie came over me. I had a feeling Conrad was sowing a few wild oats of his own. But he had showed me love where the "righteous" judged.

In his restlessness, my brother Philip begged our parents for permission to join the Navy four months before his eighteenth birthday. A farewell service was held at church, as was the custom during World War II for anyone entering the armed forces. Phil's six-foot-six frame towered over my father's slight stature. Dad turned to Phil, looked up at him with dignity and tenderness, and gave him a simple and impressive send-off: "Son, remember Jesus Christ."

Set free from the confinements of home, Phil began to experiment in the ways of the world. I knew this was risky, and that my parents were apprehensive, but my loyalty to him made me more lenient in my judgments. Although we had fought a lot when younger, in recent years he had treated me with special attention upon occasion, patiently throwing a softball until I learned to hit it squarely. He played ping pong with me until I mastered sufficient skill to occasionally beat him, which dampened his interest.

*My brother Philip
with our parents 1944*

*Home on leave 1944
Philip and Eunice*

Just when I would have benefited most from his masculine companionship, my brother disappeared into the maw of the Navy, and into a life of his own to be lived thousands of miles from me and his parents for the rest of his life. The rebel in the family was gone. I could see the worried look in my mother's eyes when she talked of her son. I felt her gaze on me with the unspoken message, "You'll not disappoint us too, will you?" I didn't need to say anything. I only needed to wear the good girl role I had already perfected. I missed my brother. I was acutely aware that my parents' focus was now fixed on me. I began to feel like an only child.

There were bright spots—Phil's visits on leave when I would walk proudly down the street beside him. His tall uniformed frame was hard to ignore. It was as close as I could get to the experience of relating to a male peer and feeling feminine. He gave me a Navy middy blouse to wear, a fashion in vogue during war years since many sailors sent these blouses to their girlfriends.

One day a package arrived in the mail from the West Coast. Phil had been in the Pacific, and had spent one weekend on leave in Shanghai. He had bought me a beautiful Chinese hand-sewn, white satin blouse, with intricately braided trim, and a long red and white taffeta skirt, carefully tailored, with matching head scarf. With it came a poem he had written. The first lines began:

> *Rose of Cathay, I found you*
> *Beside a garden wall;*
> *In Oriental splendor...*
> *So red, so pure, so tall.*

A note came with the gift:

> *This poem goes with the Christmas present. I hope that you like it. The title is also the name of your gift, my own idea, of course. Send me a picture of yourself in the dress.*

I tried on the outfit, standing in front of a full-length mirror in the bedroom. I turned slowly around, viewing my profile from every angle. That week I made an appointment at a photographer's studio to have my picture taken. When the prints came back, I saw that for a moment in time, my brother had turned me into an elegant lady. I was thrilled.

Growing Up in Wheaton College

Somehow I made it into college without ever having had a "real" date, i.e., one initiated by the male partner. I was already a confirmed spinster deep down inside, as well as a still-hopeful young woman. Other girls had "hope chests." I called them "despair barrels."

I had no idea that in terms of cultural standards, I could have competed in the social arena. When I looked into the mirror I failed to see my well-proportioned body, the bright-eyed gaze crinkling with a hint of mischief. Instead my mind concocted a distorted image of myself as someone out of style, out of step, and unsure. I wore clothes to conceal, not reveal, honestly unaware of my potential for sensuous arousal.

My first opportunity to date came during freshman orientation days. I was sitting with an informal group of new freshmen one afternoon. We were playfully, tentatively, flirting with one another. As we got up to go our separate ways, Barry turned to me and asked me for a date.

Inexplicably, I turned him down. A tumult of internal contradictions arose within me. This was my chance to enter the dating scene, a scene which was superficial in character, depending on "fitting in" by external attributes. I had learned the lesson of Proverbs 31:30 well: "Charm is deceitful and beauty is vain, but she who fears the Lord shall be praised." My heart shouted back that charm and beauty were *everything*. They mattered. Barry came from farm country in Nebraska. In my mind I labeled him as a hayseed. I was ashamed that I had succeeded in charming a country boy, obviously not one destined to be part of the campus "in" group. I was ashamed, but also confused. I could not admit to myself that I had decided no one would want to date me. The "no" was already on the tip of my tongue before anyone could ask.

I took a course in Adolescent Psychology my freshman year. The text differentiated three groups: early, middle, and later adolescence. When we came to the chapter on later adolescence—eighteen to twenty-four year olds—the class members pricked up their ears. This was about them. No one seemed to notice that I was still lost in reverie pondering the descriptions of the middle adolescent, for I was sixteen and hopelessly slow in finding my way through the dilemmas of that stage. I wondered if I would always feel too young to compete with life.

I concentrated on my studies, while maintaining strong ties with Pioneer Girls, becoming a volunteer staff person on campus directing the activities of women students who took on local clubs as a Christian service project. My summers became oases of camping, where my adolescent self could feel grown up as I counseled campers.

Dating was still outside the frame of my comprehension. I managed the dorm party the winter of my junior year by inviting the brother of a friend from camp days, someone as enamored of camping as I. This was safe. Many years later my mother told me other opportunities to date had presented themselves to me, but each time I had shunted them off. She recounted an occasion when a young man at our Glen Ellyn church had showed me some attention, even asked me to accompany him somewhere, and I had refused while standing at the train station in Glen Ellyn with my parents. I groaned aloud at hearing this. "Why didn't you tell me I was doing this?" I complained.

Mother just stared at me for a moment, flustered at my question. I suddenly sensed her own awkwardness. She was as ignorant as I was in encouraging the blossoming of young womanhood. I saw the worry in her eyes, the fear of my sexuality. I could tell that she had been a little relieved at my lack of response to these overtures from young men. I was left on my own to bumble through the maze of interactions with men, some frustrating, others comical.

There was a little of both in my encounter with Bill, my friend Nancy's brother, who approached me one day outside the college dining hall. We had known each other from the awkward days of my early adolescence through college. I admired his skill at the piano at church. I had observed his sequence of love affairs in our tiny young people's group, wistfully hoping for special attention. I watched him go off to join the Navy, and return to be part of my college class, though three years older. I was resigned to seeing myself more as a sister. I had long ago dismissed the notion that I was an appropriate target for romantic attention.

Here he was, standing in the dining hall doorway, asking if I'd go to the church banquet the following month. I said I hadn't decided yet about going to the banquet. After all, banquets cost money, and this one was formal, and it sometimes appeared to be a waste of time to dress up in a pretty floor-length gown and then sit there with a string of girls—the unsought and unwanted, in my eyes.

Bill pursued the issue, rather persistently, I thought. I had the impression he was selling tickets. I was even faintly annoyed. "I haven't decided yet," I told him. We continued to chat; Bill was a good friend and always voluble. Then it came time for him to leave. "Well, I really do want an answer," he said, mildly irritated, "because if you say no, I'd like to ask someone else."

My jaw dropped in amazement. "Oh!" I said stupidly. Each word came out separately like a telegram. "Are-you-asking-*me*-to-go-to-the-banquet-with-*you*?"

Bill looked at me, mouth agape. I felt myself shriveling in size before his gaze. "Yes," he responded dryly. The tone of voice told me any joyful anticipation he might have felt had now subsided.

"Oh, I'd love to," I replied. And went upstairs to my dorm room kicking myself.

It kept happening this way—not often—but every once in a while. I would get surprised by someone's attention because I had genuinely decided that no one wanted me. And through it all, I had the gall to be fussy. A rather pimply shy boy invited me to the biggest event of the year when I was a junior in college, and I held him off for a week before I accepted, saying, "I might be busy" that evening—which was ridiculous. No one on campus ever planned anything on the night of the Washington Banquet. But if I was going to date, I wanted it to be at least the class president or someone equally deserving. A thread of feeling that I was special lay there amid the tangled skein of self-deprecation.

Falling in Love

Dramatic changes took place in my senior year. I was president of my literary society and, as such, a member of the "Inter Lit Council." I was assigned to work together with a junior named Carlton in designing a special chapel service around the theme of social concern. My willingness to struggle over every word, every nuance, until it was nearly perfect, impressed Carl. Events transpired to continue to throw us into contact. It soon became obvious that we both were enjoying the long hours of labor on this project. The more interest in me Carlton showed, the more important I saw it was to labor even longer hours over those nuances.

We fell in love. This was it: what the magazines wrote about, the forbidden movies dramatized, my girl friends confided in hushed and excited tones over the telephone. The emotions and responses fit exactly—a cookie cutter teenage infatuation. At last I was like everyone else.

November was a flurry of intensified contact. First it was planning the chapel service, then it was holding post mortems—any excuse to stay in touch. In the midst of this, Carlton was elected president of our Interlit Council, which meant he suddenly needed a date for the annual Interlit banquet coming up soon. A studious sort, he had not planned to attend the social function. With profuse apologies for the lateness of his invitation, he approached me. "I know you probably have had lots of other invitations," he began. Was he kidding? I had one invitation, which I had accepted. It was humiliating to admit, but I knew that when the Council President thought that any of the Literary Society presidents might not receive a spontaneous invitation, he arranged one. I was positive this was the case for me, although the invitation came so far in advance of the event that it did not appear contrived. So I had to turn Carl down, more disappointed than I could express. Imagine my surprise when Carl walked into the banquet with Jessie, who had once been a part of my infamous junior high Tuggies Club, now a tall, charming woman. As Carl passed me in the banquet hall, our eyes met for an instant, then quickly dropped lest we betray our preference for being together.

By this time, Carl and I were an "item" among the members of the Council, a situation not lost on my date who vaguely acknowledged this with some embarrassment when he dropped me off at the end of the evening. "I know you would rather have been with someone else." "Oh no," I falsely protested. But I let him drop me off at my dorm early.

By Christmas, Carlton and I were spending more time together. Going home for Christmas that year was a wrench; it was also exciting to have this news of a love interest to share with family. My father listened to my story with obvious pleasure and pride. Mother was guardedly encouraging.

Letters from Carl began arriving. Writing was a more fluid mode of expression for our blossoming relationship. We could leave the unspoken and implied thoughts which every lover reads into and between the lines. On Christmas eve, a package arrived. Carl had gone to special trouble to get a jeweler to put a rush on the engraving of an ID bracelet, a gift which signaled a degree of "ownership." I was someone's girlfriend.

A tiny note from my Grandmother puts the occasion into perspective:

> *Yes, dear, you got a bracelet. That is enough at present.*
> *You don't need a diamond yet. Don't hurry.*

How did she know?

I came upon a small cache of yellowed scrids of paper in my archives recently. There were stubs to a basketball game we attended together; his witty invitation to the major social event of the college year, the Washington Banquet; a note saying "To My Mouse" accompanying a single red rose on Valentine's Day.

One night when our plans to meet for dinner were misunderstood, I accepted his apology with grace, and thought no more about it until a note arrived in my mailbox the next day:

> *A beautiful woman is pleasing to the eye;*
> *A good woman is pleasing to the heart;*
> *The one is a jewel;*
> *The other is a treasure.*

I pondered over those lines a long time. I was pleased to be seen as a good woman, pleasing to the heart. Faintly, far down inside, an irritating little question chafed: "Wouldn't it also be nice to be a beautiful woman, pleasing to the eye as well?"

I was to have that too. As president of my literary society, I had to have my picture taken for the yearbook. Carl asked to accompany me to the session with the photographer. Frantically, I pawed through my closet for something to wear. I decided to call on my friend, Lee, who had a beautiful black velvet top with a low neckline. The picture-taking session went well. On the way back to the dorm, Carl turned to me and asked, "Should I tell you how beautiful you looked today?"

My reply was swift and cutting. "No, and I hope you never will." I tried to make it sound like a joke, embarrassed by a compliment. I refused to believe the mirror he held up before me.

I soon learned to respect Carl's intense concentration on his studies. He was a conscientious, bright, pre-med student, who spent hours in the biology lab. One night he took the time to carefully explain to me the intricacies of the pig's ear he was dissecting. I tried very hard to care, but I was much more intrigued with Carl's ear than that of the pig.

One wintry evening after church, Carlton took me to his Aunt Alice's house for cocoa and conversation. I sensed I was on display before a member of his extended family. As we sat around the dining table, talking about food, Carl abruptly turned toward me with a sharp question. He tried to speak casually, but his words came out with all the force of a proposal. "By the way, can you cook?" I felt caught, a deer facing the headlights of his intense gaze. I pictured myself in a kitchen, wearing an apron, and surrounded by small children. Cooking! I went weak. I was not only undomestic; I was anti-domestic. I had determined long ago never to emulate my mother or her role. This effectively eliminated cooking and cleaning from my repertoire of skills.

I tried to muster up bravery to reply, but my voice was uncertain and thin. "I am learning," was all I could manage. In my next letter home, I wrote, "I'd like to learn to cook."

We took a walk together one evening after a church date. We were milking every moment out of the time before the 10 P.M. curfew in my dorm. Impulsively, and a bit awkwardly, Carl grabbed my hand, holding it tightly.

The Moment had arrived. At last, I had something to say "no" to, while my heart was yelling "yes." I jerked my hand, trying to get it free, but Carl's grip was strong. "Let me go," I begged, and silently cursed my tongue. Never were mind and heart more at odds with each other.

"Why?" Carl wanted to know. Our bodies were close, and my voice trembled as I spoke. "Only when God places my hand in someone's." Carl was impressed. Most girls mouthed slogans, but when the moment came, leaned back and enjoyed it. When he left me that night, it was with his fervent admiration. So I had won. But I lost. I went upstairs to my dorm room incredibly frustrated and confused.

By March, to my chagrin and confusion, other men began to ask me out. I was in a quandary, elated by the attention, but reluctant to be with anyone else except Carlton. Since we had no spoken agreement to go steady—the dating rules were cast in stone in that campus subculture—I felt I should accept an invitation to a concert one Friday evening. Carlton always seemed to be studying, even on weekends. Somehow Carlton learned of my date, and as he left me that afternoon, said dryly, "Have a good time tonight."

Carlton's "spies" reported back to him that I had apparently been enjoying my escort quite openly. When he saw me a day or two later, his comments were frosty. I was at a loss to explain how false my coquettish behavior had been, trying to cover up my desire to be with Carlton.

Gradually, I was seeing less and less of Carlton. The clutching fear of being left behind was almost more than I could bear. I began stalking the biology lab; I tried to second guess his schedule and when he would most likely appear for meals; I waited in vain for him to buzz my room and ask me out. Like a thud, my heart told me he was losing interest, which made me more clinging than ever.

One night we were together again, walking across campus. I sidled up close, letting my hand brush provocatively against his. He wouldn't take it. Finally, in desperation, I placed my hand within his. Of course, he couldn't understand, and there was small gratification from his touch. I couldn't understand either. I only knew I was losing him, and I needed to hang on.

Over spring break, Carl went on an archaeological expedition in the Grand Canyon. I stayed at school with other seniors cramming for May comprehensive exams. When Carl returned, he gave me a woven Navajo rug mat. I don't know why, for we both knew everything was over.

One more major event loomed: an Interlit Memorial Day party we had been planning together. It was to be an elaborate and inventive Treasure Hunt, which required us to place clues in obscure and arcane places all over campus. Inexorably, the day drew near. The gloom settling around our dying relationship was accompanied by a subtle but distinct feeling that the treasure hunt was going to be a colossal flop. Few students were signing up.

Carl and I went out late one night to plant the clues. I followed him like a pathetic forlorn puppy, looking for a crumb of affection or attention. Carl was distant and depressed about the impending failure of his plan and scornful of me. One clue, destined for the top of a lamp post along a campus walkway, required Carl to hoist me onto his shoulders to put the clue securely in place. Even this brief physical proximity failed to reignite the flame that had been quenched and smoking for some time. I felt frantic and incredibly sad. The magic had evaporated.

Soon after, we finally acknowledged to one another that it was over between us. I ran back to my room and collapsed on my bunk bed in tears. My trusty roommate, Ginny, turned around to face me. Her words were trenchant and tender. "Eunice, what did that brute do to you?" I loved Ginny for that.

Carlton was now out of my life, and no one else was taking his place. For years, he appeared in my dreams as an icon of my first love. I had enjoyed a taste of college romance, but only a taste. The assumptions common to college women in that era—that I would graduate with a diploma in one hand and an engagement ring on the other—were crushed. Very shortly I would be cast upon the unmarked sea of life without the guiding parameters of campus culture, and without the rich opportunities for engaging with peers—male and female. A long loneliness fell like a shroud upon me. I did not yet know much of solitude, in a spiritual sense, but there were indications of my hunger. I used to spend Sunday afternoons—a hauntingly dead time on campus—in the shadowy recesses of a stone cathedral-like Methodist church downtown. I would sit in the pews of a side chapel, watching the dying rays of sunset filter through the stained glass window. Then I would play the piano, sometimes for a very long time. Those times became a tryst with God.

I continued to find such sacred places in the years that followed. In the middle of the work day, I would hurry across the Chicago Loop to the Chicago Temple where I listened to the noontime organ concerts, pouring out my secret longings in prayer. One noonday, "What a friend we have in Jesus," reverberated through the quiet dark, piercing the wall of resistance. Perhaps Jesus' friendship was enough. A dam broke within, and love flooded in. It was a holy moment of surrender in that hour. I had little insight into my impoverished sense of self, but the hymn brought genuine comfort.

For three years after my graduation, a suburban forest preserve across the highway from my lodgings became hallowed ground where I walked and sat and prayed on Saturday afternoons. One day I had a palpable sense of the Divine Presence as I walked. I firmly believed God was telling me I was to remain single for life and that he would be my lover. Choking with agony and gasping for life, I thought I could surrender my intense longing for a mate.

How little I imagined of what lay in store for me. So I lay still on the potter's wheel, and hoped that the Divine Potter knew best. But I wondered sometimes.

five

Mirror to the Self

*"With the mirror we...
find a relationship to our own soul."*
                    Marion Woodman, *Addiction to Perfection*[1]

GRADUATION FROM COLLEGE involves wrenching changes for most people—the abrupt loss of a community of peers, the necessity of becoming independently responsible for earning a livelihood, and the bewildering plunge into a nine-to-five work world. I cushioned the blow of this transition by taking a position in an organization I knew intimately: Pioneer Girls. Working with the strong women who had been drawn to this work with girls gave me a mirror of my own developing feminine qualities.

I was already familiar with the contours of this women's world from my years in camp, giving me a built-in community of support, and developing my leadership skills. I learned that where there are no men to automatically assume positions of leadership, women are competent to direct a program, keep a sailboat in repair, perform in public, and negotiate with tradesmen.

I had begun eight summers before as a shy loner on the fringe of camp activities, but quickly emerged as a central figure, a star. I developed a distinct persona, performing zany antics in front of groups. I was never without my tattered red beanie dubbed my "Personality," and a small red notebook called my "Brains," containing essential lists of skits, songs and campfire talks ready for use whenever I was called upon. I earned a reputation as a "character" and made the most of it. It didn't occur to me that my absorption with the spotlight might shelter the hollowness of my inner life from my own inspection and that of others. I kept busy talking, planning, taking charge. I didn't stay still long enough to feel the emptiness and yearning that periodically asserted itself. I refused to admit how much I longed for a romantic relationship.

Finding a Soul Mate

I thrived on the intensity of camp life, reveling in the strong emotional connections among counselors and campers which were forged quickly in that atmosphere. One friendship stands out, because it touched me at a deeper level, my first encounter with a woman who became a soul mate. It had occurred at a camp in New Hampshire the summer before my junior year of college.

It was here that I met Jo, a counselor my age from western New York. We were both new to this camp, and worked our way into the team of veteran counselors slowly. Jo, athletically inclined, quickly made her mark in the arena of sports. I gravitated toward the musical parts of the program, and found that Jo had abilities and interests there as well. I observed an enigmatic quality about this dark-haired quiet woman, a combination of studied seriousness—especially when she had a baseball in her hand—and a love of merriment shining from eyes that crinkled with fun. We were aware of each other, but in the beginning we carefully kept our distance.

One day the news came that a wild bobcat had gotten loose from Polar Caves. Since camp was located on the same mountain range as the caves, the exciting and disturbing possibility arose that the bobcat might find its way to the area around our camp.

That night we held our campfire down the slope from the cabin area, at the base of this mountain. After the evening program, Jo and I stood around the fire ready to quash the embers and leave. We were mesmerized by the flames and as we stood watching, Jo suggested, "Wouldn't it be fun to come back and sit around the fire and wait to see if the bobcat appears?"

The thought of confronting a wild beast down there in the ravine was horrifying to me, but the idea of returning to sit around the dying embers of the campfire with Jo was appealing, so we carefully banked the fire and arranged to return after we had tucked our campers safely in bed.

Long into the night we sat under the stars, stirring the fire occasionally whenever it ebbed, and huddling near the flames for warmth. Both of us sensed a deep connection was forming as we quietly talked, oblivious of time. One morning a few days later, the counselors gathered to plan the following week, including days off for staff. Jo caught my eye and gestured, I nodded assent, and we signed up to spend the following Wednesday together. I felt shy pleasure, and a quickening of my spirit as I looked forward to the day.

It was a day to remember, not because it was momentous, but because it so naturally unfolded as a time to do a lot of nothing together. We drove into the town of Plymouth and roamed through the corridors of an impressive looking institution on a hill which we eventually learned was "Plymouth Normal School." We maneuvered our way up the narrow rutted Stinson Lake road to an ancient cemetery where we fingered fading epitaphs on moss-covered gravestones. The road finally crested on a hill where a panoramic view of the Presidential Range opened suddenly before us, the white granite outcroppings looming majestically across the intervening valley. The entire day was filled with little amusements of this sort, interspersed with deepening conversation. I was thrilled to find someone who felt and thought deeply about matters of concern to me. I found myself pouring out my heart to Jo, hesitantly at first—we were both reserved—then more freely.

The day ended at an obscure restaurant on the road to Newfound Lake known for its delicious home-baked blueberry pie. We sat there, stretching out our day's adventure by talking, reluctant to return to camp. After that day, we began spending our daily hour off together as well, reading C. S. Lewis' *Screwtape Letters* aloud to each other while sunning ourselves on the shores of Baker River.

We identified easily with each other's backgrounds. Both of us had been raised within the protection of a predominantly Christian subculture surrounding a college. We shared a similar feeling about our protected past. Both of us had felt a spurt of envy when listening to new converts testify at a revival meeting. We had listened with awe as they described dabbling in forbidden paths of sin before the moment of repentant faith dawned with dramatic force. Such clarity of conversion was unknown to us, who had believed all our lives. Our experience seemed tame by comparison.

Sometimes we talked about men, about dating and marriage. I was envious of Jo whose college boyfriend wrote her during the summer and seemed eager to pursue the relationship to the point of marriage. But Jo's attitude was detached. I knew I could never have been as casual if there had been someone seriously interested in me.

But mostly, we just talked about l-i-f-e. We poured out all our youthful yearnings and thoughts. It was the first relationship to be a mirror to my soul. It was natural to apply Rilke's poetic statement about this friendship:

> *Oh, the comfort,*
> * the inexpressible comfort*
> * of feeling safe with a person,*
> *Having neither to weigh thoughts*
> * nor measure words,*
> *But pouring them all out,*
> * just as they are,*
> *Certain that a faithful hand*
> * will take and sift them,*
> *Keeping what is worth keeping,*
> *And with the breath of kindness,*
> * blow the rest away.*

My friendship with Jo sweetened my life the two summers we were in camp together, and the letters flew between us all winter. In the fall of 1949, I fell in love with Carlton. I wrote excitedly to Jo, whose replies became markedly less frequent. Although we gradually lost touch as our life paths diverged, the flame of soul connection had been kindled. I now knew what it meant to give and receive unconditional love, not the womblike constancy and total acceptance I knew at birth, but a vibrant, intentional, reciprocal caring. It was my first experience of a strong female friendship and it nourished me.

Although I could not have named it at the time, I now recognize that my movement toward soulful attachments with others spoke of a holy longing within which is ultimately the fire of spiritual desire, the restlessness that knows no rest until it is consummated in God the Beloved. At that point in my life, I only knew to look toward marriage for the experience of unconditional love. When my relationship with Carlton petered out, that avenue closed abruptly. I was not ready for the demands of a mature relationship to a marriage partner. In fact, I had no clue as to what "being ready" entailed.

I turned to the safe world of women where I knew I would be nourished. I could peer out through the windows of that world at friends who were moving into marriage, but I remained hidden behind the skirts of my mother, who had subtly conveyed to me the powerful dangers of sexuality. And I was still caught behind the powerful image of my father, whom I adored and idealized.

I plunged into my work at Pioneer Girls with alacrity.

Working With Women

Going to work for Pioneer Girls was a natural choice for me. My contact with the organization from its inception on Wheaton College campus gave me a sense of ownership. It was a young organization yet, which allowed me to participate in shaping its fragile and uncertain future.

I walked into the organization on a privileged level as Publications Manager, an imposing title most recently held by Rachel, my mentor from Caravan days. My desk was located in the executive director's office, which accentuated my position of influence. In addition, for the first three years I lived in the home of one of Pioneer Girls' founders, Carol Erickson Smith, who kept me in touch with the fires of her continuing passion and unflagging vision for the future of Pioneer Girls.

Despite the egalitarian ethos in the early days of the organization, there were distinctions. The big one was between office and field staff. The field representative job was the glamorous one, and the most highly valued. We in the office existed to serve the field staff working on the front lines with club and camp leaders. They trudged in to headquarters every September for the annual Staff Conference, lugging suitcases, sleeping bags, craft samples, and folders of reports and program materials. They were like soldiers back from the front—from nights of sleeping on narrow living room sofas in Muscatine and Pentwater and Ukiah; taking buses to remote villages throughout their vast territories (one person had the entire West Coast); nursing dilapidated cars laden with camp supplies over back roads. They were heroines to us in the office, and we envied and admired them.

One of these field representatives, Joy Mackay, became our national director a year after I came on staff. Under Joy's leadership, we acquired our own headquarters building on Chicago's northwest side. This was a woman who knew about tuck pointing and shelving, and she managed to convince a suspicious and cautious board to invest in ownership. At the same time, Joy invited me to share an attic apartment with her near the new headquarters office.

Field Work

In 1954, Joy asked me to take on a piece of field work. The Colorado field representative was resigning, and the field was small enough to be served by someone who could visit twice a year and direct summer camp. I felt inordinately pleased to be included within the elite ranks of field staff.

I had been writing manuals for leaders; now I had a chance to test their effectiveness in direct personal contact. I took to the work easily, conducting workshops, visiting clubs, and presenting the work to pastors who were eager to incorporate the program in their churches.

I loved directing camp more than anything else. I had been at all kinds of camp sites across the country in my years in Pioneer Girls, but nothing rivaled the breathtaking rustic beauty of camping by mountain streams in the Rockies. Counseling at camp filled a gap in the lives of these women in the 1950s who lived in suburban comfort, their lives eased by the invention of labor-saving devices, but who were eager to find fulfilling avenues for their talents serving outside the home. They became young again in camp, reveling in the experience of working with other women, and developing their gifts as counselors. They conscientiously prepared their Bible "exploration" studies for their cabin group, learned a camp skill like archery or canoeing to teach. After hours they gathered in the dining hall to schmooze with one another—laugh and sing and talk as some of them had not done since college days in the dorm. They came to life, and told me so in any number of ways.

I began to find it increasingly harder to return to headquarters each fall. There were little signs of pressure in the home office. My own job assignment was changed, and there was uneasiness about Joy's style of management which trickled down to me as a person on the second tier of leadership. Soon my field work became a lifeline, allowing me to escape under-the-surface tensions that were creating a growing malaise within me. It was easy to decide to leave for a semester to enroll in Wheaton Graduate School for a Master's degree in Christian education. "When in doubt, go to school," has been my motto on more than one occasion. My thesis would be a treatise on "The Development of Pioneer Girls' Philosophy." No one was better qualified than I to do this research and the original work required. I worked on the degree off and on over a period of three years.

Growing Edges

During one of my semesters off from graduate school, I was sent on a field trip down South. It was a first foray into Southern culture for both Pioneer Girls and for me. My consciousness about civil rights was rousing from its dormancy, making me uncomfortable as I traveled. One Sunday, in South Carolina, I visited a Baptist church out in the country. As the sermon progressed, a nagging uneasiness arose in me, the sole northerner in the congregation. The pastor made a demeaning reference to "those people," adding, with a meaningful glance in my direction, "You know who I mean." At first, I was caught off guard, and hoped fervently that I did *not* know his meaning. Civil unrest was rising in the north as well as the south, but I had not encountered such direct references before and I was shocked.

I came to realize that my presence was regarded with suspicion simply on the basis of being a Yankee—an appellation I had not thought much about before. In Memphis, a kindly matron invited me to her home for lunch where she undertook to set me straight about any erroneous assumptions I might have about the fairness of her dealings with persons of color.

"I have a maid," she said, "and she does her work for me in the morning. And when it is time for lunch, I fix us both a meal. And she eats her lunch there," pointing to the kitchen, "and I have mine in here in the dining room and we talk together."

I could only stare, and swallow hard. There seemed nothing to say in reply. I looked at the doorway between the dining area where we were seated and the kitchen to which she had pointed. I could imagine the two of them carrying on a conversation at that distance, but it made me feel sad.

I was beginning to read books on race—John Howard Griffin's arresting *Black Like Me,* Ralph Ellison's *Invisible Man,* Alan Paton's *Cry, The Beloved Country.* I had an ear cocked to the progress of the Civil Rights movement. I began to realize that there was a kind of Christianity which was committed to racial justice and less insular in its attitudes. I knew I had some thinking to do; I no longer felt safely tucked into a secure world. When I read J. B. Phillips' *Your God is Too Small*, I responded with a characteristic openness of mind and heart. The vessel which held my faith was enlarging to entertain changing views of God and the church.

At the same time, I found myself in an anomalous situation in Pioneer Girls. I began to see problems in Pioneer Girls' immutable doctrine of church sponsorship which tied us closely to local churches. In the beginning, Pioneer Girls had existed on the margins of the church. The vision for a weekday activity program for girls had been birthed by twenty-year-old college students, not by clerics of a denomination. When I was a student leader during college, my focus was on the immediacy of my weekly meetings with girls. My father, like other pastors, were still content to provide programs for young people only on Sunday—Sunday school in the morning, and youth groups in the evening. During World War II a number of extra-church movements arose to supplement what the churches offered. Pioneer Girls' weekday activity program was one of them.

For a long time, these youth movements were seen as marginal, or even as a threat to the church, as young people were siphoned off into appealing programs catering to their interests and needs. Adolescence became a category to be reckoned with.

The baby boom of the 1950s changed everything. Suddenly the churches were full of growing families. Churches responded on two levels: by expansive building programs with modern educational facilities in suburban locations, and by finally incorporating the concept of "total church programming." Now the church needed us and we obligingly reciprocated by adopting the principle of "local church sponsorship" as a tenet of our operations. The rapid numerical and financial growth was heady—for churches, and for Pioneer Girls.

What we failed to see was that the tie to the church constituted a nearly insurmountable obstacle to following any vision which entailed risk. Our success was now tied to the church's destiny, because we could not afford to alienate our church constituency, lest we lose financial support. This meant sluggishness in addressing racial issues beginning to bubble up in certain areas of the work, in one case, where suburban churches were reluctant to join in a leadership training activity with racially diverse urban churches.

We began asking churches to put Pioneer Girls on their annual mission budgets. The demands of a proliferating organization and the increasing financial pressures of making it go—more staff, more publications, more travel expense, a bigger headquarters building, more typewriters and modern office machines—made it inevitable that we would unwittingly favor the mostly suburban churches which could afford us. Subtly, we drifted into comfortable contact with the established church and called it progress, maturing. In all fairness, we didn't see what was happening. But along with the church, we came to be a middle class suburban organization (all right in itself), but turned our backs—inevitably and unconsciously—on the cities, the poor, and the non-white just like everybody else.

It is characteristic of institutions that they reflect society—follow trends, but do not pioneer or set the pace out front. People and pioneer movements are fluid enough to take the risk and lead. Institutions are encumbered by a certain amount of mass and consequent inertia, so that they must conserve their values and move slowly. It is their wisdom, as well as their deficit, that this is true.

I wanted to be on the cutting edge. It is what attracted me to Pioneer Girls—its very marginality. At first I was happy to see Pioneer Girls become part of the mainstream flow of the church, no longer on the periphery, but I grew puzzled as I saw we were vulnerable to the church's weaknesses as well as its strengths. Finally I became restless and critical as the era of the Sixties dawned. I half-jokingly suggested that the organization burn its files and start over again—just to see what might evolve from a fresh look at our society as it was in the Sixties. I did not know what to do with my growing alienation. Meanwhile undercurrents of tension in the organization were beginning to surface and would inflict deeper wounds.

The Death of Illusion

A ground swell of dissatisfaction had been developing with Joy's leadership and was exacerbated by the arrival, in 1956, of Louise Troup, my eighth grade literature teacher, back from a seven-year stint as a missionary in South Africa. Louise extended her furlough in order to become Acting Director while Joy took a sabbatical to complete a bachelor's degree at Wheaton College. When Joy returned a year later, she struggled to find her place in the organization again. Louise had inaugurated an orderly style of leadership which, though more bureaucratic in certain respects, contributed to good feeling among the staff. I welcomed Louise's decision to stay on permanently.

Differences in leadership style soon transmuted into differences in substance. As the rest of us on the staff watched the churning events of those years, we hoped vainly that the organization could sustain the combination of qualities of the two persons at the top. As a person with close personal ties to both women, I felt like screaming for some rapprochement between the two of them. But such was not to be. And Louise had earned the ear of the board, while Joy's relationship to the board bred suspicion and distance.

Then a bomb dropped on my life. In a series of bizarre moves, the vice chairperson of the board, concerned to stem the tide of division developing in the organization, stepped in and forced the resignation of a trusted associate in my department while I was in Colorado doing field work. I was distraught and enraged. My authority had been completely undercut, and I felt helpless.

My head was next on the chopping block; I was summoned back from Colorado to face the vice chairperson. The usual frugality about travel arrangements was superseded by the requirement for haste. So the organization paid premium fare for the only flight available: ironically, it was Continental's five o'clock "champagne" flight, with drinks served by flight attendants in gold slippers. I had no stomach for champagne, nor for the ordeal I feared awaited me. I sat huddled in my seat, sick at heart.

During the harrowing night that followed, being grilled about my loyalty to the board, I felt like a caged animal, a prisoner in the Gulag trapped by interrogative powers too great to resist. In the morning, when the question about loyalty to the board was posed, I dodged it. I was too frightened and thought I had nowhere to go. Cagily, I asked if I had to "agree *with* board decisions" or "agree *to*." They well understood the crucial semantic escape hatch, and in fact did not want to lose me, and said, "agree to" was okay. I returned to Denver, crushed and disillusioned, and ashamed of my equivocal and cowardly surrender. It was another significant betrayal of my trust in a secure family, but a necessary impetus to dislodge me from my once-comfortable Edenic world of service and move me toward a deeper inner journey.

These events inflicted wounds in my relationship with both Louise and Joy. I felt bereft and behaved accordingly. Joy resigned, but I stayed on, although the vitality of the work had been killed for me. I no longer produced in my usual way or pace, and dragged my feet in any way I could. Louise knew I was suffering, but wisely supported me in quiet ways, enabling us to sustain a long-term relationship. It was with Louise that I collaborated in writing *The Slender Thread: Stories of Pioneer Girls' First Twenty-Five Years.*

It helped that in the fall of 1960, my Program Division moved a block down the street to separate rented quarters and I had a brief resurgence of the old pioneering spirit. I created a little fiefdom with a small capable staff of five. We were back to more primitive conditions, creaky floors, and huge unmanageable spaces without partitions that threw us into a family feeling again. And we were launching a magazine.

There were rumblings about moving our headquarters to the suburbs, to Wheaton, Illinois. My reaction was strong. I viewed this as a step backward, moving into a secure enclave protected from wrenching societal changes I felt we needed to face. I thought an urban location was essential to keeping in touch with currents of change. The move was symbolic of a much larger phenomenon occurring in the culture: the Great White Flight to the suburbs, and the consequent suburbanization of the church. As churches planted themselves in the fast-growing suburban subdivisions of Denver and Detroit, of Minneapolis and New York City, Pioneer Girls clubs went with them as part of the total church program. Now we at headquarters were also fleeing from the city.

I watched in dismay as inexorable momentum moved Pioneer Girls out to Wheaton with so many other evangelical organizations. I stubbornly refused to move to live there myself. A spirit of alienation settled over me like a cloud. I wasn't fond of the idea of having to commute twenty-six miles to work every day either.

In my way, I was slowly separating from a world that had housed me for so long, but which now provided neither comfort nor stimulus. It would take five more years before I could make the break. The fracture lines were apparent, but the vessel still held, though it seemed empty to me.

THE INNER LIFE BECKONS

My restiveness precipitated a growing interest in my inner life; I began paying attention to psychological matters. While in graduate school, I felt strongly drawn to the courses in Counseling and Group Dynamics, which were new to the field of Christian education as it had been taught at Wheaton. I made several unsuccessful attempts to engage the teacher of those courses in conversation about my confused feelings of loneliness as an unattached woman, hoping she would pick up the signals I was sending that I needed help. But she was business-like and almost brusque, an intensely private and reserved person herself. She saw me as intelligent and academically capable, but never ventured to probe on a deeper level. She could not see that my emotions were raw from an inexplicable sense of hunger for answers to inner unsolved problems I could not even name. I was ashamed to admit that I felt unfulfilled as a single woman. I thought something must be wrong with me to feel so self-deprecating and unhappy. Since I had not swallowed the cheap banality that "no woman is complete without a man," it was confusing to feel such a strong desire to be swept into the arms of a lover.

I reached out for psychological insights, reading voraciously to find a word of wisdom which might pour healing ointment on the wounds of my soul. I was grateful to discover Paul Tournier's *The Meaning of Persons* which set ajar the door into a psychological world I would later find life-saving.

John Welwood, in an article, "Principles of Inner Work: Psychological and Spiritual," describes my situation as "spiritual bypassing," referring to the tendency of persons in spiritual communities to "use their spiritual involvements to bypass certain kinds of personal, emotional 'unfinished business.'"[2] He recognizes the temptation to try to use spiritual disciplines as a way to rise above difficulties of unresolved psychological problems. A prime example was my effort to surrender a self at the altar rail, when I had never developed a strong sense of that self, especially of myself as a woman. I was surrounded with exhortations to pray and read the Bible, and had tried to teach others that God could heal our confusion, embrace our loneliness, and give joy in his presence alone. I did not understand why my own experience fell so far short of true spiritual maturity, or why my soul was so hungry.

In reality, my development as a person and as a woman had been truncated, stunted, aborted. This was an issue with which therapy is designed to deal. Now I treasure the meaning of the Greek word *psyche* as *soul,* and that God's grace and help comes effectively through "doctors of the soul" as well as through religious mentors. I was not living in a subculture which imputed much value to psychology unless it was completely framed by Scripture. I continued to be hungry, without any idea that I could be filled.

Then I met Char, a nurse on InterVarsity's Nurses Christian Fellowship staff, who was moving to Chicago and needed a place to live. We began sharing an apartment together. Char's interest in psychological issues was stimulated by her work in counseling student nurses. She decided to train to become a therapist. I finally had someone with whom to share my curiosity about the human psyche, and who responded to my restless questions with wisdom and insight.

Exiting From the World of Women

My exit from the world of women came by way of enrolling in school—my favored way of responding when hounded by uncertainty and dissatisfaction. I talked with friends about pursuing a doctorate in my field of religious education. Two of them urged me to consider a different field, possibly in secular studies, which would immerse me in new patterns of thought, introduce me to new people, and challenge me to find my way within a different world. The idea appealed. So I contacted the University of Chicago in

1964, and made an appointment to talk with a sociology professor, Fred Strodbeck.

After looking at my application, which was saturated with the limited experience of a Christian Education major in a small Christian college and seventeen years of "missionary work" in an evangelical setting, he was set to grill me and find a way to filter me out. I was obviously not University of Chicago material. But I turned wily, and my story held a few surprises. He asked about my minister father. When I mentioned his graduation from Harvard and from Law School, a subtle look of surprise crossed the professor's face. Later I would learn that Fred was a Harvard man himself, and held that institution in high esteem. "What denomination?" he queried. I hedged, and mentioned my father growing up as a Unitarian, much safer territory than the Baptist fold where he had eventually landed.

Strodbeck reluctantly took me on as a Special Student for my three-month sabbatical beginning in January of 1965, figuring that I would do the institution no harm and perhaps it might do me some good. He could not have predicted that once I got my toe in the door, I would find a way to continue on a part-time basis until I eventually registered as a bona fide doctoral candidate. Three years later I would complete the Preliminary Exams in my field with the coveted "high pass", surprising everyone including myself, and occurring shortly before I opted to discontinue my doctoral studies in favor of a more activist role in the world.

When I made that first tentative move to take a three-month sabbatical, I had little idea how much of a sea change this would create. I was restless for involvement in the issues beginning to absorb the attention of the baby boom generation just coming into prominence, and I was also looking for answers to questions of meaning in my personal life. The University of Chicago proved to be an ideal setting where these concerns could incubate. I plunged into this new academic culture, feeling at one with students fifteen years younger. Maybe it was possible to make a new beginning.

I accepted the inevitability that Strodbeck would become my

advisor. From the beginning he was determined to turn me into a typical UC student. He prodded me to move down onto campus from my northwest side apartment, so I would mingle in campus life, drink beer at Jimmy's with colleagues, become immersed in the academic environment unique to this university. I wasn't ready for that much change yet.

After a year and a half of part-time studies, I was ready to ask for a leave of absence from Pioneer Girls and registered as a full-time student for the 1966 fall semester. I obtained a part-time job working for a Portuguese archaeology professor, Pierre Delougaz, at the University's Oriental Institute, cataloguing mace heads, pendants, amulets, cylinder seals and pottery shard finds from the eighth century B.C. Professor Delougaz knew I was enrolled in the Ph.D. program in Sociology, and tried to interest me in the sociological implications of some of his finds. He would peer through his microscope at some ancient relic and enthusiastically point out some obscure characteristic imprinted on these bits of pottery. He was famous for having discovered the earliest pottery remnant ever found to depict musicians with instruments from all four major orchestral groups—strings, reeds, winds, and percussion. I tried to summon up matching fervor, but it was a stretch for me. I was too absorbed in the changes in my personal life to be able to meet his scholarly interests.

That fall, my dissatisfaction and unhappiness with my life rolled into a tidal wave, threatening to inundate me at times. Being at the University felt refreshing on the surface, but my inner discontent continued to simmer. One day Char handed me a slip of paper with the name of a good therapist on it, "in case you want to check him out," she said.

Char's penetrating wisdom in psychological matters made me open to her referral. I placed her piece of paper on the phone stand with deliberate care. I didn't know if therapy would help, but I was more desperate than ever before. I did not see the threshold I was about to cross. Unseen hands were guiding me more wisely than I could imagine.

PART TWO

Moving Into Freedom

Where the Spirit of the Lord is,

there is freedom.

II Corinthians 3:17

six

Born Again in Therapy

THE WINDSHIELD WIPERS wagged back and forth, a metronome accompaniment to my inner thoughts as I drove the highway in the rainy dusk of a May day in the mid-1960s. I gripped the steering wheel tightly, slowly maneuvering the underpasses where pools of water had collected threatening to stall my car if I went too quickly.

I was returning from a speaking engagement at a Mother-Daughter banquet in central Illinois. I had accepted the invitation reluctantly. Here I was, in my mid-thirties, never having been a mother and my record as a daughter blemished by a lifetime of periodic conflict with my mother. It was hard to know how to address such an occasion with credible empathy.

As I drove home through the rain, I began an inner dialogue with God. An underlying rumble of discontentment had begun to disturb my satisfaction at work. I carried around a load of repressed feeling I did not understand, and for which I blamed myself, thinking there was some spiritual lack. And my crushing failure to relate to men marked me as someone who was destined to live out life alone—a destiny I tried to face courageously. I drew an insistent conclusion that something was terribly wrong with me. The public façade was brave and confident, especially when I was in positions of leadership. In private, with the veneer stripped off, I felt unsure and inadequate.

What would it take to make me over into the ideal self I fantasized I might become? So many things would have to change. I spoke out loud: "I wish. . .I wish. . ." I strained to find a way to express the depths of my frustration. Then the words came in a burst of feeling: "I wish I could be born all over again."

"Born again." The words startled me, but felt oddly right, not primarily as an expression of religious conviction, but as words expressing the stark truth of my situation. Was it really possible to start over again, to erase the sickening self-loathing and make a fresh beginning?

I hesitated. I was still locked into traditional ways of thinking, meaning that my childhood experience of prayer to receive Jesus and of baptism guaranteed that I was a new creation in Christ. But that day, in the rain on the highway, I knew there was an authenticity about the experience I sought which still eluded me. I wanted to start life anew...a second chance to be me...a "me" I imagined. The "me" whom I knew at that moment in my life made me sick. Literally.

The memory of my rainy day monologue gradually faded, as I busied myself with my work in an attempt to suppress the loneliness and uneasiness rattling around in the hollow caverns below the surface of my life. In August, Char and I went on a vacation in the Colorado Rockies. One evening, we got into a harsh exchange of words over a misunderstanding. I was deeply upset—not with Char so much as with myself.

We talked on into the night, trying to unravel my wretchedness. I was crying, not unusual for me, but this time my tears suddenly escalated, becoming racking sobs, the groans of a soul in deep travail.

I stumbled across the floor, crawling as I wept, until I reached the corner of the room. My whole body shook, and I began to lose consciousness of reality, I was crying so hard. I felt crazy, clawing at the walls of the room, trying to shrivel up into the corner. I was trying to disappear.

In my distress, I managed to blurt out between sobs, "I wish...I could...vomit...myself."

I heard my own words with stunned recognition. I knew I was talented, intelligent, and had solid achievements behind me. I wrote articles, led groups, made speeches—spellbinding and warm. Yet I wanted to vomit myself. There was no farther to go, except to try, gagging, to turn myself inside out. The corner of the room symbolized that I was at some kind of end.

Char tried to comfort me out of my hysteria. My sobs eventually subsided, and finally sleep came. The next morning, the hot Colorado sun rose in the brilliant blue of the mountain sky over the cabin. I washed my face, looked from tired eyes to my reflection in the mirror, went outside and ran into the wind.

The memory of that awful night in the Colorado cabin continued to lurk in the dark corners of my mind. I could not erase it. I had tried—in my way—to kill the self I loathed.

For reasons I cannot explain, fall was often a difficult time for me emotionally; the fall of 1966, as I began full-time studies at the University of Chicago, was no exception. In November, alone in the apartment one night, I watched the movie "Lust for Life" on TV. It was the story of Vincent Van Gogh's life, done in black and white. Something about the agony and ecstasy of Van Gogh's life and art gripped me. All his flaming canvases, his orange suns and golden skies—in black and gray and white. His eyes—piercingly bright, angry and sorrowful—looked into me with empathic intensity. His passion for beauty, his aborted attempts to find love, his madness with Gaugin, cutting off an ear, and finally the haunting loneliness of his months in the mental health sanitarium at Arles and his eventual success at suicide all burned themselves into my brain. I had never considered killing myself. My urge was toward rebirth, not death. But I could understand the forlornness of Van Gogh, and I let it hurt me through and through.

When the movie ended, I turned the TV set to blackness, watched as the fine white point of light was swallowed to nothing, crawled into bed, curled into a ball and sobbed to heartbreak. These were not the hard, dry, suffocating sobs of the mountain cabin. These were warm salt tears—the years of loneliness welling up inside and pouring out. I can't say I felt no self-pity. I only know these were tears of release, not tears to further bind me up.

Something happened that night that I can't fully explain—a kind of melting. Alone in my apartment one frosty January morning, my Bible open on my lap, I sat absorbed in thought, contemplating my life. I knew I needed help, but was reticent to admit it. Without forethought, I began talking aloud to myself, gathering energy to take action.

"Well, Eunice, are you going to get help or not?" I posed the question like a challenge.

I got up and walked deliberately across the room to the phone. The little scrap of paper Char had given me was there with therapist Alan Richardson's name and phone number on it. I dialed. Then I panicked. But I had dialed. To my methodical and courteous mind, it was too late to turn back. So I let the phone ring.

The therapist couldn't see me for two weeks. "Is it an emergency?" he wanted to know. I laughed sardonically, thinking to myself, *I've waited thirty-seven years. I can wait two more weeks.*

THE WONDER OF TRANSFORMATION

To a therapy-conscious age, my shyness and trepidation about going for help may seem strange. I wasn't at all sure I could be helped in this way. Thirty-seven years is a long time to carry a burden, and I had tried every means I knew to rid myself of self-loathing. In addition to numerous trips to the altar rail in my teenage years, hours spent in the woods walking alone and crying out to God, I had tried to wrest solace from close friends in intimate moments of sharing. On my first visit to the therapist, I apologized for taking up Alan's time. "I don't know if I need counseling or not," I began.

I was sitting there, stiff and prim in a long, straight, dark brown jumper and my high-heeled shoes, trying to think why I needed help. I had a reputation to maintain, being seen as a spiritual leader, the teacher and counselor of others in my work in Pioneer Girls. Several envious women had told me that I represented the first single woman they'd met who was happy. My inner misery had been a well-kept secret.

Alan suggested we "give therapy a try for a few weeks and see." In my mind, I decided on six weeks.

During that first month, we dealt with some disturbing problems on the surface of my life: my fears and embarrassment about emotional intensity in relationships with women, the inexplicable breakdowns when I became physically and emotionally exhausted and which had required me to take leaves of absence. The relief of unburdening myself to a totally accepting human being did for me what years of agonizing prayer to God had never succeeded in doing. I felt accepted as I was in the sight of God, as mediated by this human being.

In fact, I felt so good that by the fourth week, I marched in one day and announced, "Well, let's summarize today." To which Alan replied, "Why?"

This was unlike him—the non-directive type who had been "umhmming" and supporting. It was a challenge.

"Because I'm getting ready to quit," I said.

His reply stung me to the core of my pride; I had been doing so well. "You've just begun," he said.

I couldn't imagine what else there was to deal with. Alan asked if I dreamed, and suggested I start writing down my dreams. I giggled, a little superciliously. This was Too Much. Freud. Analysis. Dreams, no less. To my surprise, when I began putting a pad and pencil by my bed at night, I found my dreams became even more vivid than usual, and I went to each session fully stocked with material.

One day, we began talking about my parents. Something in my stomach went "Boing!" "Touch me, deal with me, but don't touch my parents," was my unspoken message. I was proud of my parents—especially my father—and our family relationship. Often during my younger days I would say to my friends, "You should meet my parents; they are the best part of me," and meant it. I blamed myself for the conflicts I had with my mother.

I brought a dream into therapy one day:

I am in an apparel store, fingering the skirts and sweaters on the racks. June, a kindly and much-admired school friend is choosing a special sweater for me.

As Alan questioned me about the dream, my replies led us toward discussing my mother's role in choosing my clothes when I was young, and her control over the way I felt about my body more generally. I recounted a vivid memory from childhood:

I was nine or ten years old, sitting in the bathtub one evening waiting for Mother to come in and finish scrubbing me. With automatic efficiency, she rubbed the washcloth across my back, and then my chest, making no difference in the roughness of her stroke.

"Ouch, that hurts!" I yelled.

Mother looked surprised, gave a shrug and a laugh.

I was ashamed. I was also angry that she could ignore the faint signs of my emerging pubescence, for which I had no name.

Alan responded sympathetically to my story. Something clicked for me. Slowly over the years, guilt had grown in ever-thickening layers around my life. Now I began to experience a distinction between guilt and shame, a distinction well-identified by Lewis Smedes in *Shame and Grace:*

> *Guilt was not my problem as I felt it. What I felt most was a glob of unworthiness that I could not tie down to any concrete sins I was guilty of. What I needed more than pardon was a sense that God accepted me, owned me, held me, affirmed me, and would never let go of me even if he was not too much impressed with what he had on his hands.*[1]

I began to see how the layers of shame had formed. I hadn't consciously chosen my path. Like many daughters, my mother's ability to shame me was the most powerful. And hers was the legacy of her own upbringing, the daughter of a powerful father whom she adored, but whose punishments she remembered more than his embrace. She was scrupulously careful in trying to be a good and wise mother, but unaware of her effect on me. I suspect she saw me as stronger than I was. Though I put on a resistant front at times, inside I was desperate for her approval and more malleable to her influence than she imagined.

Sitting with a therapist who accepted me opened me to the grace of an unconditionally accepting God, even though he might not be "too impressed with what he had on his hands." Perhaps in God's eyes I was good after all. Could I trust this new realization? We were on uncomfortable ground now, but I pressed on. Perhaps I sensed already that where the pain was, relief would be waiting.

A few weeks later I came in wearing a black turtleneck sweater, a bright plaid skirt, and a simple long strand of simulated pearls looped in a knot. Alan complimented me on my appearance. Since this was the first time (and I worked hard to get his approval, some recognition that I was special), I was startled, and remarked offhandedly, "Oh, these pearls? I bought them for a dollar at the dime store."

"Some time, if you're interested," he said, "I could talk with you about some reasons women wear jewelry, and its effect on men."

Alan had made a similar offer a few weeks before, but I had distinctly not been ready then, and I had turned him down cold. I was above the silly obsession many women had with jewelry. I defended my decision to go plain, wearing simple "meaningful" sterling pieces like friendship rings and honor society pins.

Today I was ready to hear Alan. Something inside me submitted to the probing of a deeper layer. It was an acknowledgment that this sexless person I had presented myself as being was not making it. I felt terribly inferior in not knowing how to dress and adorn myself—and that was the reason for dressing so plainly. My shallow defenses rang hollow.

Hesitantly, I said, "Yes, tell me."

And so, that day, we talked. He asked me to tell him how I felt about my body and I began talking openly, even eagerly, if a bit embarrassed, about my body—from top to toe. My face was flushed, my eyes bright, my manner animated.

Alan pointed out some of the instinctive reasons women adorn themselves to indicate vitality and a feminine sensibility, and that men recognize this and feel encouraged to respond. Later I would discover some of his rationale was based on anthropological data. That day, I was not paying attention to theory. Rather all my senses were attuned with laser-like intensity to everything we both were saying.

Stories tumbled out in profusion—the way my mother had disregarded my emerging femaleness at the bodily level, embarrassments and confusion about how to cover or display my body, my desperate attempts to ignore or hide its feminine contours. I slowly saw that I couldn't accept myself until I had accepted my body. I looked down at my body a little self-consciously, and without thinking, pulled my skirt up just a bit higher. It was okay to appreciate this fine body I had been given, so emphatically the body of a woman.

By the end of the hour, I was high with excitement. When I got back to my apartment, I alternately sat and pranced around the living room, sharing the experience of that session with Char.

Then, just as suddenly, I wanted to be alone. I drifted into the bedroom, and sank down onto my bed, face down, reaching out with my fingers to grasp the quilt. It was April, and I wished very much that I could be outside lying on the moist spring earth.

I became very quiet, waiting. Slowly, surging up through my body, a powerful sensation of ecstasy came up from my toes, and through every part of my frame, filling me—full-filling me. Time stood still.

A thought overwhelmed me. *I'm glad I'm a girl.*

Why had I never said these words before? At this moment, they welled up spontaneously, my own deep truth.

"Don't be silly, Eunice. You're thirty-seven years old. You're a *woman*, not a girl."

But archly, I answered myself, "No, damn it. I can't be a woman until I've been a girl."

If I were to identify one moment in time for my rebirth, this was the moment. I lay there quiet for a long time, savoring the joy of being with my Self in a way I had never known before. A loving Presence filled the room, a space which had become the room of my rebirth.

After a time, I sensed that action was required. I leaped from the bed, flung open the closet door and compulsively began pulling clothes off the rack. Long brown and navy blue boxy garments—sensible and totally unprovocative. I folded them neatly and placed them in paper bags. "Maybe these will fit some hyper-sexed person down at the Salvation Army," I muttered softly, "but as for me. . ."

Saturday I bought a new dress. It was purple, with fitted princess lines, and fashionably short. I danced around the fitting room like a child. I was spending money on myself, and I was p-r-e-t-t-y!

On Sunday, I dressed to go to church, with an enormous bright orange flower perched on one shoulder of a tan linen dress. *How pleased everyone will be to see me today,* I thought. *Especially the men.*

As I marched up the stairs to the sanctuary, the usher was there to hand out the church bulletins as he always was. I was radiant with childlike joy. He took one look, did a double take, then exclaimed, "How *pretty* you look, Eunice."

At last. *"Pretty."* I was so tired of being good, competent, wonderful, talented, smart, and spiritual. How I'd longed to *feel pretty.* My own West Side Story. Before I left for home that day, four men had specifically complimented me on my appearance. I was attractive! For the first time, I felt in control of my life, able to elicit the responses I needed.

Over the next few weeks, my feet rarely touched ground. I loved my body—getting it ready for the day. I experimented with make-up and perfume, and bought some inexpensive jewelry—the kind which moved or dangled in some way to reflect my buoyancy and outgoingness toward life. I was deeply, radiantly happy.

I reflected, with some irony, upon my friend Lee from college days, who would emerge from her dorm room leaving it in a chaotic state of rumpled disorder, while she had adorned her voluptuous body carefully, her blonde hair cascading around her tanned face. I, on the other hand, always came out of my impeccably neat room, my hair in disarray, my clothes casually heaped onto my thin body. I took ironic pride now in surveying my bedroom with its heaps of clothes and cosmetics strewn about. I understood something about my changed priorities.

People around me began noticing. A person I had met for the first time in February, crossed paths with me again in April but didn't recognize me. I hardly recognized myself. As I stood gazing into the mirror one day, I was filled with awe. The face looking back at me was beautiful.

I had absorbed the teaching of my parents: that beauty came from within and could not be "made up" by externals, but something perverse in me did not fully accept that as hard fact. The instinct towards adornment arose spontaneously within my feminine sensibilities and I worked at it with all the energy of an adolescent. At the same time, the image in my mirror looked back at me reflecting an inner glow which no amount of cosmetics could enhance or produce.

As a teenager, I had chosen a life verse which now came back to me with peculiar force:

> *And all of us, with unveiled faces, seeing the Lord as though reflected in a mirror, are being transformed into the same image from one degree of glory to another; for this comes from the Lord, the Spirit.* (II Corinthians 3:18)

One day, as I talked with a friend in my kitchen, I said wistfully, "You know, Judy, what I'd really like is to get married. I wouldn't mind the dishes or housework routine. I'd just like to be married." There was no bitterness to my remark, though I made it in the spirit of an impossible dream. After all, wasn't I thirty-seven years old already?

Judy, petite, blonde, with delicate features, was much sought after by men. With unconscious simplicity, she replied, "I don't feel that way. I am not ready for marriage." I looked at her with incredulity and a tinge of envy. It seemed such a waste of her youthful vitality. A few days later, she gave me one of her long-sleeved blouses with soft frills at the wrist and neck. She said she always got compliments on it when she wore it on her dates and she wanted me to have it. I accepted her generosity gratefully.

In therapy that week I recounted my conversation with Judy. I told him I had discovered I wanted to be married. Alan's response was simple and spare. "If you want to, you will."

"Really?" I was startled. This was not the direction I expected the conversation to go. I began to protest protectively. "But statistically . . .at my age. . ."

"Statistics have nothing to do with it," he asserted.

It was crazy, but I decided to believe him. He had been right about so many things during these weeks. I was scared, though. If I began to count on finding a husband, what if someone didn't come along?

I decided to go public with my intentions. I had not been working full-time at my job at Pioneer Girls for two years. I finally sent in my resignation, and when fellow workers asked me what I planned to do next, I told them, "I'm going to get married."

"Oh," they said politely, but with undeniable surprise. "I didn't realize you were 'seeing somebody'."

"I'm not," I'd retort. "But that's what I'm going to do next." The brash declaration was a hard act to follow, and mystified my old friends, all of whom were single.

My five months in therapy thus far had been a whirlwind ride. At first I credited my therapist with the transformation that had occurred. Now I embraced a deeper realization that God was at work through the vehicle of therapy. I also had been a supremely ready and receptive participant, surrendering my usual defenses and allowing new perceptions to enter my consciousness. My dreams had helped penetrate my unconscious resistances.

I began winding up therapy in May. With summer approaching, I would be leaving town and my therapist. I felt ready and eager to launch out on my own. There was also a cranny of fear in my bravado. I decided to broach the subject of termination with Alan.

"I'd like to quit," I said tentatively, remembering my earlier effort to terminate, and not wanting to be challenged again. This time the response was a challenge of a different sort. "You can quit any time you like."

"But," I said a bit plaintively (his response was like a rejection and I wasn't about to be pushed out the door), "I thought you and I were going to decide when I'm ready."

"That is the best way."

"Then, how will we know when I am ready?"

Alan looked me straight in the eye, and his answer chilled me to the bone: "When you start dating and relating to men."

Of course, that was a logical and necessary next step to achieving my goal of marriage. But it was so *practical*. I'd been floating on air in a cloud of perfume and smiles, sailing through a very late-blooming adolescence, but what *hard evidence* did I have that I could attract and relate to a man, much less marry him?

For a long moment, I considered giving it all up, at the same time knowing I couldn't "go home" again. I gulped, swallowed—and walked slowly out the door, and into my car. As I drove toward the University of Chicago, I was conscious of the overflowing goodness of God. I had not yet put together my spiritual and psychological rebirth conceptually, but they were not at odds with each other at all. It was natural, at this juncture, to turn to God. I had begun to trust the wisdom of my deep desire to marry. I knew I had the capacity to bring happiness to another.

I had done my part in growing and changing, but I couldn't force a man to relate to me. Even in the liberated environment of the University, men tended to take the initiative in dating. Besides, I wanted what I had missed during all those dateless years in high school and college: I wanted men to approach me. Would they?

As I sped down the expressway, I turned the matter over to God.

At the end of class that evening, my French friend Jean (John) called me over, and asked me to join him for supper. The following day after Statistics class, Bill approached me, asking, "Are you Eunice Russell?" Jean had apparently been talking about me. "Can we go out for coffee?" We certainly could.

Bill was facing similar developmental issues to mine, having recently left the Jesuit priesthood. I knew he understood my dilemma in going through adolescent stages in relationship to the opposite sex, at the same time that we were in Ph.D. programs at a prestigious university. We began seeing lots of each other, and he became an anchor friend from that point on.

I was jubilant, and I was *d-a-t-i-n-g*. It was an auspicious beginning to a multi-stage process of moving toward the "other." Over the next year and a half, I kept moving forward step by step. Whenever I did not know how to proceed with the next step, I would lay it in God's hands—and wait for discernment, as I continued to mature.

I was absurdly out of step with the times. It was 1967, and in the intellectually progressive atmosphere of the University of Chicago, the embryonic womens' movement was emerging. I seemed to be going in the opposite direction with my obsession with clothes and jewelry and perfume. Yet I was undeniably coming home to my self as a woman, an identity that demanded expression. I plunged ahead, heedless of my surround.

Meanwhile I found myself awash with dreams that continued to help chart my course in therapy. One especially vivid one stands forever in my memory:

> *I am walking through a sunlit pine forest. The air is like Colorado, the smell of pine reminiscent of childhood scenes in New Hampshire. I am walking on the vivid rust-colored carpet of pine needles beneath the tall pines which are bending gently in the wind. The sky overhead is cerulean blue with massive cumulus clouds aloft. My parents are strolling leisurely beside me. We approach a fork in the path. I watch as my parents go off toward the right together, while I walk on ahead over a mounded rise up toward the blue sky. I know that I have been set free to make my own journey. I am leaving them lovingly.*

The dream marked a momentous choice I was making in my new

awareness of myself as an adult woman—to walk my own path, away from the powerful shadows of my mother and father. It would be many years before I could unravel the legacy they gave me. Meanwhile, I was set free to begin a new journey, one that would lead to a deeper experience of love than I imagined possible.

seven

Window to The Other

The otherness of the opposite sex is a window to the otherness of God.
anonymous

God makes us men and women both...the principal way we can experience the image of God.
Ann Ulanov, "Two Sexes"[1]

THERAPY LAUNCHED ME into new dimensions in the inner and outer world. On the inner level, I had been reborn as a woman, deeply conscious of my feminine self. On the outer level, a window had been opened to the world of men—the "other."

A new understanding of God and how God directs our lives was the inevitable outcome. In all of my changes in therapy, I had never questioned God's existence or the solid ground of my faith in God's love for me. I loved the Scriptures, but I was reading them differently—listening for God's voice to me beyond the literal words. I had been saturated with parental instructions and biblical precepts at home and at school. Now I was faced with a dilemma which did not lend itself to resolution through traditional Christian teaching as I had understood it. My long-dormant sexuality and consciousness of my womanhood had been awakened and I longed to marry. Who was God to me now? Like the petals of a flower spreading before the sun, I began opening my heart to a God who was transcendent, and thus whom I did not intimately know as well as I had imagined, the "Divine Other."

Confronting Sexuality Afresh

On a practical level, I was now confronting my sexuality head-on, finding new parameters for understanding myself as a sexual being. The old code of sexual conduct which had been instilled in me would not serve without re-examination. I weighed it against my heightened consciousness of joy in rediscovering my womanly body and asked if I could submit to an external legal constraint which was not rooted in a deeply felt place in my psyche. What freedom did I have to explore and experiment? I felt differently about my body now, more accepting of its contours and expressiveness. Old barriers against its pleasures were disappearing.

These thoughts were milling about inside one morning as I walked to work at the University. Suddenly I stopped in my reverie, intensely meditative. I put out my right hand in a gesture of surrender, unclasping my fist. I could let go of that old code of conduct. I imagined it clattering to the ground and shattering in a million pieces on the sidewalk. In its place, I sensed God quietly taking my hand. Over the months ahead, I would taste the sweetness of that touch whenever I needed it in my dating and relationships with men. My intimate connection with God was far more powerful than any code could ever be.

The summer of 1967 following my six months of therapy gave me a chance to make a new start in my quest for relationships with men. I chose to spend the summer in a coed camp on the California coast, a choice which bridged my two worlds of past and future. Camp had been a familiar and loved environment in the past, but, to participate in a co-ed situation in an exotic West Coast environment was a new adventure. I was fortunate to be part of a close working relationship with four senior staff, one of whom was Bert, a single man exactly my age.

As might be expected, I unabashedly set out to conquer Bert's attention. The new setting far from home was ideal for a test of my charms. To be fair, my inflated ego was a little "much" for anyone at that stage, but I saw it as compensation for the years of deflation

I had known so well. Now I was unashamedly and aggressively a female in pursuit. Yet, the men in my environment did not seem to be put off by this. I thought, in earlier years, that such behavior was too bold and therefore disgusting. To be demure had been the ideal. Instead, I only picked up hints of surprise and bewilderment mingled with obvious enjoyment from others.

It was a wild and wonderful summer, complete with my first romantic kiss—at the beach under a full moon after the final staff banquet. I was dressed in a backless black lace dress and crystal earrings. I found I needed to make my own feelings clear as the relationship with Bert progressed, because Bert was not so sure. "I . . .I. . .I don't know how I feel about you," he stuttered one day when we were hiking together.

"I'm not in love with you," I began and went on to acknowledge that this summer fling was temporary and a learning experience for me, but not one I wanted to continue seriously.

Frankly, the experience had been an experiment on my part, and a hopeful indication for the future. I had toyed with the notion that I should not be fussy about a mate since I was in my late thirties and the pickings were slim. This experience clarified for me that I must not settle for less than what met my heart.

Meeting Men

I returned to Chicago, having made an important decision: I was ready to make the move to the University of Chicago campus which Professor Strodbeck had suggested a year earlier. Leaving the satisfying home I had created with my friend, Char, was not easy, but it seemed important to place myself in an environment where I could circulate within a wider circle of contacts. Char and I had lived together for five very happy years, and now I needed to experience this next phase of my life unattached.

My association with Char had begun to change me, by introducing me to the field of psychology and helped me begin to reach out beyond my all-women's world. She had often encouraged me to attend parties with her which included male peers on the InterVarsity

Christian Fellowship staff. I was always awkward and unsure, but I would screw up my courage and go. Once at the party, I was as miserable as any thirteen-year-old wall flower at an eighth grade dance. I became tongue tied. I felt ugly and awkward. I wasn't dressed right. So I would wind up helping with the dishes, or talking to another hapless outcast like myself, or, if feeling relatively self-assured, getting into an intellectual discussion with a male. But I never got taken home afterwards, or cornered in a private chat, or eyed across the room and approached.

My brief forays into a coed world had made me feel it was of no use to try to force change by choices of environment. But now, since therapy, I knew differently. I could choose to live at the University, cope with the wrenching adjustment this necessitated in leaving a loving and secure living arrangement, and start to build new patterns of relating.

University life was full. I worked and studied and played—and met lots of men. I accepted all offers of dates, without regard to criteria. I needed and wanted experience, and was fortunate in finding men in the university setting who patiently initiated me into the world of male companionship without realizing how fresh and enlivening it was for me. I am sure my frank enthusiasm and free spirited enjoyment of their company won them over easily.

Most of the men available were younger. Since I was only twenty-four years old in spirit, and even younger in experience, no one even seemed to notice the age difference. I can be forgiven for acting half my age, as I was going through an exuberant adolescence, one that was much more fun than the agonies of my high school years.

I learned that my sexual instincts were well-grounded; I could say "no" as well as "yes" with equal grace. The "yeses" were wonderful for me, and the "noes" confirmed my integrity when I was being asked to move farther or faster than I wanted to.

I also met a lot of losers that year. Singles groups in two churches on the near north side were often a disaster, but I usually found a way to establish contact with the most likely man in range. I often felt giddy and high. I was often scared too because I knew what my goal was and, when it did not appear to be imminent, I worried impatiently about how long I might have to wait. I came to realize that the time it was taking was essential. I was learning so much and was keenly sensitive to my own level of readiness. I remember one young man from western Canada who showed up in my life at just the point when I was ready to date more seriously. He courted me with gentleness and feeling, and when we parted it was with mutual sadness, but no regrets.

Meeting Don

Then one day I ran into Don Schatz—almost literally—which made it a dramatic occasion. I was coming off the elevator of the building where my sociology research program had offices on the fourth floor. As usual, I was dressed carefully, in matching forest green skirt and sweater, a bright orange scarf looped over one shoulder, standing erect and a little breathless and expectant. I never knew whom I might meet each day. As the elevator door rolled back and I stepped into the hall, there was Don. I flashed him a radiant smile, one full of invitation.

I knew him as the rather intense-looking man who sat behind a desk in a psychologist's research office down the hall, and who was often in the elevators and hallway carrying cups of coffee from the machine four floors below. His clear blue eyes were penetrating and set in the midst of a cherubic pink-cheeked face. His forehead was high, and his close-cropped blond hair sparse or non-existent in spots. His frame was massive.

It was this rather intriguing hulk of humanity who confronted me that morning as I stepped off the elevator. As I smiled, Don turned toward me—he was talking with someone—and made an almost imperceptible gesture as though to speak. Just as subtly, I hesitated slightly, as though to respond, when suddenly he halted the gesture. Moving all the while the extremely short distance between the elevator and the place where he and his friend stood, I responded to his pausing by proceeding briskly—resigned that I had mistaken his intent—only to find that he reversed himself, and again started toward me with that very slight motion of the body, a starting to speak, a word from the eyes. I was instantly responsive again, and hesitated a fraction of a moment in my pace.

Three times this occurred in the space of those ten to twelve feet between us as I walked from the elevator. Yes, no. Yes, no. Yes, no. Then I was close enough, and the hallway small enough that I brushed his sleeve as I passed; the awkwardness of the situation seemed to force some contact. He turned totally away from his friend, and toward me, stopping me completely. The words he blurted out were to stop me on another level:

"There's something very special about you. I'd like to know what it is."

Of course. What a come-on! My mind raced between the two possible interpretations: the "truth" (I did feel very special), and the flirtatious undertones.

Don's friend drifted discreetly away. We were left to pursue the implications of this remarkable opener. And opener was all it was. We had a short conversation: I remember very little of it. That more or less ended it. I found out Don was a poet. He offered to let me read his work, and I conjured up images of sitting in his garret (surely a poet must live in a garret!) reading poetry and drinking wine and talking together into the night.

It never happened. What I didn't know was that not long before Don had packed his bags thinking he might go to a Trappist monastery to live out his life without benefit of the joys of female companionship. Our encounter had been a dramatic and exciting interlude in my day, but a dead end in terms of follow-through. But Don continued to appear often in the hallways and elevator all year, passing by with a "Hi" and a smile.

I became aware of the research program with which he was affiliated—a psychological testing project of Dr. Eckhard Hess, chairman of the Psychology Department at the University. Dr. Hess was becoming known for his discovery of the relationship between dilation of the pupil of the eye and interest. This finding had naturally precipitated much excitement in the field of advertising, and consequently there were a number of projects being pursued at the University that required test subjects to come in and look at slides or movies of various products and packaging. At the same time the subject was viewing pictures, his or her eye movements were being photographed with the help of a special camera. It was often Don's job to man the camera, and afterwards to run the processed film through a special machine that enabled him to measure pupil dilation. He prided himself on being "the fastest eyeball measurer in the West." As a result of this process, the advertiser could determine precisely what packaging or approach "opens up peoples' eyes"—literally.

Dr. Hess's research assistants often went scurrying into the halls to recruit available graduate students in the various research offices on the fourth floor to serve as guinea pigs in a new experiment. Being recruited was something most grad students tried to avoid. The research assistant might plead, "It'll only take a few minutes." I was more vulnerable than most, being naturally curious and enjoying tests, as well as being less deeply committed to academic endeavors.

Therefore on two or three separate occasions that year, I was alone with Don in a darkened room, looking at movies as a test subject, and Don was looking deep into my eyes—well, at least into my pupils—and taking the measure of the woman. But he made no further personal gesture toward me. Once I had to answer a short questionnaire which included a question on my age. I balked. Don looked at me kindly. "It's all right," he said. Something in his tone and facial expression said that age did not matter to this man.

I suppose it offended me that he would not ask me out. If I was so special, how come he didn't come through. It was a challenge to my newly discovered prowess as a woman.

In June of 1968, I was assigned by my research group to take a two-month trip to the West Coast to interview college and university presidents, vice presidents of academic affairs and business affairs at twenty-four schools which were part of our sample. I was a Ph.D. Fellow with the Comparative Organization Research Program headed by Professor Peter Blau, who was looking at issues of centralization and decentralization of decision-making in large bureaucratic institutions.

I was ready to get away from campus for a while. I had come to a plateau in my search for a life partner. It was fine to experiment with men who were younger, or who weren't ideal mates, or whose values were contrasting to mine, but I knew better than to get serious with someone like that. My standards were pretty high.

I tried to be realistic. I had always claimed you should choose a spouse by the faults you can live with, since everyone has faults, and some are worse than others on a twenty-four-hour-a-day basis. Also, despite my enormously increased self-confidence and my genuine love for myself, I was sensible enough to realize I had quirks too.

So I began sorting out the "essentials" from the "also desirables" in my list of qualities. I knew at thirty-eight I shouldn't be too picky. I managed to get the list narrowed down to just three main elements: someone who was open to the work of God in his life, who was intelligent, and who was strong—i.e., aggressive, principled, initiating. The criteria of strength came from my discovery through dating that I sometimes felt I was too much for my companion. It did not feel right to extinguish my own natural assertiveness, which seemed to be required. When I complained about this to my therapist, his solution was straightforward: "Look for strong men." That made sense to me.

There were many times during the two months of my summer trip west when I had lots of time to think in quiet motel rooms in strange cities at night, and my heart was gripped with fear. What had I done in setting out on this bold pilgrimage to get married? Suppose marriage was a mirage?

An old acquaintance from Pioneer Girls days—a woman who felt frustrated about her desire to be in love and to marry—posed the same question to me. "Suppose the years go by, and *nothing happens?*"

It felt like the taunt of the Devil and was the hardest eventuality I had to face. It was like doubting God, or my faith. I asked myself,

"Suppose it's all a giant hoax and I am still the Ugly Duckling, and the Magic doesn't work any more, and I turn back into a frog, and the glass slipper gets broken, or. . ."

I faced my friend's question squarely: "I'm not playing games about this. I really believe I will be married, that it is of God. And if 'nothing happens' by, say, two or three years from now, I'll seriously question the whole thing, because I am not letting God off the hook on this. I mean marriage soon—not tottering down the aisle when I am seventy." This was long before I knew how spry I would still feel at seventy!

It was a long summer, sprinkled with visits to old friends along the way whenever my itinerary would permit. More than once, friends "fixed me up" with someone. But in each case, it was only a "someone" not The One.

My last stop was at a small university in South Dakota. The month was August, the year 1968. The political scene back in Chicago was heating up in preparation for a Democratic convention that would prove historic, and I knew that many of my friends at the university were planning to take part in the protests that would fill the streets and parks downtown. I turned on the TV and watched in horror that night as the Men in Blue were flailing with nightsticks, and beating bloody the heads of protesters—some of whom would surely be persons I knew. I cried for my country. What was happening to it? My own sensibilities were attuned more to those who protested than to those in power. Patriotism had a new face for me now.

I returned to Chicago and settled back into my room at International House. Campus was still somewhat deserted. I sat down to assess my life and where I stood. The world around me was seething with the energy of protest. My sentiments had long been aligned with the struggle against racial injustice. Now, the issue was resistance to the Vietnam War, an issue I was slower to embrace. My political instincts had been either absent or dormant. My conservative background told me that the president had more information available than I, so I should trust the president's judgment. But the University of Chicago was full of sophisticated intellectuals who began to sway me with their arguments questioning the "domino theory" which supported United States' aggression on the Indo China peninsula.

Slowly, inch by inch, I began moving with the '60s throng toward a more critical stance toward authority. In the realm of education, this move made sense—to give more power to students to determine the learning process. The protests on campus were becoming more mixed as time wore on, moving from resistance to the war and the draft, to rebellion against academic structures. Our professors often joined with us in reaction toward an administration which they often felt was oppressive of their academic freedom.

In the midst of this intense political ferment, I was absorbed in the radical changes in my interior personal life. I had a finely tuned sensitivity to every minute movement toward readiness for marriage. That fall, back at the University, I knew I was at last ready to fall in love. I felt in full bloom.

It was a risky realization. I knew people fell in love, only to fall out again. Falling in love could hurt, and I'd still wind up single. Why didn't I say, "I'm ready to get married?" Because I knew I had to fall in love first and I dimly understood the necessity of placing myself in a position of risk. I could see that one reason some persons didn't marry was because they couldn't risk the leap of love—in case it didn't get returned.

A Good Jewish Boy and a Gentile Like Me

Don was one of the first persons I saw back on campus—in the elevator, of course. Was he always there? And with that ever-present coffee cup? Looking at me, he must have seen the smoldering discontent of my offense at him for not following through on the overtures he had made toward me the year before. "What's the matter?" he asked. "You look so sour."

That made me angry. He could tell how I felt. And it was another insult. If there was anything a "special" woman did not want to appear, it was "sour." But I was not able to tell him that my sourness was for him. In his presence, I felt angry that I could not captivate him, make him respond to me.

I was walking down the Midway at the University of Chicago the next afternoon, when I fell into step beside Don. As always, he was reading a book as he walked toward the lake on his habitual saunter through Jackson Park to his home in South Shore.

Something in our conversation made Don turn to me and say sharply, "I'm a Jew." He was trying to put me off, sensing my growing interest in him. He was sure this remark would do it. On the contrary, this heightened my interest. I had just finished reading Chaim Potok's *The Chosen*. Since childhood, I had been steeped in the stories of the patriarchs, the prophets, the kings, and been nourished by the poetry of the Psalms. In my tradition the Jews were revered as chosen, and I was not yet familiar with the Jewish reluctance to be so set apart, since it often meant stigma rather than honor.

Don continued, determined to put me off. "I'm a poet." I suppose this was a warning that he would always be poor. I still had the fantasy of sitting alone with him in his garret drinking wine and listening to his poetry in muted candlelight, something that was never to be since Don lived in the basement of his family home. I later visited once, saw the battered old piano near the wash tubs. Don used to sit at the piano playing absentmindedly, his latest painting mounted behind him, so he could scrutinize its reflection in the mirror above the keyboard.

Don had discovered his talent at eighteen, when an art teacher at Roosevelt University suggested that Don go to the Art Institute and check out Rouault's work. Don was gratified to find that some of his own work mirrored Rouault's style. He began a frenzy of painting, using ever larger canvases. Some of his work portrayed images of paradise, Edenic figures thick with layers of color. Other canvases depicted mounds of skulls against a black background, faces staring out of the hellish images of Holocaust which had so affected him in the photographs his uncles brought back after World

War II when Don was eight.

His family sent him to Europe at twenty-six to give him a needed break from the art scene, from his apartment buddies, and from his depressed father. He went to see Europe's art as an artist, and came back a different person, and a poet.

In Europe, museums became his home away from home. He took a memorable bus trip a few miles out of Amsterdam to Arnheim, where he slogged down a muddy road, flanked by cows in nearby pastures on one side, and on the other by statues created by famous sculptors like Henry Moore. Inside the museum were the expressionist painters Don loved and to some extent emulated: Van Gogh, Rouault, Chagall, Klee.

In Paris, he reconnected with friends who were going to Majorca, an island off the coast of Spain known for harboring artists. He decided to go along. Don describes his time in Spain as an experience of heaven and hell. He roamed the streets, delirious, feeling the angst of his life, and all that he had left behind him. He had gotten accustomed to not eating much in order to save money, so was comparatively thin.

One day he wandered into a cathedral in Majorca, a sanctuary in noonday heat. Stained glass windows let in just enough light to profile the crucifix that hung in the front arch. As he stood there gazing upward, time stood still.

He describes it as experiencing all the molecules spinning around and breaking up before whirling back into place again. At that moment he knew he was in the presence of God and some of his inner confusion and despair melted. He does not remember walking out again into the sunlight of that August day. He only knows he could no longer paint out his angst in the tortured images on canvas that were his trademark as a painter. He began using language in unfamiliar ways, speaking of Mary, for example. He wandered into an English-speaking bookstore one day, and purchased a volume by St. John of the Cross.

After a week in Madrid, he returned to Paris for a few days. While there, he began to write. Words were becoming critically important to him, partly because he had been immersed in countries which spoke other languages for so many months. While musing one day about words, he thought about the word "tree." Yes, he could paint that image. Then the word "plastic" came to his mind. He could also imagine constructing a plastic tree. The third word which appeared changed his art forever: "invisible." Strung together, "invisible plastic tree" could be written, but not painted. Writing became his art from that point on.

So Don became a poet, but not just any kind of poet. "I write religious poetry," he said to me on that September afternoon walk with a certain sense of finality. This was to be the ultimate put-off. But how little he knew me. Now I was genuinely interested.

In my post-therapy dating days, I did not ask the men I was dating if they were Christians or not. I was finding out that in my contacts with University people, there were plenty of seekers and questioners of life, and they interested me more than those who had answers. My search for love was in God's hands, and I was learning not to doubt God's wisdom in the persons who crossed my path.

So it was with a little jolt of surprise that I found myself beside this towering six feet two inch giant of a man who wrote religious poetry. At that time I knew nothing of his own peregrinations over the map of calling and faith. On his return from Europe, still reeling from the transformative experience of the church in Spain, he knew he needed to be on a religious quest. He began by becoming a student of Eastern religions. Restlessly, he questioned and floundered. A friend of the family put Don in touch with a Dominican priest who suggested that Don visit the Trappist monastery at Gethsemani in Kentucky. To a Jew, Christian faith would be the most extreme, the most at odds with the history of persecution suffered by Jews at the hands of Christians. Yet his moment of transformation had occurred in a Catholic church, so Don felt he should at least check it out.

He traveled to Gethsemani on several occasions. One time, a copy of some of his writing and drawings were shown to Thomas Merton, who then came up to Don's cell to see him and talk.

Merton was a physically strong figure, and his powerful presence left its mark with Don.

But that day walking on the Midway, I did not know all of this background. I just knew I was intrigued. Looking back now, I can imagine how very Gentile and Protestant, even Puritan, I seemed to him. Minority groups are so much more sensitively attuned to the environment, testing the waters of possible prejudice. At that point, Don was totally unacquainted with the small segment of the Christian world that has a strong tradition of revering the Jewish heritage to which it feels a strong link, and that does not blame Jews for killing Christ. Rather I had been taught that I was as responsible as the Jews of Jesus' day. Had I been there, I, too, could have been part of the taunting crowds as easily as I could have been a disciple.

That day, Don thought that by declaring himself to be a religious poet, he would effectively shuttle me off to greener pastures if I were a typical University of Chicago woman. My response may have startled him. "Oh, then I *am* interested in your poetry," I said warmly. He offered—again—to let me read some of his work.

"Ah, now it will happen," I thought. Aloud, I said, "Any time. You say when," and flipped into the House, hoping this would stimulate him to pursue further contact with me.

Later, discerning friends scolded me, "You should have said, 'How about right now?'" Never leave anything to chance!

But poetry was not to be my door of admission to Don's heart. It would turn out that I would need Don's help in extricating myself from a predicament of my own making. It is hard for me to admit some of the foolish things I did in my eagerness to move out into the world of men and romance. But the fact is, although I had unbounded confidence in my ability to handle any situation, my lack of discrimination in choosing dating partners was about to exact a heavy price.

On one of my forays into one of those ghastly singles groups in a near north side church I was approached by a man who claimed to be a Manhattan broker, in Chicago on business. Stock trading was a foreign world to me then, and I could not read his designs on me. I accepted an invitation to meet him for dinner two days later. Over the next forty-eight hours, I became embroiled in a series of events which would not only prove me naive, but also blind. I went through the drama of betrayal, deceit, and the threat of treachery in rapid succession. I learned that this man had betrayed a friend of mine by standing her up for a date the night before he and I were to meet. I sought "revenge" by deceiving him about my willingness to accede to his romantic designs on me, playing a dangerous cat and mouse game with my flirtations. Then he turned on me with aggravated hostility, posing some threat. When he apologized the next day, I gave in to his pressure to meet him for lunch at the University on his way out of town.

I called my trusted friend Char for advice. "How did you get yourself into this?" she asked. I began feeling foolish. Char was worried for my safety. "Suppose he tries to abduct you?" she challenged.

I knew I was out of my league in dealing with the situation and needed to be in a more practical frame of mind. I began hatching several elaborate schemes. I could stand him up, play his own game of betrayal. But I wanted to believe I wasn't stupid, to be convinced it was a big mistake. There seemed to be no end to my pride. The clock ticked inexorably on. It was nearly noon. I finally decided not to go ahead with lunch. I would meet him at the appointed time and place on campus, and tell him my decision, and that would end it.

Perhaps. But God had something else in mind. Slowly, I walked down the hall from my office towards the elevator. I knew Don was often to be found in that elevator. I decided that if he were there, I would ask him for help.

The elevator doors slid open. Empty. My heart sank like a rock. Down, down, past the first floor, to the basement a few steps below ground level. The doors rolled open, and I walked out.

—Straight into Don's chest! There he was, big and beautiful. He took one look at my scared eyes and said, "What's wrong? You look upset!"

How did he always know my feelings? I blurted out my problem. He was instant sympathy. He took my arm and steered me outside to his car. "I'll take care of you," was all he said.

As we pulled out of the parking lot, he muttered, "How did you get yourself into this?" I felt very young. We waited fifteen minutes for my date. Don was fully prepared to tell him off, and I was beginning to enjoy the feeling of his protective solicitousness. I was more than ready to leave after waiting that scant quarter hour in vain. Don offered to drive me to lunch. He was going to get sandwiches for the others in his lab. So we drove to a little delicatessen near his home in South Shore—the Shoreland—for a corned beef sandwich on an onion roll, and a coke.

And fell in love.

I remember it all clearly. The crisp golden October afternoon, my face aflush with the feeling of a child, my body full of the yearnings of a woman. And Don saying things to me in that strange enigmatic language of abstractions with which I have become so familiar. We did most of our communicating with body language—with our eyes, mainly. And with vague but meaningful references to unspoken thoughts and emotions. "I'm glad we connected like this today." "I've been wanting to know you better." There was a deep sense of everything being right to me. That this "chance" meeting had been arranged by some unseen hand.

We didn't want it to end. We lingered, until it became obvious Don couldn't ignore his waiting friends at the lab any more. In the parking lot back at the University, we got ready to part. When we got out of the car, we would be leaving our private world, and entering the public one of university life again. Don sensed my feeling—and his own. He reached over with his forefinger and gently touched my shoulder. Such a little thing, but it was as full of electricity as a passionate embrace. I was all shiny and warm. Something called love was beginning.

That evening, the phone rang. It was the New York broker calling from Toledo. "Where were you?" he asked with irritation. I told him I had waited the requisite fifteen minutes. Then I couldn't resist adding, "So I went out with someone else and fell in love."

Don offered me some of his poetry to read. Little did I know that his work was of a modern genre alien to my rather limited and conservative background. I was fascinated, but only because it was Don's work. I tried to make sense out of it.

A few days later, I was sitting in his office, talking about my reactions to his poetry. "There's one passage I like especially," I began. "Here, I'll show it to you," and I came over beside him and we stood together by the desk, as I pointed to the page and read.

There it was, right beside me, that big burly body. Unconsciously my own swayed close to his. I slowly stood up straight and we looked at each other, full of feeling. And then I was in his arms. We were in love.

Don always wound up at my place for supper and the evening now. It only took a scant two weeks for us both to become sure of our love. By Thanksgiving, just a month after we came together, I met his entire extended family. I was overwhelmed by the effusive hugs, the boisterous chatter, the ready wit, the special gestures that marked this warm, outgoing and energetic family. I may have been critically scrutinized but I was warmly welcomed. I could see that Don was dearly loved by them all.

Don never actually asked me to marry him. And my deciding to spend my life with him was almost done *for* me. I spent no time weighing pros and cons. I simply knew instinctively it was right. I learned a bit about his personality and character—enough to trust him completely. I saw his impatience, his indecisiveness, his abstract strangeness. Something from deep within Don drew me. He was intelligent, but more important, he had a creative fire within—the mark of an independent strong man. When I paused to consider the criteria I had developed a year earlier, I realized Don not only met the criteria, he surpassed them with his creativity as an artist, and his identity as a Jew who had encountered God.

I talked to a few friends who encouraged me to go ahead with the relationship—friends who read me well and saw the signs of an emerging love and womanness in me. My friend Irma Pickens remembered Don from their days of listening to jazz in the same clubs where her husband Willie played. "He's all right," she told me. "Jewish men take good care of their wives." I remember sitting on the floor of her third floor apartment on 54th Street, crying softly at her knee—wondering how it would be to marry a poet who didn't seem to be earning much of a living.

By mid-November, my journal records lines that sound like wedding vows:

> *Because you want to live your life for God's glory, I promise not to stand in the way of whatever it is you have to be or do in order to achieve this.*
>
> *I will live with you in honesty and authenticity, God helping me, sharing your joy and pain, unrelentingly working at resolving the difficult places.*
>
> *I leave my mother and father, and forsaking all others, cleave to you, your people becoming my people, your life my life, and our God is One.*
>
> *I love you today and I will love you forever.*

In a letter to my parents, I tried to explain the ecstasy of my newfound love.

> *The world is so new to me. I've not known love before, and so all the things familiar to others are fresh and beautiful as though I were the first person in the world to be loved. Don is very gentle, and restrained, and every contact we have has been sheer poetry. There is a meeting of spirits that is fulfilling and awesome. No regrets, and no bumps yet. I know these will come too.*

I was subtly aware of ways in which Don was like my father. As different as they were in physical frame, in background and in temperament, and in their ways of thinking, something curiously similar hovered in my consciousness. I could not place it at first.

Sometimes it even seemed to be the facial expression. Later, I realized I had married a man who, like my father, would spend much of every day in quiet reflection and writing. He would also be a person with whom I could live out all my days in a togetherness reminiscent of my parents' marriage.

I asked myself if I should have been concerned about Don's religious status and beliefs. I had been thoroughly warned as a young person about "the unequal yoke." It was Don who asked me to take my questions about him and our future to God. He surprised me one day by saying, "If you're not interested in God, then I'm not interested in you." He was the one to draw the line. He went even further, letting me know that for him, God was first, his poetry second, and I would come third. A number of years later, he confessed that the last two priorities were reversed; he would give up his poetry for me, if it were necessary. He knew I would not ask this of him.

And somehow God was not an issue. Just as we began assuming our love and trust, we assumed God in our lives. A rock-like stability began to emerge. We could count on each other through conflicts and hurts, and we were rooted in God.

One day in December Don suggested a plan: that we announce our intention to marry to our parents in March, marry in June, and in September go to Israel to live on a kibbutz. I had mixed feelings about this plan. For one thing, unknown to Don, I had told a few close friends already that I intended to marry Don—so a March public announcement sounded ludicrous. I didn't want to wait another four months.

But a kibbutz! Well, yes, maybe—but. . .? I took home Spiro's book on the kibbutz and read. As I read, I began to cry, facing the surrender of choice which would be involved in a shared communal life. I was caught in a power struggle. Was I to have my way? Or Don his? Or God? How could I surrender without denying some essential ME-ness? What did it mean? I had to see it first of all in relation to God. Then perhaps I could understand what it meant in relation to Don.

I felt tormented. *"O God, a kibbutz. Why?"* I was distraught, until an illuminating discovery occurred. I could do even this because I knew marrying Don was right for me. And simultaneously—at the same precise instant—I knew Don would not ask me to do anything I felt strongly opposed to.

That night when Don came to dinner, I began telling him my reactions to the book about the kibbutz. Before I said much at all, he saw my distress and interrupted with, "I'll not take you there if you can't go." He confessed later, "I was testing." From the vantage point of over thirty years with Don, I only partly believe him. If he was testing, it was not deliberate or strategized; it was intuitive and spontaneous. And there was always the goyim in me that he must gauge. I was realizing how very Gentile I must seem to him.

This set a seal on our relationship. Love can do anything, but love doesn't ask the unbearable. Mutual love and trust were building.

The prospect of entering into marriage raised Don's apprehensions about his place in the world of work, a place which he did not occupy securely. One evening, after an intense time of talking with Don about this, I felt that old power struggle with God, and the necessity for Don to work out his occupational future alone. Don told me that night, "I will not be the weaker of us." I felt enormous relief, nestling into the arms of a truly strong man.

※

One day, Don asked, "Where do you go Thursday nights?" I had been attending a small interracial church fellowship that met each week at the Hyde Park apartment of Don and Julie Davis. "Can I go too?" he asked. He eagerly devoured the Bible studies we attended that winter, creating a small sensation in the group with his unorthodox questions and challenges. I found it refreshing.

We announced our engagement on New Years Day, 1969, while visiting our friend Betsy and her husband Lew, a photographer who took a series of pictures of Don and me. When we looked at the prints later, we broke out in hilarious laughter. In each pose, Don was facing the camera with different expressions on his face. (I find it irritating that he is unfailingly photogenic, since I distinctly am not.) I am close beside him, looking up at him adoringly, my face mirroring his expressions exactly, one after another, in turn. Today Don still will remark wistfully, "I miss those days." I do not, but I love the memory of that bliss even as I appreciate our matured love today.

In February, we traveled to New Hampshire together to meet my parents. There was something about our time there, the intimacy we felt, the knitting of hearts, that made me realize that in my innermost being, I was already married. I wanted the outer wedding to affirm it, but the inner one was essential.

My parents warmly received Don, checking him out carefully. They were pleased I had found a life partner, though they were skeptical about "that psychologist," as my mother referred to my therapist, who had clearly brought about my change as far as I was concerned. Whenever I came out with a remark that stood in contrast to the way she had tried to teach me, or which smacked of a certain air of self-confidence, she would mutter, "That psychologist was not good for you."

I never took the bait and responded to these deprecatory comments. I was so deeply happy about the changes God had wrought through my therapy. I tried to convey to my therapist my heartfelt appreciation for our work together. One day in a session with Alan, I blurted out what felt like my own deepest truth, "You have given me back my Self."

I brought Don with me to a therapy session so that we could talk over a few issues prior to our marriage. Don spoke first: "What do I do when she cries?" he implored my therapist.

Alan never flinched as he replied, "Well, you have to realize you are marrying an hysterical woman!"

"Arrgh!" I yelled, proving the point. Don gripped the sides of his chair and gulped, stuttering, "Oh, yes, yes, of course."

Alan continued, unperturbed. "And hysterical women are never boring." Don visibly relaxed. Somehow this was the answer he wished for. And I was not displeased either.

It was our pastor, Don Davis, who married us in April—three months ahead of Don's first schedule. The day before, my parents and a few friends went with us to a West Side church—Keystone Baptist (because it had a baptistry)—in the black community, and there, as the setting sun streamed through the stained glass windows and created a halo around Don's red gold hair and exalted face illumined with fresh joy and tears, he was baptized "in the name of the Father, and of the Son, and of the Holy Ghost."

I cried then, standing near him, but on the next day, I only smiled and laughed. Though everyone else wept at the wedding—and indeed, there were touching moments for us all—I was carried away with joy. It was a culmination, a crowning, and I was radiantly, ecstatically happy. We walked down the aisle of Bond Chapel together to the cadence of an old Hebrew folk melody, and retreated back to the sound of trumpets from Handel's Messiah. "And the trumpet shall resound. . ."

As I sit here writing this and reliving it, I am filled with awe and feeling. There is no question in my mind but that God was in it all. It happened so differently from the way I'd expected, the way others had told me it would be. No dates, no proposal, no long courtship, no extensive "talking out" of matters of religious faith. I was simply in God's hands. And God was within me. That being the case, I was free to move, to choose, to act, to trust my instincts. Other people call this "finding God's will." That's too external, too impersonal. I must have God within so I can be free to move.

WINDOW TO THE OTHER

Don and Eunice

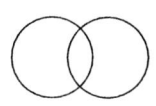

Engaged

Don Davis marries us April 13, 1969

10 Years Later

eight

The Seventies

On or about November 1968, American character changed.
George Packer, NY Times Book Review[1]

ON OR ABOUT November, 1968, I fell in love. Simultaneously the era of my socio-political radicalization began. At the University of Chicago, surrounded by persons twenty years my junior, I came alive to the swirling political currents of the times. The cresting of protest in that fateful year of 1968 served to carry me across an imaginary divide created by my age. I had long considered the 1940s to be the crucial shaping force in my life—especially World War II. Now I was more in sync with the children of my age cohort than my peers who were busily emptying their suburban nests. Therapy had made me feel young. I would find a strangely compatible home in the culture of the 1970s.

The 1960s did not fade without a mighty upheaval of violence. Chicago's West Side exploded in riots following Martin Luther King's assassination in April of 1968. On the South Side, home of a substantial African American population, disaster was averted when two rival gangs, The Disciples and the Blackstone Rangers, came together on the grassy medial strip dividing the University from the black community of Woodlawn. Slowly, like two huge army platoons, hundreds of young black men filed in order down the Midway toward each other to effect a temporary truce, agreeing to suspend hostilities and devote their combined energies to preventing the kind of destruction that was decimating the West Side.

On Palm Sunday, I was on my way to church when a police officer parked outside International House stopped me, telling me it was too dangerous to cross into Woodlawn, so I headed downtown to attend Fourth Presbyterian Church. On Michigan Avenue, I stood shocked and sorrowful as I watched a phalanx of army tanks rumble past me. The city was under siege.

Things grew worse in August when hundreds of protesters gathered outside the Democratic National Convention hall. The ensuing police riot shocked delegates inside the hall, as well as those of us watching on television across the country. I felt helpless to register my distress effectively. Voting Democratic for the first time in my life was the only gesture I knew.

By the spring of 1969, a new life began for me: I married, completed my Master's degree at the University and abandoned the Ph.D. program, and at the end of the year turned forty. The decade of the 1970s began.

In *The Seventies: The Great Shift in American Culture, Society, and Politics,* Brian Schulman makes a strong case for seeing the 1970s as more than a "wasted decade," or merely a sandwich filling between the explosive 1960s and the conservative 1980s. He calls the 1970s "the long decade," including the years 1968-1984.[2] He argues that the 1970s provided an essential breeding ground for the emergence of a new American character, one focused more individualistically on personal development and away from dependence on the public institutions of government to accomplish societal change.

The killing and wounding of student protesters at Kent State University by the National Guard in May of 1970 had a chilling effect on activism. The protesting yippies at the Democratic National Convention went to Woodstock for a summer of love in 1969, and by 1970 were retreating into rural and urban hippie communes. As the decade wore on, the counterculture of the 1960s went mainstream; the hippie of the 1970s transmuted into the yuppie of the 1980s.

Don and I gravitated easily to hippie ways: Don grew a shaggy beard; we both grew long hair; I sewed dashiki-style shirts for Don; we festooned our South Shore apartment with madras hangings and assembled funky furniture. We hosted weekend gatherings of kindred spirits at our South Shore apartment, talking far into the night, thrashing out issues looming large on the political horizon. Don had never had contact with evangelicals before, and these were evangelicals of a special stripe—progressive, socially concerned, intelligent, free spirits. The 1960s had not touched much of the evangelical subculture as we knew it. We were impatient to ignite a spark in that subculture, to incite Christians to concerted meaningful action. The passion of the 1960s still lived in us, although we failed to acknowledge we came from a basically intellectual point of view. We were more oriented toward educating and serving than storming the barricades of the bastions of power.

We tossed around ideas: performing anti-war guerrilla theatre in the park, or creating "art happenings" in church settings. Don cathected quickly to the prophetic use of the arts, because of his involvement in the 1960s era performance art movement in Chicago. He had observed that evangelicals seemed totally ignorant of modern art, so he suggested establishing a Christian Center for Urban Culture.

BIRTHING THE URBAN LIFE CENTER

Don talked about his vision for introducing Christians to the arts with our minister—Don Davis—and some folks at the newly formed interracial house church in Hyde Park we attended. Momentum began to build. Don Davis responded by adding his ideas to the mix. His passion centered around the racial divide, particularly the apathy and ignorance of suburban evangelical Christians. He wanted some way to bridge the gap between city and suburb, black and white.

Don Davis and I had been part of a little group called "Conversations on the City," which met sporadically during the late 1960s in Chicago. Originally, this group was a split off of the Evangelical Minister's Alliance, and was composed of persons whose theology was conservative, but who wanted to combine concern for social justice with the focus on personal salvation. A distinguishing mark of this smaller group was its stand on racial justice, and the strong determination of its members to stick it out in the inner city in the face of white flight to the suburbs. It included persons like Bill Leslie of LaSalle Street Church, Ray Bakke at Fairfield Baptist, Bill Bentley, an African American pastor on the West Side, and non-ministerial types like Evan Adams from InterVarsity Christian Fellowship, Phyllis Cunningham and me from Pioneer Girls.

The Conversations on the City group was a feisty lot, and tough. Some of us in the group were undergoing radical changes in our thinking. We were on a growing edge that was not yet clearly defined. Phyllis Cunningham, who was at the University of Chicago working on a doctorate in Adult Education, helped us organize a weekend conference national in scope, "Double Exposure on Race," at the University of Chicago's Center for Continuing Education. Charles Hamilton, author of *Black Power* spoke.

For some time, Phyllis had been concerned about the inequities produced in society by racial discrimination. She had gotten involved in a West Side interracial church. At the same time, she had taken some daring steps to change the racial outreach and composition of the entire Pioneer Girls program while she was in charge of the development of North Star, the international leadership training center for the organization. She met with stubborn and racist opposition on both the local level and with the Pioneer Girls board. They "weren't ready" yet. Phyl resigned, as a matter of conscience, in 1967.

Phyllis joined us in the spring of 1970 in conversations about the nebulous idea of an urban center of some sort, perhaps for the arts. She recognized in this informal cluster of friends an opportunity to move on her social and Christian concerns simultaneously. Because of her skill in articulation and organizing, she provided an important stabilizing element to the embryonic ideas and visions floating about from Don Schatz and Don Davis.

At a key point, we got in touch with Dave and Neta Jackson, who also belonged to Phyl's West Side church. They were young and resilient, and were experimenting with a communal lifestyle, sharing an old farm house with another couple in the countryside west of Wheaton.

Dave had his own pilgrimage story, beginning with an experience of radicalization that occurred while he was editor of the school newspaper at Multnomah School of the Bible and where he had espoused an anti-administration view of the Berkeley Free Speech movement. His radicalization took a steep upward turn during the race riots in Chicago after Martin Luther King's assassination in 1968. He had joined the National Guard to avoid being drafted into fighting the Vietnam War. When Mayor Daley called out the Guard to quell the riots on Chicago's West Side, Dave was put in the tenuous position of having to oppose younger members of his own church congregation who could well have been out roaming the streets in those chaotic days of turbulence. After all, the mayor's instructions to the police were "Shoot to kill."

In addition, as Assistant Editor of *Campus Life,* Dave found himself in a continuous dilemma of conscience, precariously perched in a position that was pressing him toward conformity and away from his deepest concerns. His home had become a haven for a small minority of restless, self-proclaimed radicals from Wheaton and Trinity College (Deerfield, Illinois) campuses. Just as Conversations on the City provided shelter for like-minded ministers and Christian workers in Chicago, the Jackson home became a center for conversation and encouragement for students in tune with 1960s anti-war sentiment, the growing spirit of communalism, and a host of issues spawned during that period.

On Wheaton's campus, the Jonathan Blanchard Society became the focal point of the dissidents' activities and energies. It seemed appropriate to hark back to the genuinely radical ideas of the school's founder, for Wheaton had been established, in part, out of protest against slavery, and out of strong social concerns.

Students on the Trinity campus had been caught up in the groundswell of anti-war protests. Jim Wallis, a student at the Divinity School, and a band of fellow students formed the Peoples'

Christian Coalition, which tried to raise issues connected to current dilemmas aboil in the world. Eventually, a cluster of them left along with Jim to take up residence in the poverty-stricken area of Uptown to work among people there. At the same time they carried on communications with a broader spectrum of Christian individuals and groups concerned about justice and peace. Their newspaper, which Don Schatz named *The Post-American,* provided a link with other kindred movements across the country. Eventually they moved to Washington, D.C., renaming their magazine *Sojourners* and establishing a community there.

***

A dozen of us sprawled around in Dave and Neta's living room one evening in the spring of 1970, as all of these histories unfolded. We talked about our restlessness and discontent; we sharply criticized the suburban evangelical subculture, the provincialism and isolation of Christian colleges, their blindness to the issues of war and race. We shared our vision, our ideas for some sort of focal point in the city. The urban location was essential, both for the emphasis on the arts and culture, and the preoccupation with political and sociological issues of racism and militarism.

We decided to set up a "semester in the city" type of program for students from Christian colleges in the area. Students present in the meeting named it the "Urban Life Center" and told us, "If you start this, we'll come this fall and be a part of it." That catapulted us into action.

It only took two spring meetings to launch the Center initially. We rushed in where angels feared to tread. We rented a big old church building (how ambitious we were—and blissfully blind to its unsuitability as living space), hired Dave Jackson as coordinator at a modest enough salary ($8,000), which we thought we could sustain. Phyllis used her academic contacts as leverage to talk a dean of a special division of Roosevelt University into granting credit to our students and paying three of us part-time faculty salaries to teach nine hours of courses that we added to their fall curriculum. Inner-city outposts were looking attractive and "hip" to some college administrators in 1970. We became such an outpost in the Hyde Park area.

By August we were in the church building, armed with buckets of paint, a little lumber for partitions, a load of Army surplus beds and a truckful of old, dorm-room furniture from Moody Bible Institute. Twelve of us signed the articles of incorporation making us legal in Illinois as a private, not-for-profit corporation. We emptied our bank accounts, cashed in life insurance policies and savings bonds, and poured the proceeds into the common coffers. We wrote letters to friends, asking them to invest. Only two of the twelve of us had regular jobs. We were graduate students, professional part-timers, freelancers. By September this motley crew launched the Urban Life Center. Although the fervor with which we launched the Urban Life Center was decidedly 1960s, the form it took was 1970s in character: it included a communal living component; it provided an alternative form of education giving students maximum input in establishing the criteria for grades; and it focused on individual development and consciousness-raising rather than direct activism.

We moved quickly. It's easy to look back askance at our naiveté, our lack of foresight. We paid dearly for a number of our mistakes. But we never stopped to question in those early months. Our fearlessness was our flaw, and our strength, as we moved boldly onto untrodden ground. Something worthwhile was born, that would last into the twenty-first century.

Implementing the Vision

The brief two meetings it took to launch the Center were more than balanced out by the two years it took for the project to stabilize, involving long hours of meetings. When we incorporated, we decided on a board structure that would allow us maximum flexibility and minimum interference. We wanted a working board, people who would wield hammer, saw and paintbrush; who would raise funds, determine curriculum, recruit students.

Phyllis and I came to this enterprise jaundiced by our experience at Pioneer Girls with its self-perpetuating board. We had seen two executive directors cruelly ousted, and had been subject to decisions which at times we considered out-of-touch with or antithetical to the concerns of our constituency and to changing trends in our rapidly changing culture.

So we opted for a more democratic framework. This resulted in board meetings of interminable length creating twelve sore rumps. There was always that impossible item on every agenda: financing. So many decisions to be made and we were doing it by *consensus.* Our democratic ideals were about to hang us up permanently. Students and older adults were to be equally involved in decision-making at all levels, but after two or three hours of sitting in a board meeting, students got fidgety. They'd had their say about program and living arrangements. They weren't interested in deciding whether to hire a plumber or not, or in the details of raising funds.

Old familiar attitudes of resentment came cropping up, reminiscent of college administrators. "You try to give young people a voice, but they aren't willing to take the responsibility that goes with privilege and freedom." We were struggling to provide a truly different environment from the college campuses from which students had come, with their rules and stifling of dissent. We counted on the altruism of the students to take this move into the city as an opportunity to act on the ideals we had articulated together in the spring, only to find out that when the students arrived, they descended to Maslow's first rung on the maturation scale: physiological safety, closely followed by psychological survival.

Students had said they wanted community, and we thought the vast spaces of the church building would serve adequately for this purpose, but instead it did everything to militate against it. The church education unit, where we set up living space, had cold cement floors, high ceilings, and drab green walls. The frosted windows let in the scant light that filtered down between closely set buildings and penetrated the gloom. Makeshift partitions had to be constructed to afford some privacy. Colorful posters and madras bedspreads were tacked onto the walls in a desperate effort to make it look cheerful. Dave and Neta tried to make their corner space on the second floor feel like a happy and fun home for Julian, their toddler son.

Communal living was the order of the day, but when this necessitated doing chores, there began to be immense areas of fallout and breakdown. We discovered that these young people lacked experience in sharing the work load necessary for making a community function effectively. Some lacked essential skills. Phil, a gentle long-haired blond fellow from New Jersey, decided to make spaghetti one night. He knew the ingredients, but was at a loss as to how to combine them. So the raw noodles, tomato sauce and hamburger all went into the frying pan together, until some kind female happened by and with a shriek rescued the meal from total failure. All was not lost, however, for several years later Phil embarked on a career as a gourmet cook.

The creation of a curriculum fell to some of the twelve members of the Board. Various ones of us would come to the Center for an evening to team-teach a seminar that used the varieties of expertise found among this diverse and talented board, several of whom were in graduate programs at the University of Chicago. We began using popular techniques of the Alternative Education movement—letting students set up learning contracts in order to grade themselves according to pre-set criteria which they developed. We had read *The Student as Nigger*, and other books critical of the academic process, and were as game to experiment as the students were to have us allow them this new freedom. The concept of freedom entailing responsibility was very slow to catch on among these nineteen- and twenty-year-olds. We learned the hard way.

Meanwhile, finances were perilously thin. Everything was done on a volunteer basis except for the directors, Dave and Neta Jackson. By November, we began to fall behind in payment to them.

Tensions mounted.

We had envisioned using the church sanctuary for larger gatherings, possibly arts-related, to which the university community could be invited. We hoped we could raise some income by this means. We were therefore delighted when musician Oscar Brown and his group asked to rent the space on a regular basis. The place would soon be rocking.

Alas, the cold winds of winter began to blow, and we discovered what a voracious appetite the furnace had when asked to heat an entire sanctuary area. The oil bills rolled in, but Oscar's rental payments did not. One especially ugly interchange occurred one day when Dave and Phyllis approached the woman who was Oscar's manager and asked for payment. Her response was not encouraging, so Dave and Phyl reminded her that regardless of Oscar's problems, Standard Oil Company must be paid. She looked at the two of them with scathing scorn, saying, "You *own* it!" and flounced off. Inside, they cringed. They might have termed themselves liberal, or even radical, but now they were merely "Whitey" and seen as holding the strings of power. Feeling helpless and stung with rage, they turned and walked away.

A few weeks later, Dave and Neta announced they had reached the bottom of their barrel. The dilemma was producing an alienation between the Jacksons who were bearing the brunt of the day-to-day harassment of students and oil companies and musicians, and the rest of the board who came in to teach and to engage in endless board meeting discussions about the state of the finances. At the end of the spring term, they left.

Phyllis agreed to move in temporarily. She did not want to see the project flounder; and she had the temperament and capacity to take on the daunting task of restoring some order to the chaotic environment. To meet our urgent financial needs, we began accepting live-in persons who were not students. It was not hard to find people who needed some place to hang out in those days, interested only in survival and their own comfort, rootless souls who proved destructive to the ideals of the program. We were reluctant to admit there were some unsavory things out of our control happening along the edges of the enterprise.

About this time, Don called on an old family friend, Jim Bertucci, to come in and take a look at some of the problems we were encountering in the physical facility. Jim came, and was instantly intrigued. He began hanging out at the Center. Jim was born in Little Italy, of an Italian mother and an African American father. He had taken the Italian surname and become a runner for the Mafia in order to survive in his ghetto. He was tall and lean, muscular, and could take in an entire situation in a glance, and penetrate to the heart of what was going on. He and Phyllis got along famously; something in them was cut out of the same cloth, a determination not to be beat down by obstacles. Jim got interested in the architecture of the church, climbing into nooks and crannies near the roof and familiarizing himself with the systems housed in the basement. Jim also knew how to handle some of the problems raised by our increasingly difficult clientele.

During our second year, the program took a turn. We had fewer students living at the Center from Christian colleges; instead, there were a number of commuter students at Roosevelt who were selecting our offerings of classes and coming to the Center twice a week for studies. With Dave and Neta gone, Don and I began hanging out at the Center on a more regular basis, dropping in after our work and handling various responsibilities having to do with the maintenance of the Center's program.

We continued to provide short-term programs for Christian colleges nearby. Students came in by bus for a day or a weekend. We exposed them to ethnic neighborhoods, to cultural events, to persons in positions of political influence. We had developed an impressive network of contacts: Circuit Court judges, Aldermen, artists in both classical and folk traditions, independent journalists, key community leaders in African American and Chicano neighborhoods. Sociology professors loved it. They would have been shocked to discover how close to collapse the Center was at the time. We were stunned too. We struggled blindly, hamstrung by a huge unwieldy building that sucked up our money and gave little of value back.

We hung on by a thread. Toward the end of that second year, Phyllis and I went out for lunch one day to talk about prospects for the fall which looked bleak. Should we give up the program now, and cut our losses, marking it off as a failure? This looked like a reasonable course to take, but it was against our instincts. We do not take to failure easily.

Phyllis offered to borrow money from her mother and buy a building more amenable to our needs. We would pay the mortgage payments as rent to her and cover the cost of utilities and day-to-day maintenance. She left the task of finding a suitable building up to the rest of us. We found a three-story brownstone nearby with five bedrooms. We had only two students signed up for fall. Phyl would serve as residential head, and one of our board members, Kathy Blair, would serve as residential assistant. In September, Phyllis moved in, an act of pure faith, not having seen her new home before moving day.

The building at 5004 Blackstone looked like Eden to all of us. Fully carpeted downstairs and up the stairs, with attractive multi-paned windows looking out onto Kenwood High School across the street, this was everything that the cavernous and gloomy church building had not been. It was *home* and it might be possible to create some semblance of community here.

STARTING OVER

In September of 1972, the Urban Life Center made a new beginning. Don and I had kept our day jobs teaching part-time at Roosevelt University, but we now moved the Center office into the living room of the new house, and showed up every day. We had already taken recruiting trips to the campuses of a number of Christian colleges in Indiana, Illinois, and Michigan. We started with Goshen, a Mennonite school in Indiana. The sociology professor seemed impressed that Roosevelt University had granted academic credit to students for our program. We made an impelling presentation everywhere we went, and always found a select number of students who were attracted to the idea of spending a semester off campus in the city. The restless student rebellions of the 1960s had prompted key professors and academic deans to see the advantage of providing an off-campus experience for their students. Slowly, school by school, deans became willing to write contracts whereby we would receive tuition from the school for each student who came. At last, we began to operate on a sound financial basis.

Semester by semester, enrollment in the Urban Life Center program grew. The house provided a built-in size limitation which was ideal for the building of community, and for a meaningful education with plenty of individual student contact. We no longer worked under the assumption that we could create a genuine consensual community with a new student group each semester. We renamed the house a "co-op" and instituted minimal structure and controls. We introduced a required course in Group Dynamics in order to help students adapt to the living situation with more equanimity and skill. We continued to involve board members with the students and program, but gradually the work was more and more in the hands of the residential staff and Don and me.

Jim Bertucci continued to hang out with us. He was often called to attend to a crisis, like a burst hot water pipe, and then he might putter around and install a chandelier in the dining room. We never asked where it came from; Jim was good at scrounging and salvaging items others might throw away. He began to get interested in the program we were providing, not just the physical aspects of the building where his competence so far exceeded ours. He suggested he would like to take groups of students to his old neighborhood in Little Italy and introduce them to the folks on the block, the store keepers, the tradesmen, to get a glimpse of life as it was daily experienced. He wanted students to see the local culture at its raw street level, human being to human being. He helped them appreciate the folk art, the ethnic foods, the natural barriers—bridges, railroad underpasses, medial strips— which demarcated ethnic enclaves from one another, thereby helping students make sense of what would otherwise seem alien or ugly or chaotic.

Thus began an important feature of our program, Jim's personally led tours. It was not only Little Italy Jim knew like the back of his hand. He was comfortable in the black community, in Chinatown (where he said the mafia leaders used to meet), the Mexican community, Uptown (an area occupied by new arrivals from Appalachia, among others), the posh section of the local area where Elijah Muhammad's castle-like home was located. Jim would drop students off to wander the streets for awhile, then come back and talk, full of questions coming from firsthand experience. Jim's formal education had stopped in the sixth grade, but he was self-educated and bright, and more than a match for these college students from sheltered environments. Jim's contribution to the program satisfied one of our important goals: changing attitudes of students toward the city by introducing them to it in such a way that they could overlook its stereotypical flaws and perceive its hidden charms.

Resolving Tensions

From the beginning, there were lots of interpersonal struggles among us, some of which were stimulating and provocative. We studiously avoided stating any explicit theological basis in our charter so we could remain inclusive. One of our Board members, Bruce, was writing his doctoral dissertation in New Testament at the University of Chicago. Born of missionary parents, Bruce had taken a long journey from the faith of his parents. The trail led from Columbia Bible College to Westminster Seminary to Temple University to Tubingen in Germany to the University of Chicago. Along the way, he had jettisoned much of the Christology he had been taught, and felt he could no longer in all honesty call himself a Christian. Although we considered the Urban Life Center to be Christian, we shied away from identifying with the kind of evangelical faith most of us had espoused in our younger years. I felt a strong affinity with Bruce, and was determined not to shut him out, although I was puzzled at his insistence on literal honesty about not being a Christian. We were quite cavalier about our faith, it seems to me now. It was not a stretch to include Bruce. I think he felt a little pulled by our acceptance of his agnostic position, as though we would convince him to admit something he no longer felt.

The ambiguity of our position on theology, our lack of insistence on certain spiritual practices (church attendance, daily prayer, grace at meals), and our greater toleration of unapproved habits of life (drinking, smoking, using irreverent language) placed us in a precarious position in relationship to the schools that were sending us their students, steeped in the innocence of their isolated enclaves in rural Michigan, Indiana, Kansas, and Illinois. We hoped they would not ask us too many questions, and indeed they were probably reluctant to probe too closely. They genuinely trusted us and our Christian foundation. Our policy banning sex and drugs in the house reassured them. Beyond that, we wanted to give students a greater measure of freedom than their campuses allowed, even as we attempted to create a program that required them to take more responsibility.

Other struggles were not as creative and stimulating. Our board meetings were often tumultuous, and always extremely lengthy. I shied away from directing the organization assertively with the wisdom and objectivity it needed. There were several strong independent vocal members who easily persuaded me to adopt their positions; at times I lacked the courage to stand up for my own views. Instead I kept hoping that others would support me in my position; I did not pick up the reins and lead. I was moving toward a softer approach, and more intimate contact with individuals. But I did not know that then.

Passing the Torch to the Second Generation

In 1977, a group of students came for our special January term from Tabor College in Kansas, shepherded by their Sociology teacher, Scott Chesebro, and his wife Norene. Scott and Norene liked what they saw at the Center, and over the next few months made the momentous decision to leave college teaching and come to Chicago to work with us at the Urban Life Center. They arrived in the fall and began the process of getting heeled into the ongoing program. We made every effort to include them at the core of responsibility, knowing how difficult it had been for other part-time staff members, most of whom were younger and less trained, to feel equal authority with the trio of persons who were founders—Phyllis, Don and me.

I thought things were going well. At a staff meeting in late winter, we sat down to make plans and distribute responsibility for upcoming events. I volunteered to continue writing the newsletter, figuring no one else would want to do this. Scott demurred. He would like to take this on, it turned out. I was stunned! At the time, I thought that doing this writing would keep me in the background, but Scott quickly saw that the person who wields the pen actually has a lot of power in determining how the program is presented to the wider public. I was honestly taken aback.

I argued with Scott at first, then after a moment of quiet, something shifted inside me. "Scott, the newsletter is yours," I said. Now it was his turn to express surprise. "Really?" He wanted to make sure I was not just giving in on the surface. But I was certain, deeply certain.

I had been increasingly restless in my position as director, especially since spending a year in Facilitator Training at the Oasis Center for Human Potential. My experience there had whetted my appetite for a more person-to-person role in my work, and I had become much more focused on my counseling sessions with individual students than on the administration of the overall program. Scott's eagerness to assume more control left me free to surrender my position as director unequivocally. I could feel it in my body that evening. I was exhilarated.

The Role of the Founder

I was facing a familiar and fascinating issue: the dynamics in Christian organizations revolving around leadership succession. I had observed how founders frequently made poor administrators, precisely because of the passion of their vision and their intolerance of the second generation who come on board with an interest in organization that does not seem to be quickened by the same degree of fervor as the founders. I desperately did not want to fall into the quicksand I had seen envelop such persons.

I had experienced the process of birthing a movement with others and becoming wholly given to it. Just as I had felt intensely involved in the development of Pioneer Girls and in those who were its founders, now I was heavily identified in this enterprise upon which Don and I had made indelible imprints. In both cases, I had been so identified with my work that it became play—pure exhilarating pleasure. I never counted the hours or rewards. There were so many times when my colleagues and I looked back on the early days' moments of agony with boisterous replays in conversation. These memories became the badge of "in-ness" to us as the founding group.

I also had seen the way everything got sacrificed for the cause, with the inevitable treading on toes, the falling out of friends or fellow workers, coupled with a ruthlessness of vision. I had observed moments when an insidious ingrownness began to take over, the drawing in like a turtle or a snail, a defensiveness against attacks from the outside. I was aware that jargon creeps in, the special words that defined Us, as against Them. It became easy to dismiss those whose dedication was less than total.

I was especially intrigued by the role of the founder, who ultimately becomes most closely identified with the organization. How does the creator survive the growth of the child he/she helped birth? Now that I was on the verge of handing over the reins of leadership to a second generation, I began asking searching questions:

> *What makes the "pioneer" get involved in the first place? What is the founder's genius, her unique gift? Why did she/he become pivotal? How is this sustained?*

I had watched weaknesses emerge within founders of organizations which hindered their effectiveness. Now I had to assess my own talents and liabilities. A shift had occurred in our leadership structure at the Center that altered my perceptions about my place and power. I needed to step back decisively and remove myself in some sense. The "central person phenomenon" may be inevitable in small movements like the ones I knew. It may be in the nature of new organizations to require certain predictable stages, and just as likely, it may be in the nature of a creator to find a situation where he/she can become central.

LETTING GO

These and other thoughts engrossed me as I considered the implications of our talk with Scott and Norene. As soon as Don and I reached our apartment that evening, we sat down to mull over our situation together. We talked a long time, not bothering to turn on a lamp as dusk deepened across the room. We had been increasingly restless to make a change in our lives, and now we realized we were free to leave the Urban Life Center. Suddenly our vistas widened.

Over the next few weeks, we made our plans carefully. There were elements of the Urban Life Center project that were still fragile, and we had been dominant figures for eight years. We decided to ask for a sabbatical in the fall, and use that time to check out future possibilities and make our decision. We made a proposal to the Board, promising them we would return for the January term in 1979.

An entry in my journal suggests that I was beginning to move away from my preoccupation with the arena of social action and toward a journey that would explore a more personal dimension of the inner life:

> *Will I find my new future in some exploration of self, rather than service to society? Is this the deeper, more daring trip? I am taught that it is weaker, escapist, self-centered. I must be very sure before I embark on this Second Journey.*
>
> *". . .the images and symbols of our minds introduce us to a wider world than that of our actual historic life."*
>
> *Perhaps some answers will come to me through the life*

of the imagination as I set my sails, and remain open to the winds that blow. Winds of the Spirit. Winds of my dreams.

In the fall of 1978, Don and I set sail into these winds on our four-month sabbatical odyssey.

At that stage, I did not predict the resilience of the Center in lasting over time. Thirty years later, Chicago's mayor declared July 17, 2000, as "Urban Life Center Day" in the city, in recognition of the contribution of its students and staff to Chicago in many significant ways. The resolution passed by the City Council said, in part:

The Urban Life Center has placed more than five thousand university students from around the United States in Chicago communities as volunteer interns, having contributed this year alone, over fifteen thousand hours of volunteer work.

The Urban Life Center has added to the positive development of Chicago by encouraging hundreds of its alumni to settle and work in Chicago as teachers, social service agency directors, business leaders, artists and other community leaders.

Clearly there is continuing Life at the Center.

nine

Sabbath Time

Sabbath implies a willingness to be surprised by unexpected grace. . .when what is finished inevitably recedes. . .[and we are] surprised by fruitful beginnings.
Wayne Muller, Sabbath[1]

THE FOUR SHORT months of our sabbatical were curtained by two deaths—one at the beginning, the other at the end. On a sunny August morning, we bid goodbye to Chicago's beloved skyline, and headed east. We had set aside the first month for a writing retreat in an idyllic setting in Rockport, Massachusetts, in the home of a friend who lived across the street from the Atlantic Ocean. Before we could touch down in Rockport, while traveling through New Hampshire, a phone call from my mother, now living in California, interrupted our plans. My father had been taken to the hospital, and his life hung in the balance.

Don and I flew out to California to be with my parents. I was shaken to find that my reactions were embarrassingly typical. It was the little things. Outside the hospital room, the family gathered and talked as his life was ebbing away. We found ourselves slipping into the past tense. "He was always so..." and then we would catch ourselves, guiltily, and correct it: "He *is*..." Much to my surprise, several weeks later as Mother and I sat talking in the deepening dusk the evening after he died, I noticed we were using the present tense, as though Dad were yet alive.

At the hospital, when he was so close to slipping away, we came to accept his death as desirable. He was eighty-six, and a number of bodily frailties had taken their toll, so life was far from comfortable and satisfying to him. He was not strong enough to travel, or take in cultural events, or walk in the countryside nearby, and increasingly his eyes were dimmed so he couldn't spend time with his loved books—the greatest source of stimulation all his life. He said it plainly and openly and often: "I want to go Home."

But in those weeks of waiting, Dad began to get better—just enough to make us pause. I found myself feeling anger about the good medical care he was receiving that would prolong life but not improve its quality; at best it could only defer the inevitable by weeks or perhaps months. We in the family were working hard to allow him to die—even make it easier for him to go quickly, without lingering. We were confused—and ambivalent. My husband and I had flown 3,500 miles across the country expecting a funeral. And Dad wouldn't die to convenience our schedule.

I lived with that conflict as Don and I returned to the East Coast. Three weeks later the phone call came announcing that Dad had died—at home, in relative peace, early in the morning on the very day he was to be admitted to a nursing home. Did he intuit this, and insist on dying at home?

I don't regret the timing now. Those two weeks with Dad in the hospital gave me a chance to say a meaningful good-bye while he was lucid and alert. He knew I was there, and said little appreciative things to me as I fed him, or combed his hair and beard, or just stroked his furrowed forehead with my hand.

I observed Dad intently for long periods of time, wanting not to recoil from his gaunt bony frame, so like a victim of Holocaust. His fingers and toes were purple from lack of circulation. I would rub them with lotion. After each meal, I cleaned his rotting teeth, learning how to do it painlessly. I watched him sleep, the facial contortions, the beautiful snow-white hair, the hollowed socket where he had never had sight in one eye. I wanted to know death intimately and not be put off by its grotesqueness.

I was learning by all this that the body is the shell of a person. When I flew out for the funeral, the body had already been prepared for burial. I had not seen Dad dead, and it seemed important to me to do so, although I was filled with dread in facing death's utter finality. With my mother and my brother, Phil, and his daughter, Jane, I went to the funeral home Sunday evening, where the casket was opened for us. Standing there, looking at that beautiful peaceful face, I spontaneously exclaimed, "He looks so good," something I had heard others say at such a time. I always used to wonder why it mattered, but I found that it was instinctive to want the loved one who died to look at peace.

I reached out, very frightened, and touched his chest. I was unprepared for the hard, stiff feeling of the body. I flashed on phrases I had heard: "rigor mortis," "stiffs." As I touched, and looked, I suddenly "knew" that Dad was not at home any longer in that body.

Back at the house, I wandered into the room where he died, trying to absorb the fact that he was gone. I leafed through the books on his shelf, the scrapbooks he kept, the poems he had written. I fingered his clothes in the closet, looked at the neat piles of socks and shaving gear and bow ties in the dresser drawer. There were his unpublished manuscripts neatly stacked in several file drawers, the strongbox full of envelopes, their contents meticulously labeled.

I was free to follow the instincts of my body in grieving. Each morning I awakened with a new consciousness, emerging out of a nether world of dreams and blissful healing *un*consciousness. The first morning it was to realize, "My heart aches." Some aching permeated every part of my body, but I felt it most keenly in my heart.

Upon awaking the second morning, my body felt heavy and sick to the roots. I saw that I had no control over this grieving process. I simply had to let my body do its work. On a conscious level, I voiced my feeling: *"My body is bearing within it Dad's dying,"* and remembered a similar phrase from the Apostle Paul: "I bear in my body the dying of the Lord Jesus." I wondered fleetingly if there were a connection.

The third morning, I awoke to an engulfing sense of sadness. I knew I had to get to a place where I would be free to let go, away from Mother. I walked out to the back wall behind our garden. In my mind's eye, I stood at the Jerusalem wailing wall, a satisfying end place where I could feel myself up against an ultimate barrier—death, God, whatever. I reached up with both hands on the stony surface and let the sobs come.

The body knew its rhythms. So I moved from solitude to companionship as I needed to reflect or be comforted. I could not stand the rawness of grief continually, so I cherished the intrusions of friends and their loving sympathy.

Through all of this, I was aware that my mother's experience of Dad's death was substantively different. I was tempted to feel guilty for my open expressions of bereavement. Mother would look at me with alarm. *"If Eunice falls apart... ,"* I could picture her contemplating. I recognized hers was the far greater loss. Yet I was often the one to break down openly, to talk about my feelings. I felt I should be strong, the one to be leaned on. I wasn't—not in the sense of composure and control. I became a little girl again, who had lost her Daddy.

Others in the extended family carried their mourning differently. My nephew Ted could not bring himself to attend his grandfather's funeral. There did not seem to be any adequate explanation; I passed it off as a young person's reluctance to face his mortality.

The Shadow Falls

The sabbatical had scarcely ended, and we were back in Chicago for our final month of work at the Center, when a phone call came from my brother in California. His son, Ted, had killed himself the night before at the age of twenty-six. Our dwindling family system reeled under this second shock, one more cruel than my father's death. I got on a plane and flew west, heartsick.

The story is familiar, in some ways. Ted had struggled with alcohol and drugs, and had recently come clean. His first marriage had ended and he had entered into what promised to be a very happy marriage with Sue, a woman aged forty-two with an eleven-year-old daughter who adored Ted. My brother and his wife, Betty, were optimistic about Ted's and Sue's future. There were some snarls to work out, as is always the case where an ex-husband and custody are involved. One night, a conflict erupted, and in an irrational moment of anger, Ted decided to solve the problem by removing himself. The existence of a pistol in his closet made his decision inevitably fatal.

For me, in the midst of a major life and work transition, grieving my father's death served to eclipse the shock of the suicide. I hardly knew my nephew; he had lived so far away that I only saw him and his family at infrequent intervals. By contrast, the consciousness of my father inhabited every fiber of my being. I was packing to move cross-country to New England, the place of my birth. I would be walking under the elms in Harvard Yard just as my father had done more then a half century earlier. I would be moving into an area of Boston known as Upham's Corner, named for the family of my great grandmother, Mary Eunice Upham.

So my brother and his family moved on in their lives, and so did I. A large shadow moved over the extended family and hovered there for decades. My niece, Jane, and her husband and children, moved to Camarillo to be close to her grieving parents. But the tragic event exacted its price from each member of the family over the years. It was difficult to know how to grieve, or how to reach out to those most affected. A suicide is so mercilessly public, and so devastatingly private.

I packed my sorrows and headed for Boston.

ten

The End of Ideals

BY MARCH OF 1979, Don and I were on our way to Boston to live. During our sabbatical trip in the fall of 1978, we had visited both Washington, D. C. and Boston, with an eye to starting life over in one of those two cities. While we were in Boston checking things out, we met Ben Mehrling, a man who shared our interest in alternative education and issues of peace and social justice. He made a strong case for us moving to Boston, announcing that he had bought a three-decker in Dorchester and would save the first floor apartment for us at the unheard of price of $110 a month. We had been wavering between the two cities; Ben's offer confirmed our decision to move to Boston, a city that felt more cosmopolitan to us. The university community was strong there, which boded well for bookstores and other evidences of culture. Washington seemed provincial, and dominated by the overwhelming presence of the federal government.

We were excited about the move. Don had lived all his life within a three-mile radius on Chicago's South Side. He thought it was time to discover himself in a new setting and to pursue his writing more seriously. As for me, change was in the fiber of my bones. I looked forward to establishing myself in a new surrounding, especially since it meant returning to New England, which felt like coming home.

On a blustery March day, we packed up our worldly goods, put them into a U-Haul truck, and pulled out of the snow-packed driveway of our South Shore apartment in Chicago. In the course of our travel, the snow by the sides of the road disappeared and a soft rain welcomed us as we found our way at last through the labyrinth of

Boston expressways into Dorchester, along Boston's south shore.

As we exited the last toll booth in Cambridge, out of the corner of my eye I saw a car speeding down an entry ramp and gauged my own speed accordingly, confident that the car entering would be yielding to the main traffic on the turnpike. Wrong. It zoomed ahead of us with brazen foolhardiness. It was my first introduction to Boston driving, something we accustomed ourselves to very quickly. In the end, we decided that Boston driving habits actually make good sense. It became perfectly understandable that one would sometimes need to make a left turn from a right hand lane, or proceed through a red light, and accomplish other tricks of the road for the sake of efficiency in a city that has few geometric street patterns. If it were only Boston's driving code we had to master! We plunged into our new life in Boston with hopeful naiveté, having no clue as to what lay ahead in this unfamiliar context.

We made the final turn onto Maryland Street, where our apartment was located. The one-way street was narrow, crowded with parked cars on both sides. Instead of the solid brick buildings several stories high to which we were accustomed in Chicago, we were met by a row of closely set wooden "three-deckers" immediately bordering the sidewalk, a signature of Boston's communities. Several vacant lots yawned menacingly across the street, a sign of burned out buildings. Landlords were often happy to recover their losses on a building in a poor neighborhood by arson, and there were always persons willing to do the torching. We did not know it then, but one such volunteer was sitting on the front steps of our apartment building to greet us as we pulled up in our truck. Jimmy, our second floor neighbor, sauntered off the steps and came toward us smiling cheerfully. He offered to help us unpack. Naively, we struck up a conversation, unaware that he was casing our load for any choice items that might one day be removed. I began to be a little wary when he volunteered helpful suggestions for a way to siphon gas out of somebody else's tank. He appeared to have a number of such skills on his resumé. But on the whole we remained blissfully innocent, as Jimmy chatted volubly on.

Ben told us that the previous tenant on the first floor was leaving a refrigerator for us, but there was none in sight when we entered the kitchen. We asked Jimmy about this, thinking he might know. He declared he was clueless. Upon inspection of the basement, however, we found a refrigerator in a back storeroom. Jimmy said it belonged to his uncle.

We called Ben, who was puzzled. We talked to Jimmy again a couple of times, beginning to suspect he might know more than he said. We went to a used appliance store nearby to check out prices for a used refrigerator. We made sure Jimmy knew this was putting us to a lot of trouble. Next day, he came and told us he had obtained a refrigerator for us. Taking us down to the basement, he proudly showed us a dark green refrigerator in the back storeroom. He had painted the refrigerator a lurid Kelly green and now wanted twenty-five dollars for it. We paid rather than try to confront this wily man. I painted huge daisies on the door to mask the hideous paint job.

We began to settle into our new community. We were full of eagerness and zeal to show our openness and inclusiveness to our neighbors. On one trip to the hardware store, we greeted the storekeeper by introducing ourselves as the Schatz's. He looked at us quizzically. "You spell that S-h-o-r-t-s?" he asked. We'd forgotten that rounded Eastern accent.

We went about the task of setting up housekeeping with a vengeance. We put up curtain rods, peg boards, shelves and picture hangers, endlessly it seemed to my husband who declared he knew nothing about carpentry. "Why," he once told a friend, "I can't even screw in a nail." So much for that.

There were immense hurdles to overleap: problems to solve, decisions to make. But none stuck so in the craw of our systems as the problem posed by our bathroom sink which was missing a stopper. It fell to me to solve the problem. I measured the diameter carefully—one and a quarter inches exactly. And off to the store I went.

And that is where the story should end, but instead began with a city-wide search for the Tight Sink Stopper, trying various sizes and style, none of which worked. Then I remembered Arnie, the little man on the corner in a store without a name. Every day, children hung out there after school, making ponderous choices about penny candy in the dim recesses of the crowded single-room store. All the merchandise was covered with layers of dust, but there were one-of-a-kind surprises in abundance all over, as I had already discovered when I needed a special light bulb. The proprietor made change from his trousers pocket. His counter was a rough-hewn wooden slab—indented with many metal-reinforced pockets containing treasures for a pittance.

My instincts were flawless. At first I wasn't sure, for he also had no inch-and-a-quarter stoppers, though he had one of almost every other conceivable size. However, when I laid out my dilemma to him, he spoke with authority. "Buy the inch-and-an-eighth stopper," he said. "Is it a bathroom sink? Sure, that's the right size. I been selling them here for forty-five years." Without a moment's hesitation, I bought the stopper, and was not a whit surprised to find it fit exactly when I got home.

It was to Arnie's I returned several months later, in need of embroidery floss. It seemed unlikely he would carry something so un-hardware but I must try, and it was far more convenient to go around the corner than to take the subway downtown. Arnie took one look at the sample I showed. "Sure, I got what you need," he said, and shuffled to the back of one of the narrow aisles, moved unerringly to a certain shelf holding a series of dusty little boxes. He pulled one out, and *voilà!* there were several skeins of embroidery floss, one of each of several colors. Although my demand was rare, he charged only what such an item would have brought ten years earlier when he had acquired his stock.

Kids in the neighborhood tended to treat Arnie cruelly, at the same time that they flocked to his store after school. When Arnie got annoyed, he drove some nails into his counter. "The girls come in here after school and sit on my counter," he complained to me when I mentioned the ominous-looking surface. He knew they would not be inclined to perch on top of those nails.

Arnie was a legend in the neighborhood. He was Jewish, and when others of his community had fled to safer territory, he had to stay for economic reasons. He was a bit tottering by the time we arrived, and there were times when the store was closed because Arnie was in poor health. He was rumored to have cancer. One day, the shutters came down for good. A graffiti sign appeared on the side brick wall of his store, "Arnie Lives," it proclaimed, an affectionate farewell from the kids who used to haunt and taunt him, but who counted on him to be there with his archaic assemblage of penny candy and other treats.

The Neighborhood

There were other trials, among them a reluctant furnace. We were not sure if there was an oil leak, or if some thoughtful neighbor was siphoning off our supply. We felt quite primitive and adventurous, Don wearing thirteen layers of underwear and shirts and an old navy stocking cap while he assiduously worked on his drawings. We had become accustomed to brick structures in Chicago. Now we must adjust to the greater airiness of wooden tenements.

If Jimmy was the thoughtful neighbor siphoning off our oil, which became increasingly likely, it was not his only activity of that nature. We noticed a number of long distance calls to Florida on our phone bill. The phone company checked and found that the calls had gone to a family named "Morris" —Jimmy's last name. The phone company generously gave us credit, but we were suspicious. We began hearing strange clicks when we lifted our phone receiver to make a call. Apparently someone was on the line. We asked the phone company to come out and check. I went down to the basement with the repairman who took one look at the connections and instantly dialed his supervisor. "Get out of there as fast as you can," yelled his supervisor. Clearly, something illegal was going on. Jimmy had connected his phone to our line and not only was making calls to his relatives on our line, but we now knew that his wife Shelley had been listening to our calls as well. Some of those calls had been frantic ones to our landlord because of our growing suspicions about Jimmy's activities. An enmity which had been latent was now overt.

Jimmy seemed to come and go frequently. We sometimes knew he was home because there would be a fight upstairs, often between Jimmy and Shelley's brother who would come by and stir up trouble. At the conclusion of these Saturday night fights, we would hear a ruckus on the stairs, as someone's body careened down and out the door. We had never lived so close to this kind of violence before, and we were frightened.

We were soon to learn how naive we were. We had lived in a middle class black community on Chicago's South Shore, and had experienced the usual urban difficulties common in the 1970s. Like everyone else we knew, we had been ripped off—as the saying went—more than ten times in our first decade of marriage. We treated this casually since a number of these occasions involved persons we knew: thirteen-year-old Frankie, who lived upstairs, and left his big sneaker footprints on our linoleum floor, leading to the place where a camera he admired had once hung on a hook; and José, a musician, who came over to jam one night, and left with a twenty dollar bill I had carelessly left in an open purse on a table.

Burglary did not appear to be the prime problem on Maryland Street. Rather it appeared to be a place for street clashes. A policeman once told us, "Maryland Street? When I was a kid we used to come down to Maryland Street to fight." *Great,* we thought. The street was occupied by poor white Irish families, with the predictable array of problems: alcoholism, verbal and sexual abuse, grinding poverty.

A Cambodian family moved in across the street, and we made friendly gestures toward them. Race had been an issue in our Chicago experience, and we were well attuned to it. However, here our welcoming gestures were a sign to our neighbors that we were on the wrong side of the issue. There were epithets shouted at us, egg on our window, and slashed tires. The Cambodians were not to be made to feel welcome on this turf.

Our very first week in town, we had purchased a desk from a used furniture shop nearby. The delivery arrived at dusk one evening. When the African American drivers stepped out into the street to open the back of the truck, our next door neighbor came out shrieking, "Tell those niggers to move that truck on out of here!" We were appalled. No one would have dared yell that back in Chicago. With a forty per cent black population in the 1970s, racism was more apt to be covert, though pervasive. We were shocked to find that in Boston, with a mere ten per cent black population at the time, racism was overt. Also, a sizable proportion of the black community had immigrated from the Caribbean. I was surprised the day I walked into a supermarket on Columbia Road to find that not only was I the lone white person in the store but also the only one who was not speaking French.

We did not know how to live according to our ideals in this community. Race clashed with class, and we were caught in the middle. I marvel that we stayed on Maryland Street six years, alternately enduring the heat and withdrawing in fright within our four walls.

I was acutely aware of the absence of the bourgeois trappings I'd grown used to in my South Side Chicago community. Houses on Maryland Street in Dorchester weren't carpeted. The sinks stood alone in the kitchens, bereft of cabinets. The refrigerators didn't defrost themselves. The pipes weren't all in the walls; some were in the room in plain view. The basement had a dirt floor. The dogs weren't on leash (and consequently barked less to proclaim their territory). Kids played in the streets constantly, and mothers screamed at them. Classical music, jazz, great art, discussion of ideas, going to the museum—these were for Cambridge, not Dorchester.

I was dismayed at my own reactions. I was alternately critical and horrified by my surroundings. To attempt to identify with my neighbors seemed to be totally out of the question. It appeared that "downward mobility" didn't suit me well, despite my radical Christian rhetoric.

First Sunday in Boston

By the time we arrived in Boston, we had no church home. But we decided to try again here, for we were hungry now. On our first Sunday morning, Don and I ventured out to Boston's South End to be with brothers and sisters at worship. The experience was electrifying in itself, and was compounded by all the raw emotions surrounding our uprooted state. But at such times there is also more clarity.

The sign outside announced it as "South End Neighborhood Church." It was located in a building occupied by an urban ministry called Emmanuel Gospel Center directed by Doug and Judy Hall, whom we knew by reputation. Inside, we instantly felt the neighborliness, as a friendly tail-wagging dog bounded through the foyer, sniffing out people as they entered. A lady in the third row had a small cache of biscuits that she surreptitiously distributed to the dog as members assembled.

I kept looking for some distinguishing mark of commonality. Was this a church of poor people? Of Latinos? Of street folks? There seemed to be one of every category I could identify. The organist paused between chords of her prelude to "sign" to two obviously deaf persons in the front row. Later, she interpreted the entire sermon for them. A second dog made his appearance shortly. This time he seemed to belong, for his mistress was blind. She sat in her chair, rocking back and forth.

I was struck by the variety of skin colors. Every two or three chairs, the colors changed. But still no categories stuck. Some were well-dressed; some shabby. Some faces looked gaunt and worried, a little out-of-touch. Others appeared fresh from college studies, alert and carefree.

The "sharing time" began to explain. . .or further complicate the scene. A young Puerto Rican woman, obviously new to the church, admonished us to trust God, to be patient with God when God doesn't seem to answer at first. "I asked God, 'Show me that you exist.' Our family was hungry. Then the next day at the grocery store, I won a thousand dollars in the lottery!"

Another young woman (a University of Chicago graduate, as it turned out) talked about her excitement at being at a conference for Christians in social work that past week. And then she asked us to pray about the possibility of a trip to her Puerto Rican home to meet her family whom she had never seen. I was slowly learning not to be surprised at such remarks.

A man on the far left announced he had been "dry" for a month, and off cigarettes for a week (the latter was a harder habit to kick, he said). The congregation applauded in spontaneous empathy. Across the room, a shy Latino fellow mentioned a hotline number at the city hospital, where he was then employed. "They take care of all kinds of things—bad drug trips, runaways, child abuse."

A thirties couple, married one year, told us they had been able to replace their stolen wedding bands that week. They would be showing slides of their wedding after the service, in honor of the first anniversary of their marriage.

A dignified black man with a Jamaican accent asked that we have silent prayer for Jimmy Carter, who was in Israel that day, attempting to help bring peace to the Middle East. We waited a few minutes for the commotion of latecomers to subside, before we had that quiet moment. All the dogs and children and persons with restless distraught faces were breathlessly quiet as we paused.

Before we prayed, a dark-haired woman in the front row asked that we remember her husband who was to come up before immigration authorities the following Tuesday to receive citizenship— or be denied. Many in the room understood the ominousness of that occasion.

Far back in the room, a woman with straight gray-streaked hair and a chalk-white face, lined with grief and anguish, began to speak. Tears coursed down her cheeks as she told us her welfare worker was coming to see her on Thursday. "You know the trouble I've had with my older boys. Now they want to take my younger ones away from me. They are accusing me of physical and emotional abuse."

Instantly, the pastor responded. "Thelma, you have a loving supportive family here, and we aren't going to desert you at a time like this. I'll call the welfare worker before she comes and find out what's up, and then I will come and meet with you both on Thursday if you will have me."

Another woman—a black woman—spoke up on Thelma's behalf, telling us about an incident at the child care center where Thelma's actions helped keep a difficult situation on an even keel.

I was caught between judgment and compassion. The hard lines of Thelma's face. Could she abuse the child by her side? Others seemed to trust her. Maybe, I thought, she is in the throes of change.

We bowed to pray, and the weight of the crushing burdens of this tiny congregation momentarily overwhelmed me. Physical and mental disability, poverty, injustice, oppression, discrimination all crowded together in my consciousness. I was painfully aware of my clear-eyed gaze and relatively unworn face, so free of cares.

I was torn. On the one hand, I wanted to come and live in the midst of these people. I wanted to share their love and gifts. It was obvious to me that they had these to give. Yet I wanted to run away. I wanted not to know they existed at all. I wanted to be with people who looked like me, talked and thought like me.

Familiarity and security? Or risk and challenge? I was surprised—and distressed—to find I was comfortable with neither.[1]

Finding Work

Then Don and I began the Great Job Search, a major undertaking in itself. Initially, we took low-paying jobs: Don sold art prints in a bookstore, and I typed for a temporary office service.

Don's adjustment was far smoother than mine. As an artist and poet, he was accustomed to earning money at something other than his true vocation. But I experienced instant role displacement. I'd been used to the freedom and prestige of a director role. Now I was being treated like a secretary, told to move from one chalk mark to another. The put-downs were subtle and unintended, but they were there—like the assumption that I was incapable of anything beyond blind copy work and counting spaces from the left-hand margin. My long-dormant feminist awareness sprang to life.

On my way home from work, sitting in the subway with my unknown neighbors, I began to identify with them: people who go to work every day, are told what to do, receive very little pay, and live from one pay day to the next. Meanwhile, Don and I found ourselves edging slowly but surely toward the brink of insolvency. The move out, the unexpected trips West for two family funerals, and fifteen hundred dollars worth of repairs on our aging Plymouth Valiant, plus a hungry, oil-guzzling (and occasionally leaking) furnace—all these took their toll on our modest resources.

I got scared. I began counting nickels and dimes, reading the labels on the grocery shelves (the ones that looked like algebra equations and were hard to read for a middle-aged woman with bifocals), looking for discounts and sales. When the doctor said I needed a minor surgical procedure costing seven hundred and fifty dollars, I felt the whole dam break. I wasn't worried about my health, simply how I would pay the bills, since I was between jobs and without medical insurance.

At home with Don, I sat down to reconnoiter. Why were we here? What was the meaning of this consummate concern with survival? Here I was in Dorchester, afraid we'd run out of oil before we had the money to pay for it, and that our cash on hand wouldn't last until pay day. I was beginning to identify with my neighbors more than I had intended. I began observing them closely. How did they manage the cost of oil? Were they sitting around in their houses with sweaters and socks piled on, too?

My discoveries surprised me. In the first place, no one else in Boston seemed to be used to the overheated apartments to which I had become accustomed in Chicago. I got used to wearing a few more layers, keeping active, and sending messages to my body to adjust to a lower temperature over-all. I began to see that humor, friendship, and family ties were all strong and important outlets for people on the street: an ongoing card game at the corner store in a back room, men wearing hats and swapping stories with one another;

a mother across the street, always on the front porch watching her children, carrying on conversations with other women leaning out of second-story windows; eleven-year-old Stanley, who offered to help me pick up trash and who knocked often, asking, "Anything you need at the store?"—his inventive way of earning pocket money.

I was still haunted by the tired faces of the women coming off the subway at the end of a working day. Their jobs did not confer dignity and meaning, causing a harsh but necessary separation between personal and work life. Even the menial jobs I took at first were more than some of my neighbors had. I had been busy preaching meaningful careers, but I had to live without that for a time, and was relieved to find I didn't fall apart without a professional work role.

In time, I settled into a permanent position—appealing to me because it offered an opportunity to work with women who could not easily find their way into the work force, and thus could not relieve their dependency on welfare. I became a teacher/counselor at the YWCA's Women Resource Center in a CETA-funded project in Framingham.

Here again I was forced to deal with subtle cultural differences. It was obvious to me that I was the one who must adjust, learn a new teaching style, use a different vocabulary, be more flexible. In both my home and work environments, I was faced with similar issues, which made it easier to see some common threads in the lives of the women and in my own experience. Facing women each day in our storefront classroom became a daily rebirth for me. I had come to Boston to start over again, but had not imagined the direction my new beginning would take.

We Cry "Uncle"

A change occurred one year after moving in on Maryland Street. Ben, our landlord, offered to sell us the building for $10,000, which we could pay in installments of modest size. It was a good deal; in retrospect, considering the sky-rocketing real estate market of the late 1980s and 1990s, a phenomenal one. But we did not want to own property, and in particular not this one. However, we met new friends, Dan and Paula, who needed a place to live midway between Dan's seminary on the north shore and Paula's social work job on the south shore. We were desperate to be rid of Jimmy. We suggested that Dan and Paula buy our building, and move in on the second floor, thus replacing Jimmy and his family. Our landlord was in agreement. Although he had hoped that our presence in this neighborhood would have a positive influence, by now he saw we were hopelessly out of our depth in coping with Jimmy. I had to face the cognitive dissonance of being someone who had helped convene a national conference on Tenants' Rights in Chicago in 1970, and was now helping a landlord kick someone out of house and home.

Jimmy and Shelley sensed the situation accurately when they were served notice to leave. From that moment on, they were determined to make life as miserable as possible for us whom they deemed responsible for their plight. During one night of terror, one of those predictable drunken fights occurred again, with Bobby sending his brother-in-law tumbling down the stairs. Then, still in a rage, Bobby banged on our front door, yelling for Don to come out. All my supper came up into my throat in one panic-stricken moment. I thought Don was going to be killed.

Tension mounted inside the apartment as we waited to see what would happen. I do not recall if we called the police or not; we must have, but my memory stands still at the first moment of panic. After a time of quiet, the third-floor tenant came downstairs, smelling smoke. Sure enough, a fire had been set in the basement. We got it under control, and then Don went outside and sat waiting on the back steps. He knew Jimmy would return. In a moment of crisis, Don can be unbelievably strong and calm, masking the panic within. He was determined to face Jimmy down. He peered into the darkness and soon saw the embers of a cigarette as Jimmy moved slowly across the neighbor's back yard and into our own. Don greeted Jimmy with studied casualness, and Jimmy sat down beside him. "Someone tried to set the house on fire," Don said. "Now, who would have done that?" he asked Jimmy.

When moving day came, and Jimmy and his family moved out,

Dan and Paula went into the second floor apartment. There they found a padlock on the outside of the door of a small bedroom. Chicken wire had been nailed against the window. The room reeked of excrement. We were appalled to learn that Shelley had kept her brain-damaged baby caged in a room directly above our own bedroom. Neighbors told us there had been previous reports to the Department of Social Services on Shelley for child abuse. In the wake of all that we had been through, we felt conflicting emotions of sorrow and anger, and shock. We had lived underneath that family for a year and had never known the fate of their son.

We had come to Boston full of pride for our progressive attitudes toward urban problems, our spirit of helpfulness to those in need. It had all been too much for us, and we felt defeated and broken in spirit. Now we were the ones needing help and rest.

eleven

The Beginning of a Life Work

DON AND I had worked together since we married, and longed to continue doing so, but were not sure how or where. Like a pregnant woman who feels the stirrings of a child in her womb, I had begun to conceive of ideas which I thought could take shape in organizational form. The year before I left Chicago, I had happened upon the emerging field of career education. While I was attending the spring conference of the American Association of Higher Education, I discovered in an obscure basement location a few sessions on "Identifying Transferable Skills" based on Richard Bolles' nationally known *What Color Is Your Parachute* book. I was fascinated. Not only was the material applicable to my own restlessness in my career, I had been instinctively using similar methods in helping Urban Life Center students obtain internships. I had a natural aptitude for career counseling. I had also taken a year of professional training as a Group Facilitator at the Oasis Center for Human Potential which had sharpened my skills in working with groups.

I had begun networking in the Chicago area, and discovered some practitioners using the term "Life Work Planning." The wholistic approach of blending concerns of Life with Work attracted me, and I began to offer a few workshops and individual sessions for friends as an experiment.

One aspect of my experiment turned out to be predictive of the style I would assume a few years later. After a client, Bob, had a few sessions with me, he asked if he could draw in a few other friends for our next session in order to get feedback from a more diverse group. The following week, five of us sat in our living room as Bob presented his career dilemma. We were to listen carefully, then ask pertinent and probing questions to help him think through the decision he was making. At the end of the evening, one of the other participants remarked enviously, "This was great. Could we meet again so I could take a turn?" We met five more times, so that each member of the group could take center stage for an evening, with the rest of us attentively responding. I felt a palpable creative energy in the room as we shared our diverse perspectives with the person on stage.

When I landed in Boston, a city where I was unknown, I decided to build on this beginning in career counseling and tailored my resumé to support this claim. I embarked upon the job search process with vigor and enthusiasm, one more indication that I was well suited to this field. It was in one of my temporary typing jobs that I met Renée Levine at a womens' job center. As author of a popular book *How To Get a Job in Boston,* Renée was a key contact. She recommended me to a career counselor job at the Womens' Resource Center in Framingham.

My interview there was instructive. At that epoch there were no credentials for career counseling. It drew upon the fields of education and psychology, but there were not yet qualifying programs for this burgeoning field. The interviewer quizzed me on my experience in teaching, group dynamics, counseling, and working across ethnic and class lines. For a $12,000 a year job, she was expecting strong expertise in several fields. It was easy to answer all of those questions, for I had more depth of experience than the usual candidate. I was hired.

As part of my networking, I dropped in one day at Northeastern University, where a new program in career assessment was being launched. The academic dean happened by and engaged me in conversation. Before I left, he asked for my resumé. Soon I was teaching courses in Career Assessment in their evening adult program, a job that provided a base for the next seven years while

Don and I were creating a ministry.

Meanwhile Don was doing his own exploration in the area of Christianity and the arts. He visited Mass College of Art, considering a degree program there, but was discouraged by the faculty member in charge who told him he was too advanced for what their program offered. Don set his face toward his poetry writing, and went to work at the Harvard Coop selling reproductions of art prints with characteristic ironic humor.

He asked everyone he met about the art scene in Boston, in the faint hope there might be some Christians pursuing the arts in ways that probed deeper than caricature or maudlin expression or as a tool of propaganda. He began hearing about a group of people in downtown Boston who had some interest in the arts. It was an ecumenical venture named Many Mansions. Don decided to check it out.

MANY MANSIONS

Downtown Boston had charmed us from the moment we arrived—the ancient Commons flanked by the gold-domed State House on one side, Park Street Church with its lighted spire on another, and the Episcopal Cathedral on the third. Two subway lines intersected below the surface, one of them the Red Line which connected us from our home in Dorchester to Don's job in Cambridge. Like a visiting tourist, I walked around Boston's quaint downtown area, camera strapped to my shoulder. The Commons provided me with plenty of photographic material: an old sea skipper carving wood, a tall skinny juggler entertaining the crowds, mothers with strollers and small children, vagrants sleeping off the chill of a homeless night, families riding the swan boats that sailed on the limpid stream in the adjacent Public Gardens. Something about the lighting in early morning or late afternoon caught my eye. I was experiencing Boston as a stranger, and I fell in love.

It was a scant half block from the Commons that Don found the Many Mansions enterprise. The building was wedged in between a Chinese book store and a convent selling religious icons and books. Two doors away stood the Brattle Book Shop, legendary for its selection of rare used books.

The day Don walked in at Many Mansions, volunteer workmen were scattered over the first floor of a five-story building that used to house an old shoe store. They were tearing out walls and counters and shelves in preparation for turning the first floor into a restaurant/café. A rickety elevator took Don to the second floor where the Many Mansions offices were located. He was welcomed with effusive friendliness by an assortment of volunteers—two suburban matrons bustling over preparations for the noon meal and another struggling with an archaic addressograph machine, a couple of young men in overalls battling plaster dust as they pounded down a partition. The directors, Richard Faxon and an associate, both Episcopal priests, stepped forward to introduce themselves and welcomed Don with warmth and enthusiasm.

It was almost lunch time, but first noonday prayers were conducted in a swept-out corner of the second floor where a makeshift altar stood before a row of windows looking out over rooftops of nearby buildings. A few chairs were placed facing the altar. The rest of the group sat on low shoe store stools salvaged from the first floor. A gong sounded to announce the commencement of quiet before one of the volunteers read the "daily office."

Lunch took place around an enormous square table on which women placed a huge wooden bowl of salad and a tureen of soup. One of the cooks responsible for the salad makings used to walk the two miles downtown from her home in Brookline, stopping at several supermarkets on the way, scrounging slightly damaged vegetables and fruits from dumpsters and adeptly transforming them into edible delights.

As it turned out, Many Mansions had less to do with the arts than Don had been told. It was an ecumenical venture, largely evangelistic in purpose. A group of persons from several traditions—Catholics, Baptists, Episcopalians, and others—had been meeting together to pray for several months. They wanted to establish an ecumenical presence in Boston as a means of attracting the unchurched. As part of their outreach, they envisioned using the arts in some way, principally Christian musicians. Their goals were modest.

Then the five-story shoe store building on West Street came onto the market. One of the leaders of the group had received an inheritance which he donated to the project. Modest goals suddenly expanded to match the size of the building; the name Many Mansions was chosen to fit the enlarged vision. When Don came home and told me this story, we were reminded of our days at the Urban Life Center during its inception. We knew from experience how a large building could choke the elemental vision and sap the energy, diverting it into the needs of the physical structure and the consequent costs.

Don began hanging out at Many Mansions. The warmth of the welcome drew him in, despite the anomalous character of the enterprise. He urged me to come down and visit too. The people in charge sensed we had energy and skills to contribute and invited us to take part. We realized this was an opportunity for the two of us to work together again, but we worried that Many Mansions was out of kilter with the way both of us thought and functioned in our religious lives. Its focus was evangelism, and at that time we were still the "unchurched" that Many Mansions' brochure claimed to want to reach. The leadership of priests—both Catholic and Episcopal—and the resultant subtly hierarchical atmosphere, was foreign to us. We were in the midst of lay people who addressed the leadership as "Father" with almost reverential tones. Another element was missing for me: attention to the psychological dimension as applied to spiritual growth, a strong interest of mine.

We stayed on the edges, tentatively feeling our way into the project. I had already resigned from my job in Framingham, which was supported by a temporary contract subject to governmental whims, but kept my part-time teaching position at Northeastern. Don switched from his job at the Coop bookstore to the Chinese bookstore next door to Many Mansions. At the same time, Richard Faxon asked us to come on staff for the summer, promising us a salary. We said yes.

At this precise moment, the project began to collapse. Renovating the ancient building in accord with city fire safety codes for a restaurant was proving financially impossible. The calamitous Cocoanut Grove fire decades earlier had resulted in Boston revising its fire safety code to be exceedingly stringent. In addition, there proved to be a problem in getting a clear title to the building. Uncertainty reigned. In anguish over the crumbling of his vision Richard called a meeting of the workmen and told them their work was terminated.

Life/Work Direction is Born

The corps of young persons who had been planning to work at Many Mansions were now suddenly cast adrift. What was to be done to respond in a practical way to this group who had gathered expecting to work at Many Mansions? Judie, a woman from the Womens' Resource Center, had followed me to Many Mansions and was hanging out there. "These people need a Support Group for the Unemployed," she told me. Together with Richard, the three of us convened a workshop in December of 1980, a little like the ones I had conducted in Chicago, and again at the Womens' Center in Framingham.

The participants liked it. A lot. They told their friends who in turn begged for another workshop. The second one was offered in January, then in rapid succession, a third, a fourth, and a fifth. The fire of enthusiasm had been ignited and was spreading. Undoubtedly, the high unemployment rate in the early 1980s contributed to the initial attraction of our program. By February, it made sense for us to incorporate as a legal non-profit entity, chartered by the Commonwealth of Massachusetts. We settled on the name "Life/Work Direction" and wrote a simple statement of purpose in the charter:

> *"To provide spiritual direction through an ecumenical context rooted in the historical Judeo-Christian tradition for persons wishing to integrate their faith with their whole life/work."*

On February 12, 1981, the lection for the day in the Book of

THE BEGINNING OF A LIFE WORK

Common Prayer ended with II Corinthians 4:12: "So now death is at work in us, *but life is at work in you*," which confirmed our choice of a name.

We began looking for affordable space for our fledgling ministry. A storefront around the corner from our apartment in Dorchester became available at a reasonable rate, and on the day of the annual Dorchester Day Parade in June, 1981, we moved to Savin Hill Avenue. We constituted a triumphal procession, bearing old shoe store shelving and stools, and an array of plants and beat up desks and chairs which had been given to Many Mansions in the days when there was hope of being used for its vision and purpose. While we lugged the furniture inside, rows of Dorchester drill teams and war veterans and decorated floats passed by headed for a festive community celebration on Savin Hill beach nearby.

We settled into our new work with zest. When cold weather came, we encountered the uncertainties of a sputtering furnace in our new location. As the winter winds whipped over the storefronts on the avenue, we huddled inside, wrapping layers of sweaters and coats around us. We tacked colorful quilts and blankets over a layer of newspapers on the walls, but we still shivered. And yet the stream of workshop participants arrived, week after week, coming by word of mouth from former participants. We were tapping into a hardy cohort of persons, most in their late twenties, some of whom had come to Boston expressly to engage in some form of Christian ministry.

Down the block, we made friends with Harry the Barber who recognized our plight with a malfunctioning furnace. "Psst," he said to us in an aside one cold day, "Talk to the landlord of my building. I think the tenants next door are vacating." We looked at the tiny space next to his barbershop, and wondered how we could fit all our ponderous files and desks and chairs into this minuscule space. But the price was right, and the furnace worked. We moved in, and our carpenter friend Dan ingeniously helped us create the right kind of space with partitions. It was tight, but it would meet our needs.

At Many Mansions, a lot of care had been given to serving meals, as people were always dropping by, curious to see the progress of the venture, and hospitality was highly valued. At Life/Work Direction, it was natural for me to continue this custom, taking over the preparing of meals each evening before our workshops convened. Using a two-burner hot plate, and an electric fry pan, I managed to serve heaping platters of rice or pasta adorned with colorful vegetables. A huge wooden bowl cradled a tossed salad. Dessert could be made at home and carried in. Several evenings a week, a workshop group of five or six persons would gather at our round table after work and share the meal with Richard, Don and me; then we went into workshop mode for the next two-and-a-half hours.

After five years, it began to be increasingly difficult to put a group together with five persons who had the same night free, so we began working with people individually, since the demand for our services continued unabated. Don had been feeling the disadvantages of the group experience, seeing how it tended to dilute the depth to which we might go, and he was the one to suggest that we begin offering the Life/Work Direction process—which was now formulated as an ordered curriculum—to individuals rather than groups.

Admittedly, there was a loss when we stopped meeting with groups. People loved the interaction with kindred souls. Often they asked for "advanced workshops," and we supplied them with all sorts of opportunities: a mens' group, a womens' group, a group dynamics group, a group to teach "Experiential Focusing," an Arts group, an Enneagram study group, a Post-Abortion Counseling group, a life-story group, a Spiritual Direction group, a "Bethany" group for seekers in the spiritual journey, a "Poustinia" group that practiced contemplative silence and reflection. Once a year we would throw a "bash" for everyone around Labor Day.

When the focus changed to work with individuals, people lost that sense of camaraderie with others provided by groups. By contrast, there were unexpected positive effects. The impact of three of us—Richard, Don and I—meeting with one person intensified the experience for each client. People exclaimed about the unparalleled privilege of having the undivided attention of three people for an hour a week over a period of several months. I have since observed that this way of working is effective in creating more objective feedback, different from the subjective atmosphere of therapy with its focus on the one-to-one relationship. Each mode has its place. The composition of the leadership team was crucial.

A Trinity

We were an unusual trio—Richard Faxon, Don and I. The team approach helped each of us make a unique contribution and balance one another's gifts. Of the three of us, Richard's nature was more reserved and quiet with participants, waiting for the right moment to enter the conversation with his laser-like insight and authority. He was a tender man, always courteous, and genuinely interested in the participants. Raised in a home where religion was assumed, but expressed formally, he hungered for a more feeling expression of faith. He loved to have me play the hymn, "I want to walk as a child of the light, I want to be with Jesus." Tears often came to his eyes as he sang. His personal spiritual life was saturated with prayer. Many participants approached Richard for his healing ministry of prayer for some circumstance in their lives.

Don served as counterpoint to both Richard and me, with his love of the outrageous, his total immediacy of presence, his enthusiastic hugs, his spontaneous reactions to the ridiculous. He would not be fenced in by structures or the linearity of curricular plans; he sensed the tempo, gravitated to the beat of the ongoing conversation, introduced the absurd and unexpected. He relied on Richard and me to rein him in if he got too far afield. He always greeted participants at the door with open arms, exuding warmth and love. They quickly learned that he would speak the truth unequivocally to them from that place of warmth.

So there I was with these two giants—Richard was six foot four, Don six foot two and ample in girth—the sole woman. I held my own, because these two men both knew that the work was impossible without me. I was the educator of the group, designed the curriculum, knew how to present the process to new participants in a way that made sense and drew them in. I wrote the materials, kept track of people and money, and did lots of the practical tasks that made things go.

We shared a passionate interest in the philosophy under which we operated. We spent hours talking about this, writing down our ideas, thinking through what we were doing and why. It was a productive, happy time.

The Process

Although people came to us with the presenting issue of their *jobs*, that was not our focus. We were not even primarily interested on helping them find or change *careers*—although some people did make important decisions and changes. Instead, we gave our attention to the deeper issue of *vocation*. Because we believed that a person's vocation is to become the unique self which God has created for God's glory, all our efforts were bent toward helping each person unearth that true self in all its authenticity and complexity.

The life story became our basic tool, underlying every other part of the process. People opened their hearts to us in their life stories. We were not looking for a chronology of their lives, nor were we asking for an interpretation, such as might have been derived from therapy. Instead we asked, *"What did it feel like to be you when you were growing up?"* which sent them into vivid stories of discrete events and turning points in their experience. We tried to find fruitful ways to help them look through a different lens in interpreting their childhood experiences, to see "the spiritual advantages of a painful childhood," as Wayne Muller has put it.[1] Our task was to ask probing questions, to elicit from them the unique story of their lives and help them uncover the hidden inner wisdom of their deepest desires and goals.

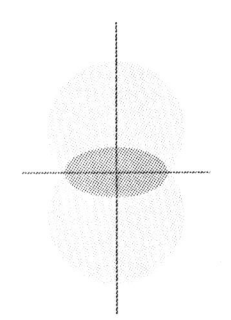

We discovered an ancient symbol which seemed to conceptualize the process we used with people. It was the "mandorla," as discussed in Robert Johnson's helpful book, *Owning Your Own Shadow*.[2] The symbol consists of two overlapping circles intersected by a cross. The overlapping almond shaped segment is called a mandorla, the Italian word for almond. It can represent any two opposites which present a contradiction—light and shadow, good and evil, the demands of inner life and outer work.

People came to us when they faced a "mandorla" transition between two states of being: between the way they lived and their ideals and values; between their self-image and the hidden reality of the true self; between the religious experience they had grown up with and the deeper hungers they felt that seemed to oppose the old religious forms. Often something had broken down which they had relied on in the past, or they were sensing a need for something new and were not clear about what it was. Some were experiencing an impasse in their outer life and work and a staleness had crept into the daily round. Whatever the case, these were all signals pointing to the need to cultivate the inner wellsprings of the soul, so that their life and work in the world might flow from a fresh source. Our work with people was much more than career counseling; it was a soul journey.

We used every device imaginable to elicit fresh insights. We asked them to draw or to write or to imagine. We made use of a few standard career inventories in unconventional ways. We analyzed their stories of satisfying activities in their past for core traits which came into play in these times, providing them with concrete, precise descriptions of their gifts. We led them to look at the "shadow" side of gifts—the ways in which their gifts can become hazards, when used defensively. It was another "mandorla" moment, seeing the way in which light and shadow are both essential elements, and that real healing occurs not in abolishing one in favor of the other, but in the acceptance of the whole self in its opposing manifestations.

The most powerful part of the process turned out to be the time we spent on uncovering unconscious motivation as elicited through the use of a unique tool called the Enneagram (a Greek word meaning "nine points").[3] I had studied the way the Jesuits and Franciscans applied Christian teaching to this map of personality and found that, more than most personality theories, the Enneagram seemed to get at the root of the matter, seeing one's gifts and problems from a spiritual perspective. In my own life, I had experienced this tool like John the Baptist's "axe laid at the root of the tree" (Matthew 3:10), cutting into my own ego structure, laying bare my underlying motivations and deadly sin.

We were hesitant at first to introduce the Enneagram to our clients because of its subtlety and complexity, but they found it so helpful, we incorporated it into our process. The Enneagram proved to be a powerful tool. It identified a person's motivations with such deadly precision and accuracy that he/she felt exposed, stunned by the recognition of their previously unconscious attitudes. The Enneagram also contained within it pathways of spiritual growth that coincided with scriptural Christian teaching. The results were life-changing for many participants. Because we presented this material at the end, it wove together the threads from the entire process on a spiritual level. Participants saw the connection with their inner personality dynamic and the way they approached issues of life and work.

Living and Working at Home

We continued working in the storefront on Savin Hill Avenue for nine years. Don and I were happier in our living space, having moved in 1985 from our Dorchester apartment to Jamaica Plain, a subdivision of greater Boston which stands out as the most sylvan, as well as including a diverse ethnic mix.

For five years, we commuted daily from Jamaica Plain, driving through Franklin Park into Dorchester, down Columbia Road which edged gang territory and which sometimes became a place for unannounced "target practice." We were beginning to long for a space to live which would also accommodate our work. In one of our infrequent newsletters to our constituency in the spring of 1990, we casually mentioned this:

> We have begun to think about finding a place for Life/Work Direction which would be more of a home environment, and which would include living quarters for Don and Eunice. The idea is in an embryonic stage, but we share it with you as a way of networking, in case you have knowledge of possible places. We see such a move as two or three years away—but one never knows.

We were pleasantly surprised a few days later when Scott Walker came by. Scott was a member of one of our first workshops when we were still located at Many Mansions downtown. He had remained in touch through the years, participating in Life/Work Direction's programs in various ways. Scott and his wife, Louise, were planning to buy a house as they awaited the birth of their first child. They offered to buy a two-family building in order to share it with Life/Work Direction and with Don and me.

Suddenly, we stood on the threshold of our long-held dream. We began an intense search for housing and were delighted to find a suitable two-family house not far from Jamaica Pond, a place where we took frequent walks. Living where we worked made all the difference—in pace of life, in the feeling of participants when they entered the space, and in the way we experienced the integration of our life and work. One early morning soon after we moved in, I arose and wrote:

> It is the darkness before dawn and I come awake, listening to a soft rain fall outside the window here at the house on Halifax Street. Soon I get up and move down the corridor, sensing the spaces as I pass, in the dim light from a street lamp outside.
>
> The prayer book lies open on the hassock in the Common Room where the three of us left it the night

before, at the end of an evening of seeing people. I move on into the sunroom office, now shadowy and still.

The faint stirrings from the floor above remind me that someone is preparing for a day of work and also that a baby will be born in this house within the next month.

I feel the Birth of our Life, our Work, and the Direction of both—in new ways—graced by this gift of space. It gently presses us into a new mold, a new way of living and being, and must affect the work we do here. I cannot live so close to my work, occupy this kind of space, without tasting deeply of gratitude and integrity. Gratitude because of the kindness of the comfort and the beauty of the place. Integrity because of presence and transparency.

After twelve years of working as a threesome, Richard retired in 1993. Don and I readily made the adjustment to working "two on one" from the former "three on one." We were acutely attuned to each other's thinking and way of working. We recognized that as a married couple, we would easily constellate in our clients the sense of mother and father. We knew it was important to hold our own distinct viewpoints so as not to present a united front which might preclude the client from making his or her own decision. We found that working together enriched our marriage because it made this dual requirement: to be sensitively attuned to one another, and yet retain our separate approaches—the educator and the artist.

February of 2001 marked the twentieth anniversary of Life/Work Direction. The time was ripe for another sabbatical, and we settled on a duration of ten weeks. Don suggested we take the ten weeks one at a time throughout the year, providing a rhythm of alternating work and rest. I agreed, for I saw this as a model for the way we might live out this season of our lives.

I began meditating on the meaning of *Sabbath*. A few lines from the writings of Eugene Peterson about the often-neglected Scriptural commandment—"Remember the Sabbath day, to keep it holy"—suggested that in the absence of attending to this important principle of taking time out, we become absorbed in our own doing and God's work is forgotten or marginalized.

> *When we work we are most god-like, which means that it is in our work that it is easiest to develop god-pretensions. Our work becomes the context in which we define our lives. We lose God-consciousness, God-awareness.*[4]

I was aware that nowhere is such a tendency to god-like pretension more likely than in work such as ours.

Don and I decided to take on the challenge of entering into this Sabbath contract with each other and with God for the year 2001 and to experience these seemingly arbitrary stopping points ten times during the year, and to see what might come up in the silence. We predicted that the quality of our lives would be changed by this practice, and we hoped that the sense of Sabbath would continue to permeate our lives long after the year was through.

It was during this year of Sabbath, that the writing of this book was completed.

twelve

The Preacher's Daughter Comes Home to Church

I HAVE A checkered history with church. In childhood, church was home to me—the place where Daddy worked. The Sunday rituals were part of the background music of family life. This smooth continuity between home and church continued during my years in Wheaton, with some added dimensions: educated professionals teaching Sunday school; superior preaching by gifted ministers; and a high quality of music directed by trained musicians. The presence of college faculty members and students assured that the congregational singing would be robust, replete with full-throated, four-part harmony.

As a Pioneer Girls staff member, I began to be in touch with a number of different Protestant denominations—Presbyterian, Methodist, Congregational, Assembly of God, Mennonite, several varieties of Baptists, Evangelical Free, and churches independent of any affiliation. Although varying in ecclesiastical structure, these churches turned out to be startlingly alike in their informal approach to liturgy, which featured the primacy of the sermon. I got accustomed to the experience of worship being somewhat accidental and infrequent wherever I went. Other agendas—the church weekday program, evangelism, missions—seemed to be more important.

By contrast, worship came easily in camp. It came in the hush descending as the evening campfire turned to embers, or in the lilting crescendo of voices singing after meals in the dining hall. At such moments, my soul soared unbidden. I was with women and girls from disparate Christian traditions, all dissolved into the unity of one body. Such experiences were rare in church.

I found it difficult to confine myself to a single denominational tradition. In this, I was the heir of my father whose attachment to his denomination often wore thin. Once he was asked to speak as part of a series on denominations in college chapel, representing Baptists. He spent much of his time emphasizing the primacy of his Christian affiliation. In English class after chapel, my teacher remarked with a tinge of scorn, "Our speaker this morning hardly seemed proud of being a Baptist." I sat smugly in the back row, knowing she had not made the connection that I was the speaker's daughter. My father's loyalty lay deeper and broader than to a single denomination.

Part of my struggle lay in the way I was beginning to view being a Christian. Instead of seeing Christian as a "bounded set"—one is either a Christian or not—necessitating evangelism of the one by the other, I preferred the concept of "centered set" suggested by Al Krass[1] which places Christ at the center and focuses on how a person is moving either toward the center or away from it. This resolved old tensions about evangelism for me. Under the notion of bounded sets, evangelism concentrated on the single dramatic decision of a person to become a Christian and too often stopped there. By thinking of Christianity as a centered set, I focused on a person's direction of movement, rather than his or her status. This accorded with my instincts in working with people. Whether a person defined herself as a Christian or not, I could come alongside her and encourage her movement toward Christ, whatever her spiritual status or formal religious affiliation.

My disaffection with church came about slowly and was in part a response to this bounded set thinking, defining persons as in or out, and in part a response to societal change in the 1960s. At that point, disillusionment with the church's capacity and willingness to address racism and sexism prompted me to question the relevance of the church as an institution. I grew critical and impatient.

By the time I had begun studies at the University of Chicago and entered therapy, I was ready for a radical shift in my relationship to the church, but was uncertain where I now belonged. I plunged into one experiment after another in rapid succession.

First I began teaching Sunday school to African American youngsters in a Presbyterian church located near the University in Woodlawn. After Don and I got married, we got involved in the newly formed Baptist bi-racial house church in Hyde Park being started by the pastor who married us. When we found we no longer fit there, we began attending a near north side Lutheran church that had its regular service in the "upstairs church" and an alternative folk mass in the "downstairs church" for the hippies and irregulars. We joined with the long-haired granola crowd, with artists and self-styled bohemians and folk musicians. We hugged and danced and sang and raged against the Vietnam War.

We were only marginally at home in any of these places. Thoroughly disheartened at the end of our three experiments, Don and I opted out of church for a while. The Sunday paper, walks on the nearby beach, leisurely breakfasts—these would serve.

Then we moved to Boston.

THE UNCHURCHED FIND A HOME

We were not searching for a church home when we came to Boston. We were "reaching for the invisible God," as Philip Yancey writes.[2] In the process, we stumbled into church by accident, or by the synchronous grace of God.

It came about one day when we were new to Many Mansions. Some visitors came by the site to talk with the Episcopal priest director, Richard. He pulled Don and me over to introduce us. "Don and Eunice are Mennonites," he explained. Don and I had been attending a small fellowship of graduate students, faculty and other professional persons from a Mennonite background that met three Sunday evenings a month in Cambridge.

I hooted. "Richard, we're not Mennonites! You can't be a Mennonite unless your name is Yoder." Then, more soberly, as I saw Richard's surprised look. "We're your *unchurched!*"

Richard was visibly shaken by the thought of two prominent staff members without a church home. Nothing more was said, until the next day when Richard came to work. His shoulders were set in a determined line, as he approached us and said firmly with the authority of someone who had listened to the Divine voice, "I think you should go to the church of St. John the Evangelist on Beacon Hill."

We were too startled to object, and we were also hungry for a spiritual home. We knew this church to be a Mission of the Society of St. John the Evangelist, an Anglo-Catholic order of monks residing in a monastery in Cambridge. Their founder, Richard Cowley, had come from England to Boston in the latter part of the nineteenth century, with the intent of developing a ministry to the many neglected and forgotten persons living in the crowded rooming houses on Beacon Hill among the very rich who also were housed there. The monks initiated a Thursday night supper where many homeless men and women learned they would find good food and a warm and thoughtful welcome from the "Cowley Fathers."

We walked up Beacon Hill the following Sunday to attend Solemn Eucharist. Six months later, we were confirmed as Episcopalians. We had found a home among Anglo-Catholics which would last through the rest of our lives.

At first everything was new to us. Neither of us had grown up in a sacramental tradition or formal liturgy of any sort, and this church prided itself on a particularly "high" Anglo-Catholic liturgy—complete with "smells and bells." The church was not yet an official parish of the Episcopal Church, but a Mission operated by the monks. We quickly sensed the pervading spirit of prayerfulness which the Brothers lent by their presence. A deep quiet settled over the sanctuary on a Sunday morning as one of the monks would preside over the liturgy and give the homily. A layman fulfilled the role of "Master of Ceremonies" to make sure that every detail of the elaborate liturgy was handled in a way that maximally contributed to a spirit of worship—seeing that the vestments were laid out, the incense burners prepared, and caring for the many tiny details that go into an orderly service. We knew we were in good hands, and entered into the silence gratefully.

THE EVANGELICAL-EPISCOPAL CONNECTION

Since Don had come from an essentially non-religious background, his first reaction to the highly choreographed liturgy was that he had wandered onto the theatrical set of a British comedy. However, he found the predictability of the structure comforting. Don had always been uneasy in a situation where masses of people gathered under the sway of a charismatic leader without the protection of a certain degree of formality. Huge televised rallies, or highly emotional appeals, evoked images of the Third Reich when huge crowds had been spellbound by Hitler's impassioned rhetoric. He felt secure under the authority and quiet dignity of the ancient Anglo-Catholic forms.

In my case, I was acutely aware that I was part of a growing cohort of evangelicals who drifted toward the Episcopal church. I asked Curtis Almquist, a Brother at the monastery who had made this transition himself, why he thought this movement had been occurring. He told me:

> *My hunch is that many evangelicals have been well-nurtured in the Scriptures, know what it is to live a disciplined and discipled life, and have a sense of vocation and ministry, but when it comes to the church gathered to worship, many are much experienced in hearing evangelistic-type sermons and singing hymns of personal piety, but do not have much of a sense of coming into the presence of God, for the glory and praise of God. The Psalms are giveaways that there is something called worship which has a kind of innate pull.*[3]

He made other suppositions, such as the palpable experience of forgiveness offered through the Sacrament of Reconciliation, but it was the substantive experience in worship that drew me.

While Don valued the richness of the Episcopal tradition, he also continued to find my evangelical friends refreshingly genuine and open to engagement in serious dialogue, an exercise he loved. Having grown up knowing of the tradition of the Midrash which allows for the resonance of multiple meanings in a single biblical passage, listening and questioning were far more important to him than having answers or settling upon a single ironclad interpretation. As a man who has allowed the winds of the modern era to sweep through his consciousness—both the horror of the Holocaust, and the ineffable beauty of poetic expression through words—he did not need to cling to a safe sanctuary of certitude in the religious community. He abhorred the Pharisaic "we-know-the-truth-and-it-will-die-with-us" attitudes he sometimes detected in the larger, generic evangelical community. On the other hand, he was acutely aware of the solidity and geniality of our evangelical friends, and treasured them accordingly.

St. John's Warts

Someone once said that "the trouble with the Christian life is that it is so daily." Something similar could be said of the church. Becoming part of St. John's would involve us in the whole ride: up the heights of spiritual ecstasy, down into the valley of mourning, and across the level plain of dailiness.

The beginnings held promise. In 1986, after five years as a Mission, we became an official parish. It was time to select a rector. We were fortunate in finding one candidate from within the congregation, Jennifer Phillips. It was more important than might be guessed that we had as priest someone familiar with the congregation, for there was a strong tendency in the parish for conflicts to arise, often over liturgy. Many of the struggles were picky and sensitive and destructive of forward movement. The church opened its arms wide to persons with various kinds of disabilities—mental, emotional, physical. In the midst of very formal liturgies, there might sometimes be a disturbance in the back because one of the incoherent alcoholic guests of the Thursday night suppers was coming by a bit early for his Sunday noon sandwiches that were handed out after mass. Persons who had been victims of verbal and physical abuse in childhood easily found St. John's a home. The need to keep the environment safe for such persons sometimes included putting up with unreasonable demands for special care and attention, especially from clergy.

The liturgy was a lightning rod. One did not tinker lightly with protocol crafted over the years under the vigilant eyes of the monks, or the Master of Ceremonies, or the parish priest, or director of music. When changes were made—a necessary thing in order to keep our experience fresh and relevant—there could be small explosions here and there. The priest became expert in putting out fires and in preventing them.

Don and I did not engage ourselves in the behind-the-scenes work of the church, for the most part. We came on Sunday morning, needing spiritual nourishment after a week of giving constantly to others in our work. We entered the worship with all our hearts, but once the benediction was pronounced, we left quickly, skipping the coffee hour where parishioners exchanged conversation with one another. Thus we avoided being part of the grapevine where news spread quickly whenever someone was upset about something. Sometimes we heard wisps of information long after a skirmish had been settled, or perhaps reference was made in the homily which indicated that there was unhappiness somewhere. We were philosophical about the tiffs and spats. I was a preacher's daughter, and my loyalties tended always toward the rector who bore the brunt of these matters.

We were delighted when the services of an especially gifted music director were secured, a member of the New England Conservatory faculty and an organist with a worldwide reputation. The choir spruced up immediately. The way in which he helped all of us to truly worship Sunday after Sunday was as profound an experience as I ever expect to have this side of heaven. He wanted the liturgy to be conducted in such a way that we could *pray* the liturgy, not just sing or say it. Needless to say, he had the full support of the rector in this, and we all benefited immensely from his thoughtful leadership.

It was not unusual for us to experience as a congregation a moment of palpable unity as we sang together. The song would swell, and I knew that we were in the presence of the Divine. Other times, silence would fall, a silence so thick one would hardly dare breathe. We were at prayer together. It no longer mattered to me what the calibre of the sermon might turn out to be; I went for the music. Fortunately, the sermons were of high quality as well. But during the musical portions of the liturgy, it was natural to worship. Never in my church life before had I experienced this so consistently nor been as deeply nourished.

Fifteen years after we joined St. John's, a new rector arrived who tragically misread the needs and preferences of the parish and attempted to make crucial changes in the liturgy, and to introduce some folk-style songs into the mass. She had been told this was a church ready for change, so she waded in, unaware of the strong traditions surrounding the liturgy and music that would resist change, especially directives from a comparative novice whose previous experience was in a vastly different setting than New England. This meant inevitable tension with the director of music, whose tastes ranged from the predictable focus on Bach and the old masters to modern composers like Messiaen, but did not include much from the folk repertoire except for carefully chosen fragments from African American spirituals used at the Eucharist at Easter and a few other occasions.

John Rutter, the English musician, once commented that "the relationship of the clergy over the centuries to musicians who serve alongside them could charitably be described as wary."[4] Wary would be too tame a term to describe the relationship that was being played out behind the scenes between these two principals. In short order, the subsequent flare-up between the rector and the music director blew the parish to bits. The Sunday after the music director resigned, the choir loft was virtually empty, and so were many pews. It was anybody's guess as to how many left, but it was anywhere from one-quarter to one-third of the congregation.

A great wail of mourning rose from within me, and was echoed throughout the congregation. I was in a state of shock. It was a death of something very precious that I had known in that place, and it had been snatched from me. I went numb. I did not want to speak of my feelings to others. I was already on the periphery of the parish, intentionally. I did not want to take sides and unnecessarily create further schisms within a congregation that was suddenly much weaker. A lot of people had left, representing a lot of talent, a lot of leadership, a lot of energy, and a lot of money. So Don and I mourned alone.

Don and I stayed through the year, doing our best to stand quietly by, neither siding with the priest nor with the departed. We hoped that simply being there was witness. I began to refer to the body of people who had left as "the Church in Exile."

Don and I knew we must leave at some point. We were unable to truly worship, and the parish was taking a direction different from one toward which we were inclined. The music was no longer as central. We left carefully, writing a letter that included these words by T. S. Eliot, who decades before had once attended our church.

> *Home is where one starts from...*
> *The way forward is the way back...*
> *We shall not cease from exploration*
> *And the end of all our exploring*
> *Will be to arrive where we started*
> *And know the place for the first time.*[5]

We decided to go home to the monastery of the Society of St. John the Evangelist in Cambridge. It was the first place I had gone on retreat, the first place where I had received spiritual direction. It was the place where Don, Richard and I had gone for a blessing as we birthed Life/Work Direction. It was indeed home.

THE CHURCH INVISIBLE

The other day, a woman came to me for counsel. She was musing about church. Her words were poignant to me: "I want to be part of something invisible."

I smiled. "You are," I said. Inside I was singing to myself the All Saints Day hymn:

> *From earth's wide bounds, from ocean's farthest coast,*
> *Through gates of pearl streams in the countless host,*
> *Singing to Father, Son and Holy Ghost, Alleluia, Alleluia!*

How could I convey to her my growing sense of the countless host? Those bonds which are far stronger than those of any single local church community? I have no explanation as to why that unseen cloud of witnesses is such an impelling image to me. I know it is composed of the same polyglot assortment of persons from every class, race, nation, sect which I struggle to understand and appreciate in my world today.

Yet when I stand and sing certain last verses of hymns in our monastery services that I attend now, my heart inexplicably melts, lost in wonder, love, and praise.

> *Hark! the songs of holy Zion*
> *Thunder like a mighty flood;*
> *Jesus out of every nation*
> *Hath redeemed us by his blood.*

Though I cannot explain it, I yield to the moment because only this image of the church is enough, the paradoxical *image* of an *invisible* church.

PART THREE

Becoming Still

Be still, and know that I am God.

Psalm 46:10

thirteen

The Inner Journey

*If we set out into this darkness,. . .we will have to
call into question the whole structure of our spiritual life.*
                    Thomas Merton, *Contemplative Prayer* [1]

WHEN I EMBARKED on therapy, a door opened into a new pathway to my inner world. I was already well-acquainted with the old pathway of introspection, which sometimes bordered on obsession in its constant, convoluted stream of conversation with myself and with God. Yet this monologue seldom yielded new insights or release. Therapy began to tap into the part of my inner world that I did not know and could not control—the unconscious. I learned that the unconscious used both dreams and the wisdom of the body as reliable vehicles for communicating its truth. Neither lied.

Thus far a lot of therapy's effect on me was external. By recovering my suppressed femininity, I changed the way I viewed my body and my sexuality, and in the way I began relating to men and to marriage. Add to this the context of the late 1960s, a world clamoring for the activist mode, not the contemplative, and it is clear that much of my attention was still occupied in the world of ego-consciousness. Even my work with dreams, always interpreted in Freudian terms and centering on a powerful transference to my male therapist, served to keep me focused on my waking conscious world which was undergoing dramatic visible change.

By the time I came to Boston, I was ready for another cadence, that of a slower quiet depth, although I had no language with which to articulate that hunger. I was beginning to hear people use a different language about spiritual life. I read Elizabeth O'Connor's book *Journey In, Journey Out*. Her description of that much-neglected inward journey struck a responsive chord with me because of my lifelong quest to unite the insights of spiritual growth with psychological wisdom.

Reconciling Religion and Psychology

One key experience became a meeting ground for reconciliation between the psychological and religious approaches that had influenced me. It was the memory of my baptism that lingered throughout my life. It reasserted itself one day in therapy when I was in my forties. My therapist had undergone advanced training in bioenergetics, a form of therapy that relies on healing through exercises designed to restimulate chronic tensions held in the body, in the jaw, the shoulders, or as in my case, the back. I was guided to lie down on a specially constructed stool—a posture that expands the constricted muscles of the chest and back. As I went backward, inexplicably a primal wail of terror arose from the depths of my being. Later, sitting quietly with the therapist to talk about my experience, he suggested that the supine position I had assumed resembled that of my baptism. I was a little shocked. Could there be a connection?

Later, at home, I lay down on my bed in the fading light of day, gazing meditatively out the window, and reflecting on my feelings and experience of the morning at therapy and of that other morning in my childhood. Memories of that cool June morning at the lake so long ago flashed before me: the waves lapping on the shore, the sunlight slanting through the pines and glinting on the lake, my father's reassuring touch as he cradled me in his arms and lowered me under the surface of the chilly water.

As I mused, another image came spontaneously. It was of Abraham offering Isaac on the altar, so similar in physical gesture to my baptism. The tears were flowing fast now. The tension and horror of that offering were palpable. A haunting question arose: Had my parents likewise "offered me up" on the altar of their faith?

"Abraham was a fool, betrayed by God," I thought. How could he have thought this was God's demand? And what about Isaac, who questioned, but who also appeared so docile and trusting? *"Isaac was a fool, betrayed by his father,"* was my despairing conclusion.

James Hillman in his essay "Betrayal," suggests that "Trust and betrayal. . . contain each other. You cannot have trust without the possibility of betrayal. Trust has within it the seed of betrayal."[2] He uses a Jewish story to illustrate. A father places his little boy on the stairs, saying, "Jump, and I'll catch you," and does so twice. But the third time, he lets his son fall, saying, "That will teach you never to trust a Jew, even your own father." Hillman counters our instinctive horror at the story, making a strong point of the spiritual and psychological necessity of betrayal of primal trust in order for a person to become fully conscious. He argues his point on the basis of the centrality of the theme of betrayal in the Christian story, culminating in the betrayal of Jesus, abandonment by God to death on the cross, because of God's love for us.

I was struggling with the issue of my own broken, primal trust— in the simple faith of my childhood, baptized in my father's arms, and in this God of Abraham who appeared to make a cruel demand. I did not know how to resolve my questions. I knew in my heart that I had been turned toward God all my life. But I was puzzled about this God who would first make a lavish promise of generativity to the father of a nation, and then turn around and ask that father to destroy the long-awaited heir.

Hillman points out that "the broken trust is at the same time a breakthrough onto another level of consciousness." He goes on to illustrate the necessity of a father, and by extension, our Heavenly Father as well, to let his children move from a primal unconscious kind of trust to one which is deliberate and volitional. I was slow to arrive at that breakthrough.

Instead I lived with my doubts and faith, holding their paradox in suspension for many years, until one day during Holy Week in St.

John's, our Anglo-Catholic communion in Boston. My evangelical Protestant tradition had paid scant attention to Passiontide over the years, so the care our church gave to the celebration of the week before Easter was refreshing and fraught with meaning. On Maundy Thursday, we sang an ancient chant-like hymn unfamiliar to me, which focused my attention on the words. One phrase stood out, describing Jesus as a "willing victim," a juxtaposition which startled me. It was not simply Isaac who had stretched out his arms to the will of his father. Jesus, who was no fool, had been a *willing victim,* and simultaneously our priest. The image of Jesus moving through the precise time we were celebrating—the Last Supper, the agony in Gethsemane, the trial, and death on the cross—was freighted with significance.

I glimpsed a new possibility of redeeming my early experience by taking it on consciously. A willing victim might be a contradiction in terms, but it was a condition Jesus had taken on for me and for the world, and I was flooded with gratitude. I was set free to receive that experience of long ago as an initiation into grace. The act had been primitive and simple at the time. Now I affirmed it consciously.

What's more, the intervening years since my baptism at age six had not been a wasteland. I was not returning to my childhood faith; I had never left it. The primal experience could stand for what it was—a mystery which I expect God to be able to unveil some day. The intervening years had their rich resonances of meaning too, the struggle to find my Self, so that I could surrender it consciously, not mechanically or in response to communal pressures. Some inner resistance melted and in its place, comprehending love overflowed, while we sang the hymn.

I could only comprehend the Abraham story through the lens of the Jesus story. Whereas I had seen surrender as arbitrary and difficult in my past, now it came bubbling up freely out of gratitude in the face of the mystery of God become human in Jesus, who in turn laid down his life willingly. To identify with such a one in surrender is to be no fool.

The lines of our wedding hymn held new meaning:

Thou within the veil hast entered,
Robed in flesh, our great High Priest:
Thou on earth both Priest and Victim
In the eucharistic feast.

The Contemplative Orientation

While on my 1978 sabbatical in Washington, D.C., I heard someone mention having a "spiritual director." I burst out laughing. "A spiritual director! Whatever would that be?" All I could imagine was that someone else would tell me what to do about my spiritual growth, and that notion was ludicrous. Surrender has never been one of my strong points.

However, because I deeply respected the person who had spoken of his experience in spiritual direction, I tucked the thought away for later reference. In Boston, I was thrown into contact with the Catholic tradition—both Roman and Anglican—which revere the ancient practice of spiritual direction and have a long history of familiarity with the practice of contemplative prayer.

Tentatively I began exploring the edges of this approach to spiritual growth, so new to me, yet ancient in the tradition. What would it be like to go on a silent retreat? As a Protestant, I was used to retreats packed with sessions and recreation and music and sermons. Could I endure a week of silence, or even a weekend? Who was I, if stripped of my powers of verbal expression and response?

I put my toe in the water by signing up for my first silent retreat at the Society of St. John the Evangelist monastery in Cambridge to learn more about spiritual direction. I edged shyly into the meeting room to have my first consultation with a monk. I did not know exactly how to begin.

Somehow I did make a beginning. Soon I became enthralled with reading and studying the lives of contemplatives—St. John of the Cross, St. Theresa of Avila, St. Thérèse of Lisieux. In spite of my apprehensions, I felt irresistibly drawn toward the contemplative mode. At first, I was discovering another tool of spiritual growth and was trying to wield it with the same energy as other disciplines. But soon the contemplative mode discovered, or uncovered, me. I was finding that it called upon a deep, inner, feminine instinct within me, an attitude of receptivity like that expressed by the Virgin Mary at the annunciation—"Behold the handmaid of the Lord; be it unto me according to your word."

So much of my training in the Christian life had emphasized the more masculine proprioceptive mode—reach out and grasp truths, establish disciplined practices, extend yourself to others in loving service. The contemplative mode to which I was being introduced embodied a reverse motion: be still, wait, receive—the stance of the pregnant woman.

I had only known "mental prayer" before, using words. Now I learned that at its heart prayer is simply "paying attention to God." Thomas Merton, a Trappist monk, became my teacher in this transition, as my battered, much-thumbed-through copy of his *Contemplative Prayer* attests. Merton describes a continuity between meditation, conceived as prayer of the heart, and contemplative prayer. He warns against the kind of meditation that is little more than "cultivated inertia" or a narcissistic preoccupation with attaining a particular experience—traps I observed among people who lacked a solid theological ground and who looked to Eastern forms of discipline without understanding their basis.

"True contemplation," said Merton, "is not a psychological trick, but a theological grace." It is "essentially a listening in silence, an expectancy."[3] Some tired, hungry place in me felt a joyful release at this invitation. Was it possible that living the Christian life was even more positive than I had preached to others all my life? During my years in Pioneer Girls I often emphasized in my campfire messages the "abundant life" Jesus came to bring. I would quote from Psalm 16: "In God's presence is fullness of joy." Now I grasped the principle of attraction to a loving God, rather than struggling to avoid distractions in order to be approved by God. It put the emphasis on a different syllable. Grace overwhelmed law, forgiveness overshadowed guilt.

I began calling into question the whole structure of my spiritual life, based far too much on effort, far too little on grace. Where once I stood trembling before the ark of God, fearful of judgment, now like Moses "with unveiled face beholding the glory of the Lord," I recognized the ark was where the Shekinah glory rested: Shekinah, "the feminine face of God."

Taking a week-long silent retreat became an annual habit for me, beginning in 1983. I always took my camera with me in order to record with its lens what my outer and inner eyes were seeing. It was new for me to enter into a prolonged period of time without a schedule, and I regarded it with apprehension at first. But soon I settled into the natural rhythms of each day, and had the delightfully surprising experience of feeling led moment by moment all day long as well as through the night watches, following the changes and chances of the weather and the instincts of my own heart. I learned to be attentive to the voice from within, even as I was becoming aware that prayer was exactly this kind of soulful listening.

A few lines from my retreat journals reflect the character of these times of contemplation:

> *A walk through morning fog until the sun slowly broke through.*
>
> *Images I stored in my heart: the still black pond, with black branches mirrored in it, and pieces of ice still afloat on the surface; trees hung with teardrops (I tasted one!); a moss-grown log; a deep thicket of tall straight pines reflected in leaf-strewn pools; the play of light and shadow in the sky.*
>
> *Gifts...*
>
> *Intercession: I thought of someone. Then, "Oh, I can bring that one to Christ." Suddenly it felt like a chore.*
>
> *Then I realized something: that my thinking itself was part of the praying, the Spirit's insight guiding my intention and discernment about that person.*
>
> *The Spirit prays in me. Then I need only leave the*

person with Jesus.

I see how the blank spaces I'm leaving for Jesus lead to insights and moments of warmth and light. Jesus is writing on the blank page of my day.

Questions of meaning come in the forest. Why do I sometimes want to just go and be with Jesus? To die? What is the meaning of my life? Its importance?

I am aware that I am to receive the meaning of my life. I do not create my own meaning. Nor am I to fill my life with meaning, which I often try to do. Receive, receive, receive.

An awakening moment:
When morning gilds the skies,
My heart awakening cries,
May Jesus Christ be praised.
Alike at work and prayer,
To Jesus I repair,
May Jesus Christ be praised.

Alike at work and prayer. . .The rhythm of both requires looking to Jesus for guidance. Action and contemplation. The end of both is praise.

I conducted a holy experiment, walking into the woods with Jesus. Whenever I felt fear, I stopped and let Christ touch me. I realized God's care, that he watches over me, will alert me to danger, so I can pause to listen to the wind, the birds, the stream, and watch the play of sunlight on the forest floor.

I stepped carefully on stones, crossing the stream, then sat down on a rock fence to sing:
Through many dangers, toils and snares
I have already come.
'Tis grace hath brought me safe thus far,
And grace will lead me Home.

It suddenly seemed a song about my life. Only, as I sang it there in the forest, I spontaneously sang it as "Faith hath brought me safe thus far and faith will lead me home." I learned something new about trust.

I am so used to being busy, and taking charge; it is very foreign to be waiting for Jesus' instructions all the time. I feel stumbly and awkward, a little lazy and often distracted.

Wed. A.M. "I will awake the dawn." So I did and went out to enjoy sunrise.

I decided on my walk that I felt dumb. And then realized I was also experiencing dumbness in its other meaning.

So, this is a time of being mute, deaf, blind. I'm on unfamiliar territory. It's uncharted. Misty. Good. . .and I'm not in control.

Sitting in a field in the sun, I learned of Jesus:
> That these days are good, though quiet.
> ("What happened on retreat?" "Nothing. And that was wonderful.")
> That today stretches out before me, yet untouched, an adventure with Jesus.
> That he made the field to glisten with dew.
> That he loved the world; he made it and that's why life here is important.

The day passes; the week passes and I do so little.
The blind man:
> "I see people like trees walking."
> "I see all things clearly."

I have the blind person's problem, seeing people like trees. I need to have another touch of the clay by Jesus that I might see others as he sees them.

I sense a smoothing out of the awkwardness I felt at first about releasing control to the Lord.

Last year my retreat ended with "Apart from Me, you can do nothing." Now the emphasis shifts to "I don't have to do anything; Jesus is in charge."

Sunset —silent grandeur—wiping away the gloom of a day of steady rain.

The liturgy last evening and again tonight had that deep silence, a quality of silence that was palpable. I am so thankful for others to share my retreat with me, though in silence. How is it that I feel I know these persons so well, though we have never spoken to one another?

A walk in dew, mist, sunlight over the fields, crunching over frost-tinged grasses.

Things came together in a sequence.

Teaching others is not so important any more, except by my life. Loving is.

I don't feel that great love for Jesus I read about in the saints. But I experience, and want to experience, Jesus' love for me. I'm impoverished in that regard.

This is the love that I'll have to give to others. I realize I want to experience Jesus' love, in part, in order to give it to others.

Then I began noticing each frost-tinged blade of grass and the droplets of dew. I laughed to think how God spent all night painting each blade and sprinkling the field with dew diamonds.

"God has made this world for me."
Then thinking on his love:
"Loved with everlasting love."
It all seemed to culminate in
"The love of Christ controls us."
That's a new emerging basic motivation.
Before leaving, two messages received on awaking and repeated in the closing song at liturgy:
"I am with you always."
"Be not afraid."

One year, Don and I went on retreat together at Nova Nada, a hermitage run by men and women Carmelite monks in the pristine wilderness of Nova Scotia. Silence deepened in this area so remote that the only sound we heard from civilization was an overflying small plane on Saturday morning.

It is hard to put into words what this experience means to me day by day. This morning I am seated in a rocking chair on the front porch of my hermitage looking out at an incredible scene—ferns, sunlit and lush, spruce and balsam gracefully erect in the sun, the lake glimpsed through them. The sun is already high in the sky, though it is just past eight in the morning. Birds of all sorts are very busy chirping, pecking, flying about, hanging upside down, chattering, singing, hopping, hunting for food. . .A soft wind brushes through the branches. Not a soul seems to be stirring elsewhere. The silence is full of sound, yet is so still.

Already, we have responded to the tolling of the bell, and worshipped in the chapel at Lauds, then eaten our breakfast of oatmeal and tea here in the cabin, made the bed, done the dishes, sketched a quick painting, and read the lections for the day.

I thought a lot about what it would be like to live like this. My question came, "What would I do here?" And this time, it seemed like a good question, for I am indeed called to "do"—to counsel and be with people, and I am sure of that. But though I am not called to monastic life per se, being here is changing my perception of who I am within my calling, and how I may be being called to change the way I work out my calling day by day. I see that our primary occupation is to know and experience God.

I am very aware of my self vis à vis others. . .and long to be absorbed, rather than so aware. Caught up. Oblivious to all but the Holy. And I know this is the work of the Spirit.

I rush ahead. Plan. Anticipate. Calculate. Imagine. I need to stop, slow down, digest, take in. I must go slowly. There is not much time.

I often encountered Thomas Merton on retreats, through the books in the retreat center libraries where I was staying. On one occasion, his words on silence spoke to me:

> *My life is a listening, his a speaking. My salvation is to hear and respond. For this, my life must be silent. Hence, my silence is my salvation.*
>
> *Interior silence is impossible without mercy and without humility. It is not speaking that breaks our silence, but the anxiety to be heard.*
>
> *When I am liberated by silence, when I am no longer involved in the measurement of life, but in the living of it, I can discover a form of prayer in which there is effectively, no distraction. My whole life becomes a prayer.*[4]

In reading Mott's extensive biography of Merton, I was particularly intrigued with Merton's interest in St. Thérèse of Lisieux. Mott commented that the simplicity and total unaffectedness of St. Thérèse made Merton's self-awareness appear crippling. Having a crippling degree of self-consciousness myself, his statement made me sit up and take notice. Mott goes on:

> *And yet here was the exact point of which she came to his rescue. She spoke of her cross. Could it be that the cross Thomas Merton had been given to carry was the same self-awareness with all of its tangle of complications, to be carried with courage and in silence? Was this to be his lasting humiliation, something to be welcomed as given? After all, the gifts of God were odd.*[5]

Could it be? Indeed! I wept, with identification and searing discovery. An odd grace, his and mine—this "self-awareness with all of its tangle of complications."

I continued to drink thirstily from Merton's words:

> *All the substance of the monastic vocation is buried in the silence where God and the soul meet.*
>
> *We have found God in the abyss of our own poverty, not in a horrible night, not in a tragic immolation, but simply in the ordinary uninteresting actuality of our own*

everyday life.

Then, in the deep silence, wisdom begins to sing her unending, sunlit, inexpressible song: the private song she sings to the solitary soul. It is his own song and hers—the unique, irreplaceable song that each soul sings with the unknown Spirit, as he sits on the doorstep of his own being, the place where his existence opens out into the abyss of God. It is the song of our own life welling up like a stream out of the very heart of God. The music which we sing with God is identical with the silence of God.[6]

Listening to the Wisdom of Dreams

The summer of 1987, I was attracted to a Dream Workshop and Retreat conducted by a Jesuit who had been trained as a Jungian analyst. The week began with a two-day workshop focused on dream work in relationship to spiritual direction. The rest of the week on retreat, each of us could work with a spiritual director on staff who helped us use our dreams in spiritual growth. I was fascinated by this approach, and had a week of vivid dreams, opening new insights into my relationship to God.

During the week I came across these words from Daniel 2 which I now realize were a prescient word for what lay ahead of me:

Blessed be the name of God forever and ever,
to whom belong wisdom and might.
He reveals deep and mysterious things;
he knows what is in the darkness,
and the light dwells with him. (vv. 20-22)

I wrote a few days later: "I am more at home in the dark than the light." I was beginning to realize that light and darkness were both essential in my life with God. I was comforted by the declaration in Psalm 139:12, "The darkness and the light are both alike to thee." Now darkness meshed with the solitude and silence I was coming to prefer. I was moving from the bright sunlight of propositional certainties to the hidden treasures of darkness, the world of night time with its womanly symbol of the moon. I was embraced by a "cloud of unknowing."

Helen Luke, Jungian analyst and founder of a contemplative community in Michigan, describes in *Woman, Earth and Spirit* the particular character of a woman's soul journey, birthed in darkness:

> *The extremes of this worship of the bright light of the sun have produced in our time an estrangement even in women themselves from the patient enduring qualities of the earth, from the reflected beauty of the silver light of the moon in the darkness, from the unknown in the deep sea of the unconscious and from the springs of the water of life.*
>
> *The Receptive does not lead but follows, since it is like a vessel in which the light is hidden until it can appear at the right time. Thus it has no need for a willed purpose or for the prestige of recognized achievement.*
>
> *If we can rediscover in ourselves the hidden beauty of this receptive devotion; if we can learn how to be still without inaction, how to "further life" without willed purpose, how to serve without demanding prestige, and how to nourish without domination: then we shall be women again out of whose earth the light may shine.*[7]

My descent into the mysterious world of dreams was reflected in the pictures I took that week. The album of pictures for this Dream Retreat contains misty pictures, as though I were looking out upon a world clouded in fog, shadowy spaces, close-ups with blurred backgrounds, ending with a snapshot of a speed limit sign "10 M.P.H." and a penciled note underneath, "Slow me down, Lord!"

My initial dream that week was a classic, forecasting the direction of my process. I was at a wedding, full of anticipation, hope, and joy. Apparently, something was struggling to integrate deep within me, an inner and spiritual marriage. During the week, I read in the Song of Solomon, "By night, I sought him whom my soul loves." (3:1) A dream fragment that night was filled with intimations of the sensuous love language and the search for the Divine Beloved about which I had been reading:

> *Somehow Don and I have gotten separated. It is night time and we are in Oak Park. I have "lost my beloved." And I sought him. I drive down a number of streets and lose my way. I meet a group of children and ask them directions to Myrtle Street, for that is a street I know. They point down over a hill to a lighted street below.*
>
> *"Oh yes," I say. For I recognize it. I must make my way down over a steep hill on foot—finding my way, and avoiding the precipice parts.*
>
> *The scene fades.*

How far down I must travel in my inner journey, I did not know then, and did not need to know. It was to take me down a steep descent, and I would barely avoid the precipices. But that summer, I only knew I was enthralled with the possibilities of dream work, and knew I wanted to incorporate it into my work with counseling others on which I was embarking.

Another dream later in the week seemed to build on the inner work I was meant to do:

> *A group of buildings have been taken off their foundations and turned a quarter turn so as to face in a new direction. The base structure is exposed, as the foundation has not yet been filled back in or landscaped. Also, buildings have been removed to relieve congestion and provide open space.*

Underneath a picture I took of some scaffolding which had been erected for building repair at the retreat site, I wrote: "The structure of my life has been turned. The intent is naked. Uncovered. Visible."

Attending to dreams made me more conscious as I awoke each morning. I began to feel as though God were speaking to me in those dim half-waking moments before I came fully alert to the day.

Next morning's thought came as a question from deep inside me: *"Who is to help me in my work?"* I paused a moment, waiting for the answer, which came just as clearly: *"She."* This I felt to be the Holy Spirit. I dozed off again, only to awaken with the message: *"Mrs. Fagswell."* Apparently, I was also to learn something about the Divine sense of humor which often manifests itself in dreams, in puns and word play, in ridiculous juxtapositions which cleverly hide the more brutal realizations from us until we are able to bear them, and prevents us from becoming falsely pious.

At home after the retreat, I affirmed the decision I had recently made to begin accepting clients for counseling. I had been approached by a number of women, and in the past had referred them to therapists in the area. Now both my colleagues, Richard and Don, told me, "Eunice, these women are asking to work with *you*."

It made sense now. I had been prepared in so many ways for this new work with individuals. In addition to my initial experience of therapy at age thirty-seven, I had undergone bioenergetic therapy and a year of professional Facilitator Training where I had been introduced to a number of other modes of therapeutic intervention. I knew I did not want to undertake the professional training necessary to obtain therapist credentials; that role was not exactly right for me. In Boston, I had enrolled in a Jesuit-sponsored Spiritual Direction Supervision Group, and although I received plenty of affirmation there, I did not fit into the role of spiritual director either, at least not in the way this is usually understood.

I decided to establish my own identity in the context of Life/Work Direction and to obtain supervision from Russell Holmes, a former Carmelite monk who was a trainer of Jungian analysts. I began meeting with Russell twice a month, unaware that this was about to change everything.

fourteen

De Profundis: Breakdown and Breakthrough

The human mind and heart are a mystery; but God will loose an arrow at them and suddenly they will be wounded.

Psalm 64:7

How LITTLE I realized the enormity of the step I had taken in intensifying the exploration of my inner life with God. I had stepped off the edge of a cliff, with no idea where I might safely land.

Typically, I began by immersing myself in books, starting with the writings of Carl Jung, and proceeding to works by authors influenced by his thought. I bought tapes. I attended lectures at the Jung Institute. I drove to Pennsylvania to participate in a workshop led by Marion Woodman, author and analyst with a special interest in feminine psychology. I found concepts in Jung's writings that accorded with my understanding of spiritual growth as a Christian. So I picked and chose what fit into my framework—the journey of the soul toward union with God—and discarded what seemed a fruitless exploration of esoteric ideas.

Jung's notion that the natural gravitation of the soul is toward growth made sense to me, as I observed my own process and that of my clients. The doctrine of original sin was still lurking about, but I could not hold it in the same spirit that it had been communicated to me by others. Instead, Jung's insistence on the admission of elements of light and shadow fit my experience, and gave me a way to address both in my own life. I did not need to substitute Jungian thought for that of theologians. I simply let it enrich the mix.

Because I was working with Russell, whose part-time work was directing the training of Jungian analysts, I wanted to take advantage of his expertise in working with dreams. I waded in eagerly, fully, naively. My dreams began coming thickly and with impelling images. Something was moving at a deep level within me. After a year of supervisory work, I asked Russell if we could meet weekly rather than every other week. In his eyes, this meant that I was embarking upon my own analysis, not just supervision of my work with others. I didn't grasp this until one day Russell commented, "When you started your analysis. . ."

"What?" I shrieked. I had not planned to "be in analysis," and in fact dismissed its value. I had taken an uncalculated but deliberate step down, and I kept falling. Russell encouraged me to draw my dream images, and I followed his urging, producing a stack of intensely passionate drawings over the next three years. I began to live in that increasingly familiar world of my own unconscious, and found it richly textured, hauntingly grotesque, elaborately complex, in turn.

Meanwhile, my body gave in to the strain, mirroring the breakdown of the predictable ego structures that had faithfully maintained me for five decades. I began experiencing one strange symptom after another. From doctor to doctor I went, searching for cures. I felt tormented, pursued by some unknown hound of heaven, as first one part of my body erupted with a symptom, then another. I was a textbook case for a procession of post-menopausal symptoms. Drying of my skin produced psoriasis, lichensclerosis, vaginitis, and broken finger nails. It was easy to identify with Job in his suffering from severe skin problems.

My malaise went beyond the surface symptoms. Something was awry in my soul. God was asking for my attention. As with Job, an attack on the body was a sure way to accomplish this. I was not in control—for me, an untenable situation. I shared Job's distress at my insomnia as well.

> *When I lie down, I say, "When shall I arise?"*
> *But the night is long,*
> *and I am full of tossing till the dawn.*
> *I will complain in the bitterness of my soul.*
> *When I say, "My bed will comfort me,*
> *my couch will ease my complaint,"*
> *then thou dost scare me with dreams.* (Job 7:4, 13, 14)

One horrifying dream placed me on an island:

> *I am on an island whose surface is tan-colored gritty gravel. Little stick-like palm trees are all over. The appearance is arid and barren. A man is driving his car around recklessly, and I become very alert. I feel he is a sadist. He chases me with his car. We have various interactions, and along the way, he gets into my purse. I am very angry and order him not to and finally he obeys.*
>
> *I walk up beside his car, which is made of wood and has striation marks along the side because it has been burned. This man is very destructive. I try to get away from him.*

The dream reflected the drying out of my whole body, and the sensation that I was fleeing from attack by a series of physical symptoms. No part of my body was exempt from the onslaught. My life felt arid and barren at the same time that there was a certain recklessness in my feverish pursuit of new insights about the world of the unconscious. I was a little crazy. Every time I went to the doctor with a new symptom the diagnosis was the same: it was some condition related to stress. My very identity, symbolized in the dream by my purse, was being challenged by this hostile invasion by the strange man.

With Job, I roared my complaint to God:

> *Why hast thou made me thy mark?*
> *Surely now God has worn me out*
> *And he has shriveled me up.*

He set me up as his target;
his archers surround me. (Job 16:7, 8, 12, 13)

I imagined myself as a helpless creature on a theatre stage, with God the Archer shooting arrows at me, symptom after symptom. I would dodge one arrow, only to be struck from another angle, then another, and another.

I took refuge in Psalm 88:

O Lord, my God, my savior,
by day and night I cry to you.
You have laid me in the depths of the Pit,
in dark places, and in the abyss.
Your anger weighs on me heavily,
and all your great waves overwhelm me.
I am in prison and cannot get free.

I sought refuge in reading *The Dark Night* by Carmelite monk St. John of the Cross,[1] interpreting my experience as a dark night of the soul. A journal entry reflects my growing anguish:

I awoke. My body felt totally wired. Then I experienced nausea from deep down throughout my body. A feeling of crying came up from within, but dry of tears. I began to feel sicker and sicker.

"My soul is in torment." It was a struggle to awaken enough to write notes. I had a strong feeling of revulsion.

"I'm not doing anything to deserve this." Then tears came.

I tried not to disturb Don. I wanted to be alone in this. I know that Don and I are to walk alone in our journeys for a time.

I feel I am going through a trial by fire that is inexorable and unavoidable. I feel an inner grimness about it. I don't want to wildly fight it, nor is it fun to contemplate or anticipate. There is no way to steel myself against it either for I have all kinds of vulnerable openings physically and psychologically. Jobean feeling! The Almighty has infinite resources for getting at me.

Finally, in desperation for physical relief, I contacted an alternative health clinic. As I anticipated, they determined that my wild variety and persistence of symptoms indicated a deteriorating immune system resulting in a severe yeast infection. They drew some blood to authenticate this diagnosis, and sold me a lot of expensive vitamins to begin my treatment.

The vitamins were wonderful, and I began feeling better right away. I doggedly began following a stringent diet which excluded wheat and dairy, and thus all my favorite foods. When the blood test came back, I began a regimen of a powerful drug powder called Nystatin, which tasted terrible. I was on the drug for five months, when I finally made the decision to refuse another dose. The clinic practitioner warned me that my symptoms would return. Instead I began losing a serious amount of weight and began to suspect the drug had been poisonous to me.

One day, walking through a department store, I stopped abruptly before a mirror, aghast at the gaunt skin-and-bones image staring back unhappily at me. I stood there riveted for a moment before I fled in shame. I had seen someone I did not recognize, and she looked like a victim of Holocaust. For a person who has been very image-conscious all her life, this was a wake-up call.

In a session with Russell that week, I recounted a dream about a "skimpy" person. Russell identified the "skimpy" theme in my dream as an anorexic strain, that my ego was objecting to the part of me that was starving myself. He said that the anorexic aspect was part of the "mother complex" since it is the mother who feeds us at the start of life. He suggested that I take a ten-day experiment of eating freely what I chose, and not be so obsessed with diet. I responded with extreme emotion. I stormed and pounded the floor in rage and shed retching tears. I did not know how to express the extent of my frustration and anguish but I sensed I could do this with Russell. My desperation subsided and I knelt before him asking for a funny blessing on my head. I hugged him on the way out the door, in terror of what lay ahead.

Around this time, I was sometimes obsessed with the idea of dying. In church one Sunday, we gathered at the altar to anoint a young man who had recently undergone radiation treatments and looked as though his cancer was spreading to other parts of his body. Because I had such constant problems in ways that resembled AIDS—weight loss, fatigue, skin problems—I sometimes felt I was dying, and though I basically did not want to die, there were moments when the idea appealed to me.

That afternoon I went to a movie without knowing that it was about AIDS—"Longtime Companion." It affected me strongly. Afterwards I stopped to walk around Jamaica Pond and read. I "happened" to dip into Christina Grof's *Stormy Search for the Self*[2] and came upon a section that talked about experiencing "symbolic death," and how a person in spiritual crisis longs for detachment to the point where she thinks she is literally going to die.

That resonated with me. I felt I was undergoing an "ego death" where old modes of existence must die to make way for new growth, the death of old personality structures.

I wrote in my journal:

> *I awaken to the consciousness that my soul is longing for God.*
> *"When will you come to me?"* (Psalm 101:2)

> *It is not for healing that I long. It is for the Healer. It is an interior longing that will not be satisfied with anything less. In some ways, I can't imagine it being satisfied short of Heaven.*

My insomnia, plus my growing attention to dreams, meant that much of my energy was poured into my night life. Often I would awaken because of physical discomfort, and rise to record a dream. Drawing images of my dreams and inner feelings had a soothing effect on me so that I could fall asleep.

My dreams were recording my inner journey, speaking in a

language I was learning to hear and grasp. I was on a descent, both in my unconscious life as portrayed in dreams—so many dreams took me down, to a cellar, a valley, a riverbed—and in my conscious life, as I was learning the art of guiding others in their inner journeys, a work that required I engage in my own spiritual process. I found the two parallel, and that even in the darkest times, I was given grace to continue working with others in their descent into darkness. I was sure that it made a difference in my empathy with others' pain that I was walking through my own "valley of the shadow."

This was new territory for me. Grof calls experiences like mine "spiritual emergencies." She has observed others going through a similar crisis, and because ordinary therapy does not have adequate tools to interpret spiritual phenomena, the person undergoing the experience feels insane.

There was an underlying physical element in my case that added to my craziness. I had been diagnosed with adult asthma at forty years of age. At that time, asthma was treated by pills which went directly into the bloodstream. I noticed that after taking my nightly pill, in a short time, my brain would feel wired and I would get anxious, my thinking addled. I am now astounded as I read my journal of those years and note the frequency of incidents where I felt crazy. Since modern asthma treatment uses inhalers, there is no longer a surging of medication through the bloodstream, for which I am deeply grateful. At that time, I had no explanation for these "seizure-like" moments.

BREAKDOWN AND BREAKTHROUGH

Eventually I had to name my experience a *breakdown,* a total spiritual breakdown. Something within me had to be reconstructed from within. Halfway through my ordeal, I attended a workshop at the Society of St. John the Evangelist monastery in Cambridge, conducted by Jungian analyst Ann Ulanov and her husband on "Breakdown and Breakthrough."[3] I listened mouth agape as Ann described spiritual breakdown. It was my experience in explicit detail.

So this was normative! It is a deeply spiritual life passage, she said. Breakdown occurs because we have come to the end of our ways of getting through to God. It hits us from our blind side and points to some "dropped stitches" from our past, some part of our lives we have failed to live so far. The breakdown feels bad precisely because we are becoming conscious and no longer denying that something is wrong, or lost.

When Ann talked about how breakdown is often signaled by symptoms in our body, my own physical suffering took on a new dimension. I had stubbornly clung to the notion that my ordeal was somehow something sent by God, but I had no framework for understanding its meaning.

Ann suggested that at the heart of this process is a "crossover" from seeing God as subjective object—"You are there for me"—to seeing God as objective object—"You are the Person You are." Old images of God collapse, the God we have needed God to be.

The experience of the separateness of the objective God, though painful, was also a relief, for I was clearly not obliged to be in control. I had become empty of my own ideas of God. My subjective pictures of God were too small, not commensurate with my present need.

At the nadir point, Ann said, we experience the silence of God. God appears to be a deaf mute. Jesus' last cry at the cross took on fresh significance: "My God, my God, why have you forsaken me?" We must trust that the experience of God will come back on its own. The Divine Lover will come in God's time to say to us, "I want to give you Me, so that you can be a whole passionate woman." The new comes to us in a form we do not recognize, just as Jesus' first resurrection appearances were a surprise. The women were the first to receive, and it is our own inner feminine which awakens to the new perception of God.

"God can always barge through the unlockable door," Ann continued. Once inside, everything changes. I could hold the resurrected Christ with open palms, not the closed fists of doctrinaire certainty. I could begin to live at the borders of the unknown, leaving space for the "Surprising God."

Again, it was Job who met me in the place of breakdown:

> *My spirit is broken.*
> *He breaks me down on every side,*
> *and I am gone,*
> *and my hope has he pulled up like a tree.*

But it was also Job who held out hope for me:

He will complete what he appoints for me. (Job 17:1; 19:10; 23:14)

OPENING TO MY INNER WOMAN

I was learning to love the darkness, greeting it with a line from an old Simon and Garfunkel song, "Hello, darkness, my old friend." One night, unable to sleep, I got up to draw. I needed to make vertical motions in various colors, the dark shades on the left and light pastels on the right. The drawing reminded me of my inexplicable and transformative experience in therapy in 1967, the sensation of life coursing upward through my body as I lay prone on my bed.

I had no name for that experience at the time, but now I was given a dream which seemed to offer a meaning and also to pertain to my present circumstances. The dream symbolized the process of initiation of a young girl into womanhood. A young girl was lying on a bed, surrounded by three women: her mother, a dark haired woman and me. The dark-haired woman was waiting to initiate the young girl into womanhood.

I made a drawing of the young girl being initiated, her body stretched out on a bed, her rounded buttocks exposed to view. I could feel the ceremonial solemnity of the occasion, the tender solicitousness of the mother figure standing nearby, and the quivering expectancy of the young girl. I remembered my own experience years before: the pulsating spiritual-sexual energy resting in my body at the base of my spine, and being released in a moment of overpowering sensation as it moved upward through my body and exited from the top of my head. My own initiation into womanhood had taken place in my therapy twenty years earlier, but the ecstasy and mystery were still palpably present to me. Now the dream seemed to be signaling another initiation—into something I could not yet name, a quality of spiritual consciousness.

Who was the dark-haired woman who was going to do the initiating? I thought I found a clue in reading Marion Woodman's descriptions of the "Black Madonna"[4]—a dark maternal figure who appears in the dreams of many women (and some men). I made connections to my life on three levels:

First,

She is the awakened positive mother who is constellated after the purging of the negative mother complex.

I was in the process of entering into a new phase of work with women which required the awakening of my long-dormant maternal qualities. My strong opposition to the "mother complex" had to melt in order to allow an inborn but repressed ability to nurture flourish. Black Madonna energy represented that earthy sensibility which was cut off from my consciousness growing up, perhaps not so much by either of my parents as by the religious environment reinforcing a negative view of feminine earthiness. My intellectual self had thrived, to the detriment of full development of my own positive mothering qualities.

Second,

The Black Madonna is black because she has literally or figuratively been through the fire and has emerged with an immense capacity for love and understanding.

The fire was an all too familiar metaphor in my current life experience. I only dimly saw that its fruit would be manifest in a capacity to love. Already, I was becoming more able to simply sit with clients in their suffering, without having to fix everything or reassure too quickly.

Third,

> *Black Madonna is nature impregnated by spirit, accepting the human body as the chalice of the spirit. She is the redemption of matter, the intersection of sexuality and spirituality.*

It was my body—the temple of the Spirit—which was speaking to me with such urgency during these months, and which thereby was insisting upon being acknowledged and honored as giving voice to deep inner wisdom of the unconscious. It would take a lifetime to mine the mystery of this integration of matter and spirit.

Around this time I was given another dream that spoke to this mystery.

> *I am driving along a road in a wilderness recreation area. I am headed toward "Pioneer Lodge"—an Indian medicine lodge, which holds the mysteries of healing. As I continue, I drive through watery sections, some quite deep. My vehicle appears to be amphibious for it has no difficulty navigating.*
>
> *I come to a forest glade where there is considerable water. I have been noticing a number of animals. Each appears, one at a time, and is identical, the size of a large dog or cheetah, but furry and gray like a woodchuck. Though I initially have some apprehension, I see that the animal is benign and poses no threat. When it goes into the water, it develops a large snout and looks like a hippopotamus. I find it amusing.*
>
> *In the glade, I manage a U-turn, brushing quite close to one of the animals. I drive back to the lodge and park. Inside there are all the signs of life—a cozy interior, but the person in charge is not home. I remember using his towel.*

Working on this dream with my analyst, I drew a picture of the animal, which he suggested might be "my" animal the way shamans have a symbolic animal as part of their healing. The animal, when in water, developed the snout, a sign of having a "nose" for the unconscious. Intuition. *I can trust my instincts in counseling others,* I thought.

As we talked, gradually the analyst pointed out how my intense relationship to my own father had inundated me with "too much spirit" and that my dream was compensating by having me enter the forest and the watery places (signs of the feminine) and encounter the furry animal. The simple words, "too much spirit," uttered softly by the analyst, reverberated within me as deeply true. Something broke free inside me, allowing me to go into the feminine at a deeper level than ever before.

At the same time, another movement was occurring within me, though I did not name it, a journey that would take me toward an encounter with Jesus at the cross.

At the Cross

In February of 1990, I went on my usual week-long silent retreat. On my way to the retreat center, I stopped at an art gallery in downtown Boston to see an exhibition of Ernest Barlach's sculpture. His work always affected me viscerally, and today was no exception. Rain was pouring down outside as I walked into the gallery, moving from piece to piece through the tiny basement studio. I came upon one particularly poignant piece of a beggar woman seated, head faced downward in a pose of abject despair, a shawl draped over her head. I stood in front of it, riveted, tears flowing freely down my face and off my chin. The person in charge of the gallery stayed at a discreet distance, puzzled that this visitor was so undone by the obscure little statuette in one corner.

I chose my spiritual director for the week carefully, knowing I was at a nadir point physically and spiritually. Sister Debbie was a nurse with a naturally compassionate nature. I felt she would be able to deal with my frayed spiritual sensibilities and precarious physical condition.

But even Debbie was shocked at the degree of distress I was manifesting. On the second day I sat with her saying over and over,

"I'm sick. I'm sick. I'm sick," and without any more warning, vomited into her wastebasket. I protested quickly, "I'm not sick, I'm not sick," determined not to give in to the nausea. I was ashamed and despairing. At lunch that day, which was eaten in silence, I sat opposite a woman whose eyes were full of pain. She never flinched as I sat there eating my salad with tears streaming down my face. As she left, she patted my shoulder in an understanding gesture.

A day later, I wandered into the lounge where I noticed a shelf of tapes. Idly, I picked one that had no clear title and took it back to my room. A cool, clear, feminine voice drew me as I listened. I huddled close to the tape recorder as the words ground into my soul.

> *If you say to me, 'You're a failure,' I'll have to kill you because you are threatening my life (my defense systems). If a person tries to convince me of this, she is trying to be God. Only God can convince me of this, and has the right to ask me to drink that cup to the bitter dregs, to go through that kind of martyrdom.*

I knew what she was talking about because I had been recently introduced to the Enneagram, which helped me identify myself at Point Three on the diagram, the type concerned to protect an image of efficiency and effectiveness in professional life and relationships. I had an endless hunger: to be admired, to make an impact, to be seen as more than I really was, and never to be seen as a failure. The core of my compulsion was the "deadly sin" of deceit, not just the deceit of lying which I had learned as a child, but the clinging to a false self—the image I craved to see reflected in the faces of my admirers.

The tape was talking about persons afflicted with this compulsion:

> *It's hard for a person [who needs to preserve her self-image of success] to be a Christian, to need to be saved. We are frightened if we don't know what to do, if we can't fix things. We read the Gospel and correct ourselves, improve ourselves. We do it by willpower. We don't need a Savior for a very long time in our lives.*

> *There will come a day when we can't do it by ourselves
> . . .the greatest day of our lives, though it doesn't feel like
> it at the time.*

Could this be my day? It didn't feel like a great day in my life at this moment. One sentence caught my attention:

> *Only these persons know what failure is, and can drink
> the cup to the very dregs.*

For many months I had been gripped by a sense of abysmal failure: I was up against something I could not control. My body was defying me. Like Job, it was the one thing that had succeeded in stripping me of my usual facility in being on top of everything in my life. I felt naked and defenseless, stretched out on the cross with Jesus. I pressed my ear closer to hear some word of hope.

> *The moment of liberation comes in darkness and desolation. Failure is the one reality we cannot be in touch with without experiencing terrible pain, foreboding, a fear that our life is over and we are going to die. We drink that cup of death to its dregs.*

There it was: my own present reality—the terrible pain, the desolation, the death to the effective person I had always been and prided myself on. In my mind's eye, I stood looking at Jesus on the cross, pondering what I would have felt at that moment. What would have been the hardest to bear? Had I been on that cross, it would have been hearing the taunts of the crowd that would have rankled me: "He saved others; himself he cannot save."

This was what Jesus had gone through for me. The Son of God was willing to experience the ultimate humiliation of failure. Jesus, the divine healer, became identified with my brokenness to the point of a death that demanded being forsaken by God. As Douglas Hall has written, the cross "should be seen primarily, not as a divinely managed human sacrifice to a righteously wrathful God but as God's own solidarity with the creature,"[5] a compassionate and merciful identification with my human condition.

That night, I awoke in the stillness before dawn and drew an image of the cross, then listened to the haunting beauty of the "Pie Jesu" from Lloyd Webber's *Requiem* ("Lamb of God, you take away the sins of the world, have mercy on me") and part of Bernstein's Mass. Then I slept.

Next day I wandered out onto the retreat grounds to the cemetery where a huge crucifix was displayed. Three men were digging a grave as I stood nearby looking at the figure of Jesus, feeling inexpressible love for "those glorious scars."

> *Those dear tokens of his passion*
> *still his dazzling body bears,*
> *cause of endless exultation*
> *to his ransomed worshippers;*
> *with what rapture, with what rapture*
> *gaze we on those glorious scars!*

For the first time, in a mysterious place within, I was at the cross with Jesus.

Changing the Way I Worked With People

My perceptions of myself as counselor were being radically changed by my ordeal. For one thing, I no longer saw my work in the world as in itself my primary vocation. Rather I knew that in the ministry to which I had been called, it was my own inner work that provided the only valid basis for my vocation in the world. So my inner journey became a primary focus of my life and work.

I had to learn to resist a deeply ingrained instinct for making a visible impact on others by what I said and wrote and did. I had wanted laser-like insight, to be able to reframe issues for people in innovative and powerful ways. I had wanted to touch others, make a difference. All these motivations had to die.

I had a dream about Mike Wallace of Sixty Minutes fame that I entitled "The Taming of the Shrewd."

> *Mike Wallace, another guy, and I have come to our house. My mother and father are there. We are talking together. At a certain point I realize I haven't introduced Mike to my father. I am standing behind Mike's swivel chair, hands on his shoulders. I turn him toward my father and introduce him saying, "I don't know how to pronounce your last name." (Wallace was only his stage name.) I am massaging Mike's shoulders. It was just the right touch—strong, yet deeply loving and tender. Everything felt totally natural.*

I saw Mike Wallace as tough and smart, a shrewd interviewer who cut to the core with those he encountered and who used his blend of Jewish irony and realism to good effect. I could also see that he was softhearted inside, though he preserved a hard exterior. The warm feeling in the dream lingered long after I awoke. The connection in the dream between Mike and my father was significant, representing two kinds of masculine strength upon which I should draw. The presence of both mother and father represented a healthy integration of my masculine sensibilities with my more tender feminine side.

I needed a mingling of the strong and tender in my work with counselees. My shrewdness needed taming. Russell had been quick to point out my inflated approach to counseling—working too hard to understand the clients' process cognitively, attempting to deal with too much material. He would caution me from rushing in where angels feared to tread, trying to use my newly discovered insights to help, to fix, to make a visible difference. Once, in exasperation, he looked at me steadily and offered sage advice: "Eunice, we just sit here and take money."

A major shift occurred in the way I saw my work with the women who came to me. I could finally acknowledge they were often asking for my mothering instincts, not some abstract knowledge or stunning competence. I surrendered to this inevitability at a time when my own mother was approaching the age when she was beginning to look to me for support.

Now I needed to become ready to mother my mother.

fifteen

Mothering My Mother

A CLASSIC TRANSITION awaited me—the crossover from being the daughter of my mother, to mothering her as my daughter. As with every development in my life, this change was delayed, both because I needed space and time to experience my separateness as a person, and also because my parents had a heritage of longevity in their favor which postponed the time when my mother would become dependent upon her offspring.

For more than a quarter of a century, beginning in 1951, my parents had lived out their love story in retirement as a couple again, free of family responsibility. To Dad, retirement meant the opportunity to pursue his first love—writing. Over the next twenty years, he produced six, full-length novel manuscripts, three of which were published. He worked on numerous non-fiction pieces as well, including one on the Gospels, and another on his years in China. Intermittently, he was asked to serve as interim pastor in churches in New England. This entailed four major moves and home purchases, until they settled in Epsom, New Hampshire, the town where I was born.

It was in the Epsom church that my mother, in her sixties, inaugurated a Pioneer Girls club for pre-teenagers. My father was relieved to see her plunge in with enthusiasm, as he had worried that with her loss of role as pastor's wife, she might feel bereft of meaningful work. He knew his writing would keep him fully occupied. He needn't have worried. Mother took to club leadership readily. At the age of seventy, she signed up to become a counselor at

New England Camp Cherith in Maine. She was affectionately nicknamed "Mom Mouse" in recognition of my camp moniker. The campers and staff admired her pluck and made sure she could manage the exertions of camp life.

Mother's hands were rarely quiet as she busied herself with the house, her club work, and sewing for her grandchildren. She kept a bird feeder stocked outside the kitchen window. She never failed to take her daily walk, come snow or wind. She studied healthy nutrition, and made sure Dad ate well. When his diabetes necessitated major changes in diet, she bought a scale and weighed everything he ate with exactitude, and adapted her own eating regimen to his to make things easier.

During my last season at North Star, Pioneer Girls' leadership training center in northern Michigan, my parents had come for a week. Mother sat in on the classes with great interest. In all of her contacts with Pioneer Girls, she was recognized and respected as a leader in her own right. I had to take a second look at her, not as my mother, but as another girls' club leader like the others who had traveled great distances to train at North Star. When she decided to introduce herself as "Mom Mouse" I didn't know whether to be embarrassed or pleased. I may have underestimated the degree to which she was proud of me, and sat in my shadow as well.

My marriage in 1969 made it easier for me to achieve a natural and more comfortable separation from my mother. In addition, the geographic distance from my parents helped accentuate my process of individuation apart from my family of origin. While Mother was still healthy and strong, she and Dad moved to California to be near my brother and family for a time. This felt right to all of us, for I had been the sibling to visit home often through the years. Now they could be near their only grandchild, Jane, and her family as well.

After Dad died, I became acutely aware of my mother's welfare. I watched from a distance of three thousand miles as she picked up the reins of her life with courage, sold their home, and moved into an apartment with the help of my brother and sister-in-law. She was in her eighties, but clearly her life was not yet finished. She sent me a picture a photographer had taken of her.

Amy Dyer Russell at 85

I responded with warmth:

I love the picture you sent. I hugged it to me and cried for pleasure. You have a beautiful face, all the lines and wrinkles that life has put there. You're a loving wonderful lady, you know, and the camera can't lie.

On one occasion when I was in California visiting Mother after my father's death, the two of us were returning home from an errand, sitting in the car talking. Without looking at me directly, eyes fastened on the windshield, she haltingly asked me outright a question that had been under the surface ever since my changes in therapy which had made her suspicious of my spiritual condition. "Exactly what *do* you believe?" The words sputtered out.

As I began answering, trying both to be truthful and to reassure her of the firm foundation of my faith, she murmured, "I think I'm going to be sorry I asked."

For a moment, the old familiar panic seized me. Here I was again, hurting my mother. But I took a breath and replied softly,

"Why don't you hear this as an expression of my trust in you, that I am telling you the truth?"

It was a tiny breakthrough for us both, and I wondered fleetingly if it was in part possible because my father no longer stood between us.

The conversation continued on a strong positive note, as I began encouraging her to have hope and expectancy in her future life as a widow. "Mother, you have no idea what may lie ahead of you. You may find avenues of growth beyond your imagination. You may be able to *soar!*"

Soon, we went into the house. The conversation had affected me deeply, but I was unsure about Mother's reaction. I went into the living room and busied myself with a puzzle. Then I heard the shuffling of Mother's feet in the hallway. She was holding a tiny booklet, which she thrust into my hands.

"Look," she said, pointing to the image of an eagle and one word splashed across the cover, *"Soaring."*

She understood. It was a rare moment of harmony which I would treasure long after she was gone.

Taking Mother In

Six years later, Don and I began suggesting that she consider moving back East near us. Her origins were in New England, and it was still home to her. She gradually warmed up to the possibility. In the spring of 1984, my brother and his wife made a long-anticipated move from California to Oregon.

"Well," mother said to me over the phone. "I guess I had better move East now!" I told her that providentially, that very month an apartment had become available in our building.

Although my choice to invite Mother to live near us was deliberate, both Mother and I knew we were embarking on dangerous territory that would evoke our pattern of conflict. Neither of us understood why tensions inevitably arose whenever we spent time in each other's company. Marion Woodman suggests that the transition of the mother-daughter relationship that occurs when the mother reaches old age poses a challenge for the resistant daughter.

> *The daughter, feeling guilty because she is hostile toward her aging mother, may need to examine her own victim-tyrant complex. This old woman who once seemed omnipotent is now losing control.*
>
> *The daughter can become angry and act like a tyrant, or she can become conscious and break the cycle. An uneasy truce may tremble between them. Both may mellow if they surrender to what is.*[1]

I fervently desired the mellowing option, though our past experience was not a hopeful sign. We had a history of stubborn antagonisms that did not seem to be the exclusive fault of either of us, but the peculiar mix of the worst of each of us. We were two strong women with a natural desire to control. My mother found it difficult to let go of her deeply held convictions about matters both trivial and profound, and I could not bring myself to graciously yield even in inconsequential matters.

Some of our sharpest differences centered around our preferred ways of relating to God and developing spiritually. Each of us felt strongly *right* in her way and inevitably judged the other as less in some way, not merely different. It seemed to me that Mother would be happier and freer if she could stop trying so hard and could relax in God's unconditional love. She, on the other hand, wished my language, dress, tastes in preachers and churches, were different. She wanted me to enjoy certain familiar books and habits. I admired the way she kept her mind sharp by reading and watching C-Span, which she followed religiously (in more than one sense) but her receptors were tuned to only one point of view—pretty far Right. Even the candidacy of born-again Jimmy Carter could not pry her loose from her Republican partisanship.

Caught between our strong differences in matters consequential and inconsequential, love was often lost, for both of us. We were busy judging each other and being harsh and critical and impatient (me) or sensitive and easily hurt (her) which effectively quenched expressions of love between us.

My mother's and father's religious experience had differed sharply. My mother's tenuous hold on faith contrasted sharply with my father's sure trust, based on a clear conversion in his twenties. Here I could identify with her, for I too had been raised in a loving Christian environment and both of us had come to identify as Christians—get baptized and join the church—as a natural part of growing up. It distressed me that Mother was wracked with doubt about her spiritual standing before God. I saw her uncertainty as reflective of her early experience of having been robbed of a strong sense of her own father's feelings for her, accentuated by his early death.

Her spiritual doubt was exacerbated by her literal interpretation of Scriptures. She would find a verse that seemed to indicate that once a decision to follow Christ had been made, no one could "pluck [her] from God's hand." Then several pages on, she would come upon remarks that seemed to indicate that persons who were "once enlightened" might fall away and find it impossible to be "renewed unto repentance." This apparent paradox tormented her. She searched endlessly for some definitive explanation which would clarify a position on which she could rest. I early observed that literalness can drive one crazy.

I knew it had helped Mother to develop spiritually when our family moved to Wheaton in the late 1930s. Suddenly, we had been inundated in a stream of evangelical fervor that swirled around the college. I remembered our first Sunday night in town, sitting in the College Church sanctuary, which was filled to overflowing with students and townspeople, their strong voices reverberating with the well-loved hymns we would come to know by heart. My parents were swept up in the warmth, the ardor of spiritual expression. My mother forever afterward marked those years in Wheaton as a crucible for the transformation of her sense of what it meant to be a Christian.

But the fervor could not always hold during darker times later in life. I was aware of times when my mother's tears came easily, as she struggled with a pervasive feeling of not being "right" with God. She frequently quoted the words of Jeremiah 17:9, "The heart is deceitful above all things, and desperately wicked," words which sounded an ominous knell in my hearing. Eventually, she was willing to name these times "depression," though she was opposed to seeking professional help. My naturally buoyant spirit made me impatient with any sign of Mother's sadness. After my father died, she was more open about her depression. She wrote me:

> *I have been trying to think of the many reasons I have to praise God, instead of feeling somewhat depressed. The future doesn't look as hopeful as when I was younger, but how thankful I am that God cares and that He has given me so many warm-hearted and caring friends. Also, there are always so many things to do to keep me from thinking about being lonely.*

I was startled when she once told me she had decided to join a "Self Confrontation class" at her church at the age of ninety-three! She admitted she confronted herself often—she was highly introspective—but she thought the class might help objectify the process. But she always looked solely to spiritual causes and cures; the psyche was alien territory to her.

This mother of mine was determined to keep growing, a characteristic I proudly share with her. Ironically my mother's "towering power" was a mirror to me of my own potential. I identify with the words of Samuel Bak, the talented Jewish artist from Vilna, who, with his remarkable mother, survived the Holocaust. His life was so literally bound up with hers during the war that it made it difficult for him to make the necessary adult separation when he needed to. He wrote in his memoirs about the necessity of resisting his mother's attempts to direct his life as he grew older:

> *It was no small accomplishment for a young man to withstand the effect of my mother's towering power. I had to find ways to establish my own balance. That I succeeded at all speaks greatly in her favor. One could also argue that by letting me oppose some of her positions she forged*

my character and indeed endowed me with many of her own traits.[2]

My own mother was less willing to let me oppose her positions than Mrs. Bak, but my character was certainly affected positively by the continuing necessity to develop my own strength.

During all those past years of holiday home visits, I only knew the limited view of my relationship to my flesh and blood mother. I did not know about a "mother complex," I just knew my relationship to my mother was plenty complex. The classic Electra complex was alive and well—in love with my father, at war with my rival, my mother. We had played it out over the years with tears and tenderness. My father stood by, either unaware or helpless to intervene. Or perhaps he was reluctant to relinquish his position of adored father.

I prayed for grace and a sense of humor to move through this life passage. I knew the subtle inner pressure on me to become a kind of spiritual Super Mom caretaker, responding with loving attentiveness and total devotion. I had never been a mother, and had watched with admiration as friends of mine had taken on the selfless tasks associated with rearing children. I was not sure I was up to that sort of sacrifice. My feelings had the added complication that I was not mothering a child. I was mothering a grown adult who was to some extent under my control, but who still needed her independence, and also had demands. Now she was to live under my watchful eye. The ultimate complication for me was that this grownup was the woman who had birthed me—my mother.

Mother moved into our apartment on the first floor of the three-decker building in Dorchester in 1984, and we moved to the second floor. It boggles my mind that she was able to adjust from sunny suburban Camarillo, California, to the narrow noisy street in an area of Boston known for its poverty-stricken households and delinquent children. These were rough days for us all, but I struggled to make them as pleasant for Mother as possible. I helped her set up her furniture, find grocery stores, choose a local church, and make a home for herself.

A few months after she moved to Boston, a dam broke for both of us. I suffered a severe attack of asthma, landing in City Hospital for a five-day stay. When I returned home, I was lying on my bed resting, when I heard a slow clomp-clomp on the back staircase. I knew Mother was making her painstaking way upstairs. She entered my bedroom, sat down beside me, and with tears, said, "I'm so sorry you got sick. It's all my fault."

I briefly considered agreeing with her heartily, but refrained. She went on. "I was trying to turn you into Emmet," she confessed.

At last I felt she had insight into our dynamics. I had also failed to take sufficient notice of her adjustment to widowhood. Something melted between us.

DISCOVERING THE MOTHER WITHIN

This severe asthma attack was a clue to a deeper need I was facing. In terms of psychosomatic theory, asthma is sometimes considered to be "the suppressed cry for help from the mother." When I sat down with Don to talk about this, he replied, "You don't understand *The Mother.*"

"Mother of God?" I asked, mystified.

He explained that I needed to encounter the *mother principle* at a deeper level. Carl Jung attributed "only a limited aetiological significance" to the personal mother. He contended that the strongest influences do not come from the mother herself, "but rather from the archetype projected upon her [which] invests her with authority and numinosity."[3]

I had no concept of the Mother as an archetype. Jung elucidates:

> *Archetypes are those primordial images in the unconscious common to people in every culture and time and which exert a strong influence on our conscious lives.*[4]

The mother archetype is perhaps the most common example, and contains opposing elements: the loving nurturant mother, and the "terrible mother." Since archetypes usually appear as projections on another person, I had to face the way I had imprisoned myself by my powerful negative projection on my own mother. By devaluing her maternal solicitude, I had contributed to the inevitable provoking of misunderstanding and quarrels. I slowly came to admit I was guilty of this projection, and I also discerned that Mother's mode of parenting had unwittingly invited the projection.

Now I was beginning to see my need of dealing with this because of my vocation in counseling others, which required quantities of that nurturant mother-love I had so long resisted in my mother and repressed in myself. I needed to look at the confusion in my counseling between my reaching out to help others and my need to feed myself. I often tired myself responding to others' needs. Like the infant who cannot tell where she ends and the mother begins, as she suckles at her mother's breast, I had been merged with my mother, but negatively. Jung once said:

> *Women with a negative mother complex often miss the first half of life; they walk past it in a dream. But they have a good chance in the second half of rediscovering life with the youthful spontaneity missed in the first half. Though a part of life has been lost, its meaning has been saved.*[5]

This shed light on my own experience. I reasoned that in my case something might have gone awry in my separation process, making me emotionally insatiable in my younger years. I had eternally looked for *The Mother* everywhere—in the nurturance of my father, in emotional closeness to women friends, and even in my marriage. As this realization sank in that day talking with Don, I began to sob.

I sat quietly focusing on those insatiable needs, trying to note what I felt deep inside. Longing, yearning, hunger, an ache. Heart ache. I asked myself, *"What's behind it?"* The answer came: Fear of loss, fear I can't hold onto what will meet my need, so I must magnetize others which means that persons can't come freely. So I must produce a continual high energy level to be unfailingly winsome. No wonder I was often exhausted.

During the night the words of Psalm 131 came with new force:

I still my soul and make it quiet, like a child upon its mother's breast; my soul is quieted within me.

I knew that a weaned child is able to get her own nourishment, fill her own hungers, and thus leaning on a mother's breast has a different meaning for such a child. I could image myself being drawn up on God's bosom, close to God's mother heart. The asthma quieted as I leaned upon El Shaddai, the Breasted One, God the Mother and Nourisher. Could I lay my needs, my gasping, my urgency at Jesus' feet?

Gradually, in the years of attending to my mother's needs, the old animosities thawed, and I gained some balance in my relationship to my mother. The work I had embarked upon in my spiritual journey and in analysis proved crucial in this regard.

The Journey Home

For the first two years, Mother stayed in the Dorchester apartment. Born and bred a country girl, she found urban life exhausting and ill-fitting her temperament and grew increasingly restive. She also knew she must prepare for a time when she might need care.

We discovered a retirement facility located in the town in Epsom, New Hampshire, the town in which she had lived when I was born, and again with Dad in retirement. On a June day in 1986, we moved her to her last home, an independent apartment in Epsom Manor.

The timing was fortunate, for eight days later a fire broke out in the building next door to the apartment on Maryland Street where she had been living. Flames leaped across the narrow, five-foot walkway between buildings and licked hungrily at the wooden structure we had once called home. It was declared a total loss. The Dorchester years were finally over for her and for us. Mother only remarked dryly, "Well, I guess I moved just in time." We fervently agreed.

In Epsom, she was delighted she could be near a lifelong family friend, Mabel, and to discover that another dear friend, Bernice, lived at the Manor as well. Bernice was legally blind, and Mother took pleasure in visiting with her often, reading books to her and chatting about common concerns. Bernice was one of those angels, like my father, who was rarely moved to criticism, and thus endeared herself to my mother, who was plagued by her own strongly planted instinct to focus on what was wrong with a situation rather than what was right.

At ninety-one, Mother was amazingly energetic and healthy. She took regular walks, followed the news on the public television channel, and participated in church activities. Slowly, she became more frail, her eyesight dimmed, and she was sometimes in pain. When Bernice and Mabel died within a year of each other, Mother's energy took a sharp downturn. The will to live was going.

Don and I drove up to Epsom often, trying to oversee her needs as well as we could. We had endlessly hashed over Mother's situation of needing more constant care, and we knew she would have preferred us to provide the care.

At that time I was attending a Wellness Group at my health center. During one session, we were given an assignment to write a letter to someone we needed to forgive. It was to be written as a spiritual practice, and not to be actually mailed. The letter I knew I needed to write was to my mother, asking her to forgive me for not being able or willing to take care of her in the way she would have liked, and in the way that daughters are often expected to do. I wrote:

Dear Mother,

I want this letter to be a heart letter, not a form. I want to ask your forgiveness for not being able to take you in and care for you in your last years of life.

The problem for me is that I do not want to do it, so maybe what I am really asking for is forgiveness for that, for my revulsion against the idea of caring for you. I know that to care for you from that place would be poison for us both.

> *I know you look around at someone like Mabel whose daughter Myrtle cares for her so devotedly and tirelessly, and you are envious. I could never do what she does, and when I picture myself in that situation, I can hardly fathom what would have to happen in me to be able to. My life and personality are so different from that way of life and being.*
>
> *So I am sorry I can't do what you desire, not in the sense that I wish I could, but in the sense that I can see how deeply disappointed you are that you are not able to command and control your destiny any more.*
>
> *But of course that is what we all face as we move towards dying—letting go. I would like to let go of guilt now in regard to not caring for you. Will you forgive me, Momma? (I've never called you that.) Will you? It would free me up to love you at last.*

Mother had an option at the Manor: to move into the Assisted Living Unit. Instead she made a rash decision to move into the home of a young woman in town who lived in a tiny house with two young children, and who had to work days. It was my mother's last desperate attempt to be personally cared for. The young woman may have welcomed the additional income from taking Mother in, but she was unprepared to provide the kind of care Mother was beginning to need. We went up to spend Thanksgiving Day with Mother and saw that a change would have to take place. We contacted the Manor and arranged to move Mother back into a smaller apartment.

Soon the Manor staff were contacting us, worried about leaving Mother on her own. In December, she landed in the hospital. When she returned, she was obliged to move into the Assisted Living Unit. These moves had resulted in our disposing of most of her furniture. Mother could see that we were dismantling her life. She finally turned over her financial affairs to me to handle—a major relinquishment, for figuring out her finances had kept her lucid and in charge for all these years.

In March, her weakened condition necessitated another hospital stay. This time, the doctor phoned us that the end was near. Her blood pressure was eighty and falling. I contacted the funeral home. Back by her bedside, I could say my goodbyes, and feel peace as she slowly ebbed away.

But the doctor had given her antibiotics. Strangely, she began to rally. I despaired that Mother's healthy body would ever let go. She came back to the Manor, this time to the Nursing Home Care Unit, which Mother detested. All of her Yankee pride at being self-sufficient arose within her frail frame. But there was no alternative.

She went through two more grueling months lying in her bed, feisty as ever, alternately resisting the nurses who tried to get her to eat, and docilely accepting the ministrations of those who served her and the friends from the church who visited regularly. Any residue of resentment of my mother was drained out of me as I watched her vital energy seep out. She refused food, determined now to be allowed to die.

On a Saturday afternoon in May, 1991, the nursing home called to tell me they thought she was dying. Don and I drove up right away. We remained in contact through Sunday, and on Monday morning they called again, sure she would die that day. I arrived at around 2 P.M. Mother had transferred her dependency to a young woman from the church who had visited her daily and who was devoted to her. I saw that in the last stages of dying, Jesus' remark about biological family applied. "Who is my mother and my brothers?" My Mother now had the loving attentive daughter she needed.

As dusk settled over the room, and a nurse administered another morphine injection to ease her pain, Mother raised her head and looked at us without really seeing us. In a slightly louder voice, she spoke with authority: "One last thing I want to say: I am thankful for God's love in Jesus to me." Then she resolutely turned her body over. She did not rouse again in our presence. We left in the evening. She died the next day at noon, ninety-five years old.

A memorial service was held at the church in Epsom, where I

had been brought as a newborn sixty-one years previous. There were friends there from three states, as well as the church folk. We picked up the last of Mother's things from the Manor and drove back to Boston.

Two nights later, I had this dream:

> *Mother called and we talked on the phone. Then it turned out that she is calling from within the house.*
>
> *I see her pulling out a chair in the garage to sit on. Don and I go downstairs to help arrange it. As we are there, I mutter sotto voce, "The Witch of Endor has come home." Mother partly overhears and says, "What?" I quickly pun and say, "Which?...When?" to cover.*

The dream seemed to speak of the Witch-like haunting quality of the Mother complex within me, which I distanced from by punning. The Witch was the Mother in my house, not the external mother who had died.

In June, we traveled to California to lay Mother's ashes beside my father's grave in Camarillo. On our way, we stopped in Chicago to visit with Don's family. Stepping through the metal detectors in O'Hare before taking our flight to California, the alarms went off. I looked back at the official who was fingering the small brown package containing Mother's ashes. I burst into tears. "That's my mother," I cried. Don stepped in quickly to explain, and soon a kindly assistant was reassuring me.

I told Don I couldn't believe my mother was still objecting to my treatment of her.

At a memorial service graveside in Camarillo, I felt more free to speak about my ambivalent relationship to my mother. This congregation was composed of younger persons, most of whom had known my parents in their eighties. I was able to pay honest tribute to my mother, while indicating some of the nuances of our relationship that were difficult. Her marriage to my father had been supremely happy; yet I recognized how hard it must have been for her to live in his shadow for much of their life. My father was universally accepted and adored, and he had grown up with a certain strength of ego my mother lacked. She constantly felt that people were kind to her because of him. And to be truthful, this was sometimes the case. She had many warm friends who loved her dearly, and there were also those who came athwart of her strict and unforgiving rigidities.

The other trial given my mother was to have birthed two children who spent a lot of time and energy resisting her. A line in my baby book in my mother's handwriting says, "She is strong-willed, and has a mind of her own." I used to marvel at that, having felt that I had succumbed to her will most of my childhood. Standing there in the cemetery beside the urn of her ashes, I could feel how deeply I must have disappointed her.

She has cast a long shadow. Having spent so much energy fighting her influence, I have had to spend a commensurate amount of emotional energy in connecting with the inner motherliness in myself—something I eschewed for a long time, since I had so completely rejected the idea and ideal of Mother. Her legacy to me is strong. I can be grateful now, for I realize that my best ministry to others in counseling comes out of this lifelong task: learning to live in harmonious relationship to Mother.

In modern parlance, it has been a "piece of work," but a work of peace eminently worthwhile.

sixteen

Life With a Jewish Christian Poet: For Better, For Verse

MARRYING THE FIRSTBORN son in a Jewish household was a gift I never took lightly, nor did his family. In the beginning I was probably surveyed with some apprehension, although his parents, George and Sally, and sister, Penny, hid it from me and I was oblivious, so in love was I. The evening Don and I announced our plans to marry, his father sat me down in his study to formally welcome me, treating me with engaging courtliness. I surmised that he was relieved his son had found a wife with good breeding and intelligence and that he admired my acumen in the world of work for what it might bode for Don's achievement in that arena. He had little comprehension of Don's vocation as an artist and poet. He himself was a lawyer who finally fulfilled his lifelong dream of becoming a judge, only to be tormented with clinical depression for which there were less effective cures at the time.

Sally, like any Jewish mother, let go of her son slowly. He had been her mainstay during the years of her husband's severe depressions, and Don's marriage to me meant she was losing her son's constant presence and care. Sally herself had been bereft at the age of eight, losing her mother to the 1918 flu epidemic. Her father had been at a loss to deal with her and her twin brothers, so he boarded them with a succession of relatives and friends. Sally said her happiest times were the years spent in a Catholic orphanage, which made her congenial to the marriages of one brother to a Catholic, the other to a Protestant. It also meant that Sally was less opposed to Don's finding a non-Jewish wife.

Sally became a legend among her community of friends and relatives. She was Gracie Allen to anyone's George Burns, and accomplished this artlessly. In her younger days, she had been a beautiful princess, having learned well the art of charming others in order to be accepted in the many homes where she was placed. Everyone who knows her has a "Sally story" featuring one of her characteristic malapropisms. Her quirky humor was never contrived but came up without guile. "Every time I talk," Sally told me one day, "I go off on a tantrum."

Don loves to tell the story about Sally sitting in Penny's kitchen one day and idly watching the garden. Suddenly a crested bird swooped down and landed on a post. "Oh look!" cried Sally. "There's a cardinal!" A moment of puzzlement came over her face. "But it's *blue!*"

Her son-in-law Stu tells of the time he took her to a concert that turned out to be less than pleasurable. Next morning he phoned her to apologize. "I'm sorry I took you to that concert which turned out so miserably."

"Oh, that's all right," Sally protested.

"No," Stu persisted. "It was a bad concert and I don't like taking you to things you don't want to go to."

"That's all right, Stu. Sometimes I like to do things I don't like to do."

In the early days of our marriage, we were traveling one afternoon with Sally in the back seat of our car. Sally was chiding Don about something. I don't recall now what, but she was usually concerned about two things: what he was wearing (she had given up on changing his preference for long hair), and how he was earning money. She could never fathom that his work at the Urban Life Center counseling students was a real job, because it was a position we had created. To her, work in an art gallery or as a doorman were real jobs because they came with a regular paycheck from an established institution.

On this particular day, hearing her criticize Don, I rebelled and spoke up. "Sally, stop criticizing Don. I don't want to hear that anymore." I spoke sharply, and an uncomfortable silence followed.

A few minutes later, I felt a soft gloved hand on my shoulder. "We're still friends, aren't we?" she asked in an uncharacteristically small voice.

"Of course," I responded with warmth, grasping that tiny outstretched hand. The two of us had crossed an invisible barrier. Goyim could have chutzpah too and it was all right.

Sally's humor could have bite, too, but the marvel of it was how unconscious she was about its impact. Once we were gathered at the funeral of a family friend. Before the procession to the cemetery formed, Stu came over to Sally and whispered in her ear. "Sally," he began. "I am not going to be able to go out to the cemetery with everyone because I have to go back to the office."

Sally looked up at him affectionately, "That's all right, Stu. Business before pleasure."

Sally came to visit us when we moved to Boston. I suspected she wanted to check out the suitability of our circumstances, which might cause question in the days when we lived on Maryland Street in Dorchester. When she asked how we were, as she did often, I sensed that she was concerned primarily over our financial and physical comfort, although she insisted our choices were fine with her "so long as you're happy." And she genuinely meant that, though her definitions of comfort were more upscale than ours at that point.

It was her daughter, Penny, who lovingly attended to Sally's needs as she aged, obtaining the best of care and devoting time to her as the end drew near. Sally basked in the attention, retained her humor and feistiness to the end, and we are sure she allowed herself to die the one time Penny and Stu were away from her side spending a weekend in New York City celebrating their wedding anniversary. We all knew she was making it as easy for Penny as she could.

Don mourned in his characteristic way. He dedicated a small booklet containing a long poem to his mother, and the other two women in his life—Penny and me. A year later, he directed and produced an artistic performance piece at a local museum based on another of his poems as a Kaddish tribute to his mother. He placed a small urn of some of her ashes in the center of the space to mark the occasion silently, since museum authorities were nervous about anything that might be construed as a religious ceremony. We think Sally would have appreciated the tribute, done in this unorthodox fashion.

The Poetry of Our Life

I knew I married a poet. After all, that was Don's introduction of himself to me in the beginning. He knew better than I did what the cost of that might be. Marrying a poet was a natural move for me, since my father also wrote poetry.

But I had not reckoned on Don, who was not like anyone else I had ever known. In those wild crazy first days of our romance, Don would bring his trumpet over to my apartment in the evening, and hunch down on the floor in my room to play free jazz by the hour. I was content to listen, happy to be in his presence, though the jazz genre was new to my ears. I could try to interpret this man by every conceivable category at my disposal—his Jewishness; his identity as an artist, poet, and musician; his favored firstborn son status; his abstract way of speaking—but nothing computed in those terms.

I knew I could count on him, not in the sense of being monotonously repetitive and predictable, but in the sense of being *true*, being utterly and forever himself. What I saw was indeed what I got, and at every moment in time. But with him, each moment was fresh and might mean he would disagree today with what he had stated with brash authority yesterday. And he wanted to be able to disagree again tomorrow. Don't fence him in. He both infuriated and intrigued our peers on the Urban Life Center board one time when he declared, "I just want to be able to *not* be a Christian on Tuesdays!"

At times we would engage in passionate conversations about Don's work as a poet. One of these heated up to fever pitch one day as we talked about our two worlds. Don posed a question to me that felt climactic and ominous: "What is a poet?" I fumbled about for an adequate answer, appalled and frightened at the space between us at that moment. I sat there tongue-tied.

Later that same day, a friend came in. We put the same question to her. She was meditative for a brief moment, then said, "A poet is someone who loves words." Don's response was immediate and strong, "Yes!" I felt twice as dumb. An impelling question arose: What was it about this New England peasant preacher's daughter that had attracted this postmodern poet? How did a member of urban intellectual Jewish culture tolerate this incurably romantic woman who cried at movies and during hymns at church?

We were alike in our intensity, Don about his art, and I about my psychological and spiritual explorations. In practical matters, my competence kept our daily life on an even keel, both in our counseling work and in providing nutritious meals. Don's temperament gave him the necessary detachment to support me in my times of struggle with physical symptoms and night terrors, allowing me to follow my solo journey when this was essential. I understood and completely accepted this separateness. To me, "*every* man/woman is an island." A journal entry records a moment of stepping apart from each other during my ordeal of the dark night of the soul:

> *Today I walked in the arboretum, mostly alone. Don sat in the shade. He told me at breakfast, almost harshly, that he is having to pursue his separate path (poetry) and not keep up with my journey, either by reading, or being a sounding board.*

> *The tone was hard to hear, not so much the contents. I feel cut off or as though it took extra energy for him to cut himself off. I felt numb, silent, unable to respond.*
>
> *In the arboretum, I felt as alone as I ever remember feeling, and the old familiar gag-in-throat soreness arose. I walked in the trees with my camera, only taking pictures of tree crotches, and cried aloud. All I could get out was a continuous desolate chant of the one word "I"—"I"—"I"—"I-sland." I am alone in what I am going through. It is different from loneliness. It feels whole. But deep, and alone.*
>
> *At home now. I feel humble, small, wanting to remain hidden. Not deflated, and in opposition to inflation, but desiring hiddenness.*

A little later, during the week we spent together on retreat in Nova Scotia, I was given a wonderful dream fragment which became a benediction on my soul journey, and on the particular character of our marriage. I marked how Don and I were in the sea, swimming separately, while at the same time there was an image of a woman alone who felt at home under the sea. This exemplified the way Don stayed near me during my solo journey during those turbulent years in the abyss.

Our separate togetherness does not fracture our marriage, but opens it up to a deeper togetherness, a togetherness of soul. As I sit here this afternoon at my computer, Don is two rooms away tussling with his latest poetic opus. A cord of energy and love binds our hearts. And when we come together in a few hours, we will talk or be silent, touch or be each in his/her own space, going through the predictable motions of eating or walking or taking a bath by candlelight. It is very different not to need each other, but to *want* each other.

We do not process our relationship psychologically very much. There is a deep underlying assumption between us that has been there from the beginning. We seemed to know very soon after we met that we would be husband and wife, so we worked things out with that assumption firmly in our minds and hearts. I cannot imagine anything more secure. God is between us forever.

A JEWISH CHRISTIAN

The essence of Don's poetic endeavors has to do with his dual identity as a Jew and as a Christian. For years, he lived in the shadow of images he first saw as an eight-year-old in 1945 looking at pictures of the death camp at Buchenwald. As he grew into manhood, he saw that his Jewish peers were assimilating into the society which gave them new respect. They were achieving status and wealth through this newfound acceptance, born of the outpouring of sympathy for the terrible tragedy of the Holocaust.

Don turned instinctively and resolutely from this path of worldly success, immersing himself in jazz. His uncle ran the Sutherland Hotel Lounge on South Drexel, where all the jazz greats hung out in the 1940s. He got Don to run sessions for him, thus introducing Don to a wonderful world of innovation in a music that was evolving from that spot.

Later, he turned to performance art, fascinated by the "Happenings" popular in the early 1960s with their emphasis on the unexpectedness of chance and the absurd. When he discovered painting, he began working out his existential terror and angst onto large canvases. He had a show at the well-respected Hyde Park Art Center in 1958. When the medium of painting dried up for him, he turned to poetry, which took deep root and continued throughout the rest of his life.

It was in poetry that Don worked out his dual identity as a Jew and as a Christian. An underlying beat in much of his poetry lay in his reworking of the Jewish experience, and in particular the Holocaust. I have watched him over the years trying to exorcise this element in his work by moving to a comic absurdity in his poems. This more humorous genre will placate his muse for a time; then abruptly he will find himself turning back to writing more somber pieces about the darkness of those World War II years in Germany and Poland and Russia.

Oddly enough, both Don and I feel a connection to the Jewish experience. I cannot explain how it is that when I read a line in the Psalms, such as I did yesterday, "God led us into the wilderness, and sustained us," that I believe the "us" refers to me. Not that I feel Jewish; I do not. But their history is so much my own as a Christian. Don says, "Christianity is a sect of Judaism." I understand that viscerally. From the time we first met, we found we could talk on the same wave length, Jew and Gentile, but both Christians.

It is then significant that the deepest beat in the heart of Don's poetry emanates from that fundamental decision of his life—to become a Christian. Don's complex relationship to his dual identity is exemplified in many of his poems, such as these:

> **With the Children**
> *No, this long ritual*
> *I can not stay Jewish;*
> *This full ritual*
> *I must go out in the other Pale.*
>
> *Into the future Pale*
> *Spreading through Sabbaths*
> *Generations,*
> *Blessed and sleeping.*
>
> *The children await me,*
> *Bathing their child.*
> *No holidays contain me;*
> *I will not stay Jewish.*
>
> **Christianity: Unconditioned**
> *Judaism's a rigidness now.*
> *Temple is inviolate.*
> *Out at God, among the forces*

> *Her destruction is found.*
> *Where the true, elemental "turning"*
> *Cuts well into dominion*
> *The Temple lies, immutable.*
> *Her freedom, since, lies there.*
> *Converted into religion*
> *And religiosity;*
> *While over her lost immediate*
> *Christ life is shining.*
>
> **This is My Shul**
> *This is my Shul: what is melodic,*
> *What exists in painter,*
> *In apprehensive sky,*
> *In possible stars of curlicue.*
>
> *This is my Service: smelling the Evening,*
> *Cutting the patina with my spacious prayer,*
> *Plucking the Cantor,*
> *Snatching man's helter-skelter voice.*

Becoming a Christian allowed Don to break free from past definitions of religious experience and to affirm his upside-down values—the belief that the "other world" is the essential one. The Jerusalem in Israel is not his ultimate reality, but the Jerusalem in the human heart, and the new Jerusalem of future glory. He sees how Judaism, as well as Islam, and some aspects of Christianity, become mired in materialist assumptions: "do these rituals and get the reward." For Don, that kind of gospel was exploded when Jesus was crucified and refused to become just another interesting rabbi.

In the days following the terrorist attacks of September 11, 2001, we both had to reassess our faith, and take a hard look at the three faiths at war in the world: Islam, Judaism, and Christianity. What was truly radical now? Was it to effect change through physical means—dropping bombs, or sacks of wheat? How important was land, a shrine, a holy place? Some of the themes in my own spiritual journey emerged with new clarity: the essence of my faith rooted in that "other world" as my home and the necessity of remaining centered in the inner life of union with Jesus as I went about daily tasks.

For Don this meant collecting the entire body of his poetry into a single volume entitled *Fear Itself*. He is writing now from a reinforced awareness of his Christian home in the new Jerusalem. He signs his work with the name "Isaiah Israel," as indication of where his soul abides.

CELEBRATION OF FAITH AND LOVE

The celebration of our twenty-fifth wedding anniversary in 1994 became the occasion for a special trip which entwined our two heritages into a single unified strand. We had seen Pierre Sauvage's film *Weapons of the Spirit* and read Philip Hallie's *Lest Innocent Blood be Shed*,[1] both of them about the little Huguenot village of Le Chambon sur Lignon that had sheltered thousands of Jews during the Nazi Occupation of France. It had been of incalculable comfort to me to know there were some Christians in Europe in World War II who had stood firm in their faith and followed through on the consequent actions of that faith, when so much of civilized humanity caved in before the Nazi juggernaut of power. "Let's go to France, and to Le Chambon!" The trip instantly turned into a pilgrimage.

I phoned Philip Hallie in Connecticut to get more detailed information about families that might still be living in Le Chambon, and whom we could contact. We wanted to be able to thank someone face-to-face for their gift of love and preservation. Philip gave us the names of Ernest and Rose Chazot, who had been mentioned in his book.

The week of Passiontide, 1994, Don and I flew to southern France to spend two weeks in Provence before heading north to Le Chambon. We arrived in Aix-en-Provence on Maundy Thursday.

Walking down the street from our hotel at dusk, we heard singing. We followed the sound into an immense, cathedral-like sanctuary where a service was going on. Apparently the choir and congregation alike knew the chants and hymns, for the singing was strong from both quarters. There must have been a thousand people attending, all of them intentional about their worship. As is the custom everywhere, the service concluded in darkness and silence, as the sacrament was carried back through the church to the altar of repose. We received this first night's experience as a token of God's blessing on our pilgrimage.

We returned for the Good Friday service—also solemn and ending in darkness—and for the Easter Vigil (La Paque) which began outside the church late Saturday night in the rain. A huge bonfire was lit, then the Pascal Candle, from which we lighted our own candles and went inside in procession. We will not soon forget the power of the beautiful music we heard during those evenings, and the worshipful quiet brooding over us all.

We spent most of our first two weeks in the heart of Provence at a beautiful guest home near Bonnieux. We wanted to absorb country Provençal life, to be rested and in a stable situation. The crowning glory of the house was the view—an uninterrupted one of the entire Vaucluse plain and the Luberon Mountains in the distance, even snow-capped Mont Ventoux; and on the other side Marquis de Sade's castle atop the hill on which the village of LaCoste rested. From our windows we could see the vineyards, the greening of the countryside, the approach of weather—clouds and sunlight. And we heard the whine of the "mistral"—that Siberian wind that whistles down the canyons and across the plains with such fury.

From this home base, we went forth daily to visit the quaint villages of Provence, navigating the narrow winding streets to the hilltops on which most of them are perched, dining in tiny cafés, spending quiet moments in the great churches or an abbé flanked by fields of lavender, finding Camus' gravestone, buying lunch at a village open market on fair day, sitting in parks watching the old men play "boules", climbing atop the red rocks of Roussillon to see a double rainbow, living the much slowed-down pace of the countryside. We found Picasso's chateau on the forested slope of Mont Sainte Victoire, before circling around to the southern face where Cezanne painted the sunlit mountain rising abruptly from the stark plain. There was one moment of nostalgia in Salon de Provence, where we paused in the square to listen to jazz coming over loudspeakers from a shop nearby, feeling back home again for a moment as we listened to familiar tunes played by American jazz artists.

On the eve of our wedding anniversary, we splurged in a full Provençale restaurant meal. Our host made reservations for us in the one restaurant he patronizes, on the outskirts of Roussillon. Aside from German house guests and the family of the chef, we were the only patrons that evening. The conversation around the table took place in three languages, with amazing success.

Of course the quality of the meal helped. The French style of eating is very leisurely. Edmond, the chef, mingled with us as we ate, eager to please us with his cuisine. It turned out that Edmond was also a jazz buff, and he and Don were able to connect by just saying names of jazz musicians. Don even succeeded in telling a truly international joke, by putting in the name of a jazz musician at just the right moment, with the appropriate connotations, so as to make everyone—all three languages—laugh!

The next day we left the Vaucluse and headed north into the mountains toward Le Chambon. The road was shrouded not only by fog but also the dark forests on either side, as we climbed the sinewy trail of the rivers. The deciduous trees were still a wintry black, but there were an increasing number of evergreens.

I had expected Chambon to be a tiny village, a scattering of houses in the central area, and then farmhouses on the hillsides around. But we soon found that Chambon is a kind of sports center in that area, and the village is really a small city, buzzing with Protestant capitalist energy. As we drove around the village looking at the farmhouses, we wondered which ones provided protection for Jews. In the center of town, we saw the public square, where

Gestapo soldiers strutted, and often looked the other way, for they did not particularly want to fulfill their duty and arrest the peace-loving folks here.

After a nap—the drive in fog and curvy mountainous terrain had been tiring—we sallied forth. We wondered how we would find Ernest and Rose Chazot. But miraculously, there was a telephone listing. We didn't dare phone, because of our poor language skills, and we had been told they were not English-speaking. So instead we found the neighborhood where they lived, and with help located the house. They were not home to respond to our knock, so I began laboriously writing a note in French to leave, when they suddenly drove up, returning from a visit to their relatives.

Ernest and Rose were an elderly couple, kindly grandparent-like folks. Many years had passed since they sheltered a Jewish family from Vienna in their home during the war. Graciously, they invited us inside, lit the fire already laid in the fireplace, and we began to speak as best we could across the language barrier. I knew enough French to convey to them that my husband was Jewish, and that he had been affected by images of the concentration camp as a young boy, and had been writing poetry to honor the memory of the Holocaust. I told them we came to thank them for what they and others in Chambon had done for Jewish refugees during the Nazi Occupation in World War II. As I spoke, Don and I both wept. Just as the book and film indicated, the Chambon folks are modest and unassuming about what they did. Rose Chazot made it very clear that what they did is what everyone should do as a Christian, "C'est normal."

Next morning, we found the present pastor of the church—the designation is Reformed. In this case the ethnic background is Huguenot, a group very familiar with religious persecution, having suffered throughout history for their faith. He explained again to us that what the folks did years ago was not extraordinary.

Reluctantly we drove out of town, heading toward Chartres and Paris. We would always remember our visit to LeChambon. It was a wonderful way to spend our wedding anniversary.

Don in Provence on the road to Picasso's château

At home together in Jamaica Plain

It has also been a wonderful way to spend my life—this life with Don and with God. It continues...

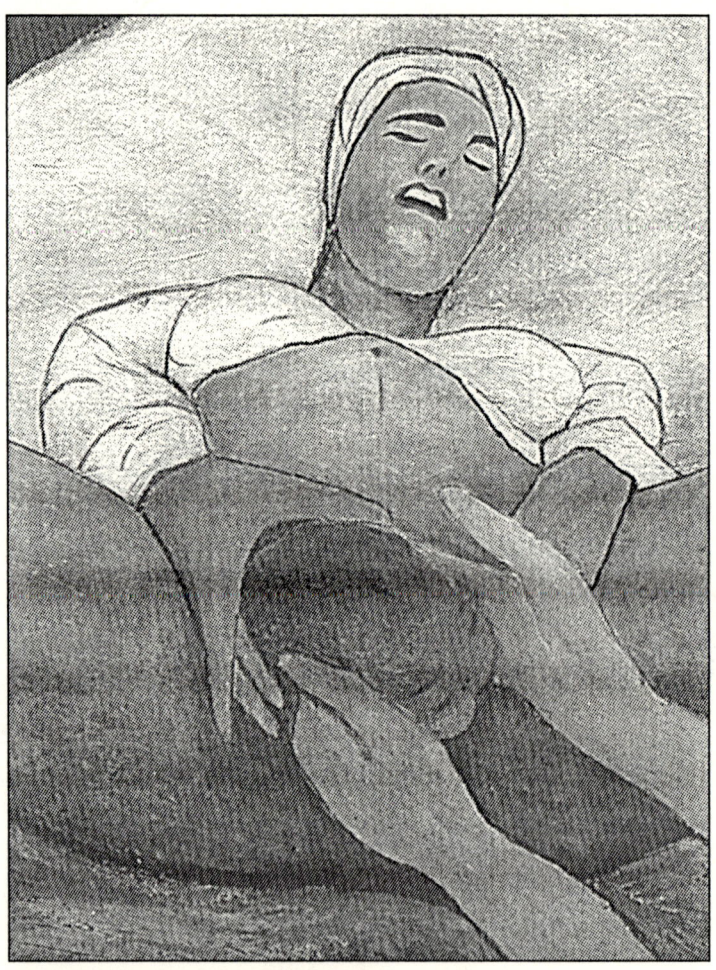

"Nativity" by Brian Willmer, SSJE
Inspired by a painting by Jonathan Walker
Used by permission

Epilogue

IN THE END it is Christmas where I encounter rebirth.

I have just come from the Christmas Eve vigil at the monastery, walking out onto the strangely silent, student-free street in the frosty air. The echoes of the songs linger in my memory, one line etched on my heart with new force.

> *Mild he lays his glory by,*
> *born that we no more may die;*
> *born to raise us from the earth,*
> *born to give us second birth.*

Second birth? Did you say second birth?

The cover on the service bulletin this evening was a reproduction of a painting done by one of the monks, Brian Willmer, who was inspired by the work of artist Jonathan Waller. Instead of the usual image of a slim, beatific woman hooded by a blue cape, gazing in adoration at her infant son, Brian has placed Mary before us as though on a birthing table facing us directly. He has depicted a darker-skinned woman, her hair in a turban, and most searingly frank, her bare legs spread wide, as the head of her newborn baby comes toward us, emerging from her distended belly. A midwife's hands are cupping the child's head, ready to guide its descent. Mary's eyes are closed, her lips apart in a voiceless cry.

I am astounded at the courage of this depiction, linking motherhood and the birth of the Son of God at this crucial moment. It evokes in me a torrent of nameless feeling.

I reflect upon my own experience of pregnancy, not physical but spiritual. Beginning to be in touch with Mary had been a reminder that God wishes to bring Christ to birth within me.

Perhaps I have been "born again" in therapy, in one sense, but it now is clear that Christ is being born again within me. That imagery fits my experience exactly.

❦

At home New Years' Eve a week later, I am listening to a CD of the Cambridge Singers led by John Rutter. Our wedding hymn, "Love Divine," is among the songs being sung. The final verse crescendoes:

> *Finish then thy new creation*
> *Pure and spotless let us be;*
> *Let us see thy great salvation,*
> *Perfectly restored in thee.*

At this instant, the puzzle of all my life unfolds in these simple lines: why it is that certain lines of hymns move me so with their imagery of dazzling glory and sublimity in the new creation. It is then that I will at last "see thy great salvation, perfectly restored in thee."

Now I can own that word *salvation* as mine. I am coming home to the mystery of my own experience of being saved. I see that I have been filled with longing all my life for that "great salvation"—which is future to me in my human limitations, but eternally present to God. I am being saved now.

This illuminates the magnetic power of my life verse:

> *And all of us, with unveiled face, seeing the Lord as though reflected in a mirror, are being transformed into the same image from one degree of glory to another; for this comes from the Lord, the Spirit.*

The final lines of the hymn roll out:

> *Changed from glory into glory,*
> *Till in heaven we take our place,*
> *Till we cast our crowns before thee,*
> *Lost in wonder, love, and praise!*

EPILOGUE

All my life has been about change. All my life has been about being saved, in the sense of allowing God to finish this new creation he brought to birth in me in so many ways: primally in my baptism, then deep in my psyche during therapy, and finally in the crucible where Jesus walked with me in the fire of deep inner work in the dark night of my soul. I say "finally" but who is to say? Another quarter century could easily await me yet, given the history of longevity in my family tree.

It is good to pause now at the end of my "three score years and ten" and recount the overflowing goodness I have been given by God, who is mother and father to me but so much more. So much more.

ACKNOWLEDGMENTS

WRITING A BOOK has changed my reading habits. I now take extraordinary interest in the "acknowledgments" section. I have profound appreciation for the cooperative nature of the endeavor, starting with my trusty Macintosh computer which appears to be crash-resistant and forgiving in other ways. What did writers of a mere three decades ago do without this marvelous machine that can intentionally blip entire segments of one's life into the trash in a nanosecond, and can leapfrog one paragraph before or after another with startling ease? I am caught dumb with gratefulness. I remember my father pecking away on a manual typewriter, and laboring to correct carbon copies.

As always it is People who deserve the most credit, beginning with the cluster of friends who waded through one of my stumbling first drafts. So a heartwarmed thanks to Judith Carpenter, Emma Lou Henning, Mary Anne Klein, Grethe Brix Leer, Norm Leer, Zondra Lindblade, Carolyn Metzler, Janet Piggins, Stephanie Smith, Lee Troup, and Louise Troup. In addition, three published authors, Lyn Brakeman, Philip Yancey, and Elizabeth Hoekstra, supplied feedback at crucial points. Each one made a difference in the final outcome of the book.

Finally, I turned to my trusted colleague at Life/Work Direction, Carmel Cuyler, for final words of wisdom and feedback, knowing she has a rare understanding of the place this book occupies in my vocation.

I asked Wheaton classmate Bill Petersen (now a Senior Editor at Baker House) for help in navigating the world of Christian book publishing. He never failed to respond with grace, as well as practical advice and names of contacts. When I decided to self-publish, Bill was the one to reassure me that Tom Freiling at Xulon Press was reliable and would come through on the remarkable promises that can be made due to the shrewd use of available technology and the internet. A good friend and artist, Janet Piggins, gave me design suggestions.

My husband Don stood at a respectful distance as I labored on this project through 2000 and 2001, always encouraging, sometimes cautioning. I rarely asked his direct advice, and he was reluctant to intrude upon a process he realized was essential for me. But I know he was proud of me, and helped me stay poised between confidence and humility as developments in the writing, revising, and publishing unfolded.

One of the unexpected side effects of this foray into my past has been a series of delightful re-connections with friends from half a century ago. Writing for permissions from a few of the "players" on the stage of my life and of this book put me in touch with the life trajectory of several persons I have not seen for years. In the process came the sad news that my therapist, Alan Richardson, who played such a crucial role in my life, had died four years ago. He deserves the tribute of this mention of him.

So many of the persons important to my life story are not mentioned by name in the book. Betty Gardner, Barbara Peterson and Alison Short Miles come instantly to mind—all of them intimately woven into the fabric of my life and sensibilities while I was on Pioneer Girls staff:

Betty, a stalwart volunteer leader in Denver during my years of field work there, stayed loyally in touch during my years of change following therapy, a time when some other acquaintances discreetly withdrew into the background for a time waiting to see how things would turn out. When I married, it was she who flew across the country to sew my wedding dress and help serve the wedding meal.

Barbara introduced me to the overwhelming importance of words, first through her poetry, and later in her letters, always winningly articulate and stimulating. She once gave me a slender leather-bound volume of poetry by seventeenth century mystics, including George Herbert and John Donne. I came to understand later why their poetry touched us both so much.

Alison and I wrote reams to each other over the years, letters full of puns and philosophy and intimate confidences. "The two of us have easy risibilities," she said once, by way of explanation of our bond. I mourn now that Alzheimer's has stolen her memory of those happy years of association.

Time and space fail me to tell of unnamed others: Les and Pat and Marlynn, and Bunny and Mary and Lois and Fred and Thea and Linda, and Florence and Peter and Barb and Milré and Lou, and Alvera and Paul, and Vernon and Joe and Leigh.

The poet who said, "I am a part of all I have met," spoke truly. I must reverse the phrase: "All I have met are a part of me."

Chaim! To life!

Eunice Russell Schatz
32 Halifax Street
Jamaica Plain, MA 02130

erschatz@aol.com

BIBLIOGRAPHIC REFERENCES

A Goodly Heritage
[1] Naomi Lowinsky, "Mother of Mothers: The Power of the Grandmother in the Female Psyche," in *To Be A Woman*, ed. by Connie Zweig, (New York: St. Martins Press, 1990), p. 87.
[2] Marie-Louise von Franz, *The Feminine in Fairy Tales*, (Dallas, Texas: Spring Publications, 1972), p. 105.

Uprooted
[1] James Hillman, "Betrayal," in *Loose Ends*, (Dallas, Texas: Spring Publications, 1975), p. 66.
[2] Father Andrews, S.D.C., *Love's Argument and Other Poems*, (London: A. R. Mowbray & Co., Ltd., 1922), p.78.

Mirror to the Self
[1] Marion Woodman, *Addiction to Perfection* (Toronto: Inner City Books, 1982), p. 99.
[2] John Welwood, "Principles of Inner Work: Psychological and Spiritual," *The Journal of Transpersonal Psychology*, 1984, Vol. 16, No. 1.

Born Again in Therapy
[1] Lewis Smedes, *Shame and Grace.*, (San Francisco: Harper Collins, 1993), p. 80. Quoted in Philip Yancey, What's *So Amazing About Grace?* (Grand Rapids: Zondervan, 1997), p. 36.

Window to the Other
[1] Ann Ulanov, "Two Sexes," in *Men and Women* edited by Philip Turner (Cambridge: Cowley Publications, 1989), p. 19.

The Seventies
[1] George Packer, "The Decade Nobody Knows," *New York Times Book Review,* June 10, 2001, p. 6, reviewing Bruce J. Schulman's *The Seventies: The Great Shift in American Culture, Society, and Politics* .
[2] Bruce J. Schulman, *The Seventies: The Great Shift in American Culture, Society, and Politics* (New York: Free Press, 2001).

Sabbath Time
[1] Wayne Muller, *Sabbath: Finding Rest, Renewal, and Delight in Our Busy Lives* (New York: Bantam Books, 1999), p. 37.

The End of Ideals
[1] "First Sunday in Boston," *The Other Side,* (Philadelphia: 1979), pp. 32-34.

The Beginning of a Life Work
[1] Wayne Muller, *Legacy of the Heart : The Spiritual Advantages of a Painful Childhood* (New York: Simon & Schuster, 1992).
[2] Robert A. Johnson, *Owning Your Own Shadow,* (HarperSanFrancisco: 1991), chapter 3.
[3] Full treatment of the Enneagram may be found in these works: Don Richard Riso and Russ Hudson, *The Wisdom of the Enneagram* (New York: Bantam, 1999), Richard Rohr and Andreas Ebert, *Discovering the Enneagram* (New York: Crossroad Publishing, 1990), Helen Palmer, *The Enneagram* (New York: Harper, 1988),).
[4] Eugene Peterson, "Christ Plays in Ten Thousand Places," *Perspectives,* June/July 2000, p. 9.

The Preacher's Daughter Comes Home to Church
1. Al Krass, "Maybe the Problem is in Our Heads," *The Other Side,* May, 1980, pp. 43, 44.
2. Philip Yancey, *Reaching for the Invisible God* (Grand Rapids: Zondervan, 2000).
3. Curtis Almquist, Society of St. John the Evangelist, personal letter, 2001.
4. John Rutter, unknown source.
5. T. S. Eliot, "Little Gidding (V)," Four Quartets, *The Complete Poems and Plays,* (New York: Harcourt Brace Jovanovich, 1971), pp. 144-145.

Inner Journey
1. Thomas Merton, *Contemplative Prayer* (Garden City, New York: Doubleday Image Books, 1971), p. 77.
2. James Hillman, "Betrayal," in *Loose Ends* (Dallas: Spring Publications, 1975), pp. 63-81.
3. Thomas Merton, *op. cit.*
4. Thomas Merton, source unknown.
5. Michael Mott, *The Seven Mountains of Thomas Merton* (Boston: Houghton Miflin, 1984), p. 184.
6. Thomas Merton, source unknown.
7. Helen M. Luke, *Woman, Earth and Spirit,* (New York: Crossroad Publishing Co., 1981), pp. 11, 12.

De Profundis: Breakdown and Breakthrough
1. St. John of the Cross, *The Dark Night,* in *The Collected Works of St. John of the Cross* (Washington, D.C.: ICS Publications, 1963), translated by Kieran Kavanaugh, O.C.D. and Otilio Rodriguez, O. C. D.
2. Christina Grof and Stanislaus Grof, *The Stormy Search for the Self,* (New York: St. Martin's Press, 1990).
3. Notes from workshop on "Breakdown and Breakthrough" conducted by Ann and Barry Ulanov at the Society of St. John the Evangelist, Cambridge, MA., March, 1989.

4 Marion Woodman, *The Pregnant Virgin*, (Toronto: Inner City Books, 1985), pp. 100, 122.
5 Douglas Hall, McGill University, addressing Covenant Network of Presbyterians Conference, Atlanta, GA, November 5, 1999.

Mothering My Mother
1 Marion Woodman, "Conscious Femininity: Mother, Virgin, Crone" in *To Be a Woman,* ed. by Connie Zweig, (New York: St. Martin's Press, 1990), p. 100.
2 Samuel Bak, *Painted in Words—A Memoir* (Indiana University Press with Pucker Gallery, Boston, 2001), p. 465.
3 C. G. Jung, *Four Archetypes,* Princeton University Press, 1959, p. 17.
4 Ibid., p. 5.
5 Ibid., p. 33, also quoted in Marie-Louise von Franz, *The Feminine in Fairy Tales, op. cit.,* p. 88.

Life With a Jewish Christian Poet: For Better, For Verse
1 Philip Hallie, *Lest Innocent Blood Be Shed,* (New York: Harper & Row, 1979).